SENSITIVITY
TRAINING
The Scientific Understanding
of Individuals

SENSITIVITY TRAINING
The Scientific Understanding of Individuals

HENRY CLAY SMITH
Professor of Psychology
Michigan State University

McGraw-Hill Book Company   *New York St. Louis San Francisco Düsseldorf*
Johannesburg Kuala Lumpur London Mexico Montreal New Delhi
Panama Rio de Janeiro Singapore Sydney Toronto

SENSITIVITY TRAINING: The Scientific Understanding of Individuals

1 2 3 4 5 6 7 8 9 0 D O D O 7 9 8 7 6 5 4 3

This book was set in Univers by Black Dot, Inc.
The editors were Walter Maytham and James R. Belser;
the designer was Barbara Ellwood;
and the production supervisor was Joan M. Oppenheimer.
The printer and binder was R. R. Donnelley & Sons Company.

Library of Congress Cataloging in Publication Data
Smith, Henry Clay, 1913–
    Sensitivity training.

    Published in 1966 under title: Sensitivity to
people.
    Bibliography: p.
    1.   Group relations training.   2.   Social
perception.   3.   Empathy.   I.   Title.
HM133.S68   1973   301.11   72-10309
ISBN 0-07-058481-8

CONTENTS

LIST OF TABLES

PREFACE

How can the ability to understand people be improved by training? The question has gradually taken over my life as a psychologist. It started with a study more than two decades ago on the influence of participation on classroom learning. My colleagues and I were puzzled to find that while participants were more intelligent, independent, and informed than nonparticipants to begin with, they did not benefit from their participation. In a follow-up study, we were surprised to find that students did not particularly care for or benefit from classes run along democratic lines. The results of a third study left us increasingly puzzled and surprised: The students who were most enthusiastic about their participation in small discussion groups learned the least from them. As these studies progressed, our interest slowly shifted from a search for the best methods of teaching to the question "What should be the goal in teaching psychology?" We became convinced that developing the ability to understand people was the answer. Since then our efforts have focused upon clarifying the nature of this goal, finding ways of measuring progress toward it, and developing methods of facilitating this progress.

As in the first edition, this book is concerned with improving sensitivity. In a similar manner, the search for answers ranges over many theories, methods, laboratory and field findings, and experiences in T groups, classroom instruction, and clinical training. Again, the reader I have had most clearly in mind is one who wants to do something about sensitivity, that is, to expand knowledge, to measure the success of training, or to try new ways of training.

However, the change in title from *Sensitivity to People* to *Sensitivity Training* reflects fundamental changes in the present edition. The tail has become the dog. The first edition gave only unsystematic attention to training, whereas here observational, theoretical, nomothetic, and idiographic training problems determine its organization. Formerly the focus was upon sensitivity as an outcome; now the focus is upon the processes that lead to sensitivity. The earlier book implicitly assumed that there was only one valid way, the scientific way, of understanding. While the stress still remains upon scientific understanding, it is explicitly contrasted with equally valid artistic, practical, and, particularly, rationalistic ways of understanding.

Problems of sensitivity concern many people in many fields. Consequently, I have tried to make my ideas clear to those who are not psychologists. Sensitivity training is the daily concern of those involved in educating clinicians and counselors, executives and labor leaders, or college students to understand people better. To achieve this goal, sections of the book are organized in pairs of chapters, the first presents theories and facts about a sensitivity component and the second traces their training implications.

The most visible change is the addition of many scales and tests. These make complex abstractions more concrete; they serve as rough models for measuring and training; they may be used as research instruments, and they also clarify the text that makes frequent references to them. The most invisible, but profound, change is the influence of the work and ideas of the philosopher Ernst Cassirer. The occasional references only suggest my indebtedness.

It is a pleasure to thank the graduate students at Michigan State University whose understanding, help, and M.A. and Ph.D. theses pervade the book: Wallace Berger, Ernest Bruni, Robert Forsythe, Burton Grossman, Ward Harris, Gerald Hershey, Ronald Johnson, Sherwin Kepes, James Linden, John Miétus, James Mullin, Kenneth Price, Jack Shook, David Silkiner, Morris Spier, Don Trumbo, John Wakeley, Daniel Wegner, and Albert Zavala. I am indebted also to the School of Labor and Industrial Relations at Michigan State University for providing time and assistance needed to complete this work.

HENRY CLAY SMITH

EDUCATION FOR SENSITIVITY

CHAPTER 1

SENSITIVITY

EVERYONE wants to understand others: The parent his child, the minister his parishioners, the novelist his characters, the businessman his customers, and the therapist his clients. Our ancestors lived in small societies and saw few people. We, however, are becoming part of a complex world society of billions. More and more, we spend our days with others and with the problems created by living with others. As a consequence, the ability to understand others has grown in importance as a goal of education.

How can this ability be developed? The question dominates this book. To begin with, we define varying ways in which we understand others, explain how sensitivity differs from other kinds of understanding, show how it can be measured, and consider its components.

WAYS OF UNDERSTANDING OTHERS

To "stand" means to assume a physical posture. To *under*stand is to assume a mental position, to view the world from a particular position. The failure to discriminate the quite different positions we may assume has created considerable confusion in sensitivity training.

Figure 1 pictures four hills from which we may look at others: the rationalistic, the artistic, the practical, and the empirical. The bigness of the rationalistic and the smallness of the empirical suggests the relative dominance of these views in our usual thinking about people. The rationalistic approach is also pervaded by the subjective: "Of, related to, or determined by the mind, ego, or consciousness." The empirical view, on the other hand, stresses the objective, what is *independent* of mind, ego, or consciousness. With these distinctions in mind, we consider these varying mental postures in more detail.

Rationalistic Understanding

Rationalism, philosophically, is the opposite of empiricism. The rationalist acts as if his subjective impressions were a source of

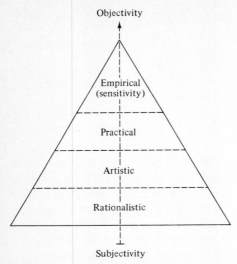

Figure 1 Ways of understanding a person

knowledge superior to and independent of empirical facts. He acts upon beliefs that have not been checked against such facts. Moreover, he believes that they do not need to be checked. He is, therefore, more interested in ideas than in facts, more loyal to his religious faith than to science. The empiricist puts his faith in what he can see, hear, and touch. He believes that valid knowledge can only be obtained by checking his subjective impressions against objective facts.

Rationalistic understanding, as we shall use the term, is *the degree to which a person FEELS close to, sympathetic with, and understanding of another person.* Here are some everyday examples reported by three college students:

> My oldest sister, who is twelve years older than me [sic], and I just don't get along. But when my grandfather died and she came for the funeral, we were really close for awhile. She knew that grandpa meant a great deal to me (much more than he did to her) and that I felt very sad about his death. She gave me spiritual strength and made me feel a lot better. For awhile we really understood each other.

> I had known Barbara for a long time but I never felt I understood her. But one night when she left dinner I saw that she was crying so I followed her to her room. She talked about things that get all of us down: unsympathetic parents, rotten grades, being forced to choose one boy friend and let the other go. Each was a petty trouble, but together they overwhelmed her. I pitied her but I didn't really feel close to her until she said, "This is all so shitty—I think I'll wash my hair." And she brought me with her so that together we could scrub her hair till it squeaked. I understood her then because she dealt with her personal problems the same way I

did. She forced them into herself until they hurt so bad that she had to physically comfort, to mother herself.

I really felt understanding for a person when I took a "blind walk." I was blindfolded and given instructions not to talk. I set out with a girl I had met only minutes before and we proceeded to walk across campus. At first, fear was the dominant feeling but this was erased by my understanding that this person was there and she cared enough to hold your hand and guide you across busy streets and up and down stairs. We walked for an hour and when I finally took off my blind-fold I was ready to ask her to marry me! To me, she was the sweetest thing on earth, when only an hour before she was nothing to me.

Rationalistic understanding is emotional, personal, and highly satisfying. The *only* measure of this kind of understanding is subjec-tive, i.e., we understand a person when we *feel* we understand him.

Philosophically, some are more rationalistic than others. Morris (1956) compared the rationalistic versus empirical values of college students in India, Norway, Japan, China, and the United States. Indian students were the most rationalistic; those in the United States, the most empirical. In rationalistic India, the physical body is viewed as an illusion and the spiritual body as reality. When Indians die they are cremated and their bones crushed to permit the release of the real body. In the more empirical United States, great efforts are made to preserve the material body.

Indian or American, psychologist or nonpsychologist, people are extremely rationalistic in their approach to other people. If 0 is taken as a purely rationalistic approach and 100 as a purely empirical one, it seems that few ever get above 10. An incident in the life of Galton (1909, p. 276) suggests the ease with which the rationalistic view can assert itself even in a scientist:

I had visited a large collection of idols gathered by missionaries from many lands, and wondered how each of those absurd and ill-made monstrosities could have obtained the hold it had over the imaginations of its worshippers. I wished, if possible, to enter into those feelings. It was difficult to find a suitable object for trial because it ought to be in itself quite unfitted to arouse devout feelings. I fixed on a comic picture. It was that of Punch, and I made believe in its possession of divine attributes. I addressed it with quasi-reverence as possessing a mighty power to reward or punish the behavior of men towards it, and found little difficulty in ignoring the impossibilities of what I professed. The experiment gradually succeeded; I began to feel and long retained for the picture a large share of the feelings that a barbarian entertains toward his idols, and learnt to appreciate the enormous potency they might have over him.

The rationalistic view asserts itself with similar ease in scientific settings. Masling (1957) asked eight graduate students to give the Rotter Incomplete Blank to two attractive girls and to interpret the results. Unknown to the students, the girls were asked to act warmly in half the examinations, coldly in the other half. The girls were also instructed in how to act warmly ("act interested in both the test situation and the examiner, make him feel comfortable and accepted") and how to act coldly ("be formal, disinterested, make him feel awkward and incompetent"). The Rotter test consists of a series of incomplete sentences like the following:

I feel . . .

Back home . . .

The best . . .

The personality diagnoses from the test are based on the answers given in completing the sentences. To make the answers constant, the two girls memorized the same answers and repeated them when the students gave them the test ("I feel *depressed,*" "Back home *in Indiana,*" and "The best *time is right now*"). The following is a typical interpretative sketch of the same girl making the same response when she was warm to a student and when she was cold:

Girl Is Warm:
She feels part of the family group . . . enjoys school very much . . . seems to be very conscientious and recognizes deficiencies within herself which she is trying to remedy . . . positively oriented toward the future . . . sensitive, introspective . . . likes people.

Girl Is Cold:
She has little insight or definition of her problem . . . frequently expresses considerable tension . . . goes on crying jags and feels sorry for herself . . . feels depressed . . . compulsively sets exacting standards for herself . . . lack of sympathy for others . . . uncomfortable in strongly affective situations and solves her problems by ignoring them and denying their existence.

In general, the author concluded, ". . . when the present subjects acted warm to an examiner, more positive statements were made about them than when they acted cold." The differences occurred in the face of the fact that the students were trained to be objective, were in a professional situation, and were interpreting the results of a semiobjective test.

The same person acting in the same way is judged differently when he is given a warm rather than a cold reputation. Three classes at the Massachusetts Institute of Technology were told that their regular instructor would not be able to attend and that a substitute would conduct the class (Kelley, 1950). They were also told: "He is twenty-six years old, a veteran and married. People who know him consider him to be a rather (_____) person, industrious, critical, practical, and determined." In some classes, the blank was filled in with the word "cold"; in others, with the word "warm," although it was the same instructor. Results: Less than a third of the students participated in class discussion when the instructor was described as cold; almost too-thirds participated when he was described as warm. After class, the warm instructor was rated by the students as more sociable, considerate, informal, and humorous.

Even the words "warm" and "cold" associated with, but not describing, a person seem to influence our judgments. Cofer and Dunn (1952) first had a group of fifteen students learn a list of words beginning: "Between, present, *cold*, . . ." and then had them rate twelve people from their photographs on eleven different traits. Another group of fifteen students followed exactly the same procedure except that "warm" was substituted for "cold" in the list. The group that had learned the "warm" list rated the people in the photographs as more altruistic, less restrained, more humane, more humorous, and more good-natured.

The goal of understanding, from the rationalistic view, is to intensify, illuminate, and harmonize one's emotional impressions of another person. The goal of scientific thought, on the other hand, is to discover relationships between one thing and other things about the person that result in more accurate predictions about him. The scientist seeks to eliminate personal, emotional, and subjective elements. From the rationalistic view, the idea of predictive accuracy seems cold, mechanical, irrelevant, and often incomprehensible.

Artistic Understanding

Rembrandt painted more than seventy portraits of himself. One in his forties suggests a sense of superiority and sardonic humor, one in his fifties his strength of character, and one in his sixties his declining vitality. Unlike the rationalistic Rembrandt, the artistic Rembrandt was not concerned with what he felt about himself but with what he actually looked like at each of these ages. Unlike the scientist who abstracts for the purpose of prediction, Rembrandt was concerned with compressing for the purpose of intensifying the immediate visual reality.

Artistic understanding, then, is *the degree to which a person is aware of and responsive to the visual, audible, and tangible aspects of a person.* Unlike rationalistic understanding, which stresses inner realities, artistic understanding stresses outer realities. Like the rationalist, however, the artist places his faith in his subjective impressions as the ultimate test of his understanding.

Who are the people who have high artistic understanding? Several hundred Yale students took an art judgment test consisting of 128 pairs of pictures projected by means of slides. The pairs were of similar theme and content. However, one of each pair had been unanimously chosen by a panel of fourteen art experts as reflecting greater artistic understanding. The same students also spent three hours taking a wide variety of personality tests. The scores of low and high scorers were contrasted. The following is a thumbnail sketch of a typical high scorer (Child, 1965):

. . . A person of actively inquiring mind, seeking out experience that may be challenging because of complexity or novelty, ever alert to the potential experience offered by stimuli not already in the focus of attention, interested in understanding each experience thoroughly and for its own sake rather than contemplating it superficially and promptly filing it away in a category.

Artists are often pained and bored by the empirical view. They see the scientist as impoverishing the complex reality of the person in his quest for predictive accuracy.

Practical Understanding

Practical understanding is *the degree to which one person can influence another to behave in a way that the first person desires.* The practical motive dominates this illustration (Coyle, 1955):

Mr. Coyle, I don't want to criticize you as a psychology teacher but you haven't taught this class one thing about how to fool an employer about our qualifications for the job—or how to pad our job resumes—or, for that matter, how to cut angles in general.

In one of several efforts to develop value consciousness, if not values themselves, Coyle assigned *What Makes Sammy Run?* as supplemental required reading. Subsequent class discussion of this book and polling revealed that a substantial majority considered Sammy "a pretty good guy," "smart," "nobody's fool," "definitely not a sucker." Several volunteered that they had learned a lot from Sammy that "would come in handy." The three or four students who spoke out against Sammy's values or "unifying philosophy of life" were "slychologized" by their classmates as being "jealous" or as lacking "the courage Sammy had."

The desire for practical understanding is not, of course, limited to exploitative situations. The mother may want her sick child to take medicine, the husband may want his fat wife to eat less, the teacher may want his student to learn, and the therapist may want his client to be more assertive. All these relationships have in common the aim of producing some immediate and objective change in another person. Here is an example of practical understanding reported by a college student:

My brother, Terry, and I were planning to take our vacations together to Montreal. We had everything planned except whose car we were going to take. I decided that we would not take my car. Since he is older and does not live at home, he would be a hard one to convince and besides that he is stubborn. I volunteered my car for the trip and told him about everything that was wrong with it: It needed new tires, motor tuning, and carburetor adjustment. I told him that it might delay our vacation and that he would have to share the costs of any repairs since I could not pay it all. Terry decided that we would go in his car. I really understand him.

The practical and the empirical are allied. What the practical man does in an unconscious, unsystematic, or incomplete way, the scientist does in a more conscious, systematic and comprehensive way.

Empirical Understanding

Empirical understanding, the focus of our concern, is *the degree to which one person can predict another person's feelings, thoughts, and behavior.* To discriminate it sharply from other kinds of understanding we shall refer to it as *sensitivity.* It is from an empirical view that Sherlocke Holmes and his brother, Mycroft, looked out of their club window at a dark man passing along the street (Doyle, 1965):

> "An old soldier, I perceive," said Sherlocke.
> "And very recently discharged," remarked the brother.
> "Served in India, I see."
> "And a non-commissioned officer."
> "Royal Artillery, I fancy," said Sherlocke.
> "And a widower."
> "But with a child."
> "Children, my dear boy, children."
> "Come," said I, laughing, "This is a little too much."
> "Surely," answered Holmes, "it is not hard to say that a man with that bearing, expression of authority, and sun-baked skin, is a soldier, is more than a private, and is not long from India."

How well the brothers understood the man depends upon the accuracy of the predictions they were making.

Predictive accuracy is not merely one test of empirical understanding, or even just a good test of it. It is, ultimately, the *only* test. Did Einstein understand the physical world? The answer lay in the ability of his theory to predict the course of the stars. Did Keynes understand the economic world? The answer lies in the ability of his economic theory to predict changes in the economic world. Did Freud understand man's psychological world? The answer lies in the ability of his psychoanalytic theory to predict human behavior. Wilson met this test (Cobb, 1944):

> I remember well, when acting as a clinical clerk at Queen Square for Kinnier Wilson, I saw him present a new case to a group of students in the out-patient clinic. I was seated at the table taking notes, Wilson was standing, having just dismissed a patient, and there was an empty chair beside my table. Wilson rang for the next patient, the door opened and a man entered, followed by his wife. He walked across the fifteen feet of classroom, smiled at the students and at me, and sat down. Wilson turned to me instantly and said, "Write G.P. (paresis) as the diagnosis." Probably my jaw dropped, for he went on "Well, Cobb, what else could it be? Here is a middle-aged man coming to a nerve clinic. He enters the room smiling, pushes ahead of his wife, does not take off his hat, takes the only chair without asking and likes an audience!"

Subsequent neurological and serological facts supported the correctness of his diagnosis.

In sum, our concern is with sensitivity, the empirical understanding of other people as measured by predictive accuracy. This concern does not assume that it is the only kind of understanding; it does not assume that it is the most important kind of understanding; it does not assume that empiricists have superior sensitivity. It does assume that sensitivity cannot be reduced to any other kind of understanding. It does assume that sensitivity has its own high and particular human value. And it does assume that sensitivity training requires that empirical understanding be as sharply differentiated from other kinds of understanding as possible.

These assumptions may be easy to understand in the abstract, but they are hard to practice. We do not act as if there were different ways of understanding people. The confirmed rationalist sees his understanding not only as the most important but also as the only kind. In turn the practical man, the artist, and the scientist each see their particular kind as the only kind. Each of us is daily and energetically engaged in the fruitless task of reducing other kinds of understanding to our kind. In this confusion of understandings, sensitivity (empirical and scientific understanding) is in the worst shape, for it is the most recent and the most fragile stance man has developed from which to view the world. Peirce (1957) defined the fundamental hypothesis of science as: "There are real things whose characters are entirely independent of our opinions about them." It was hard for mankind to accept the fact that the shape of the world was entirely independent of our opinion about it. It is still hard for us to accept that what a man is and will do is entirely independent of our opinion about what he is and will do. Our opinion of him may or may not fit the facts. However, the correctness of our opinions does not *determine* the facts. To repeat: It is to the development of this empirical kind of understanding and to the ability to discriminate it from other kinds that this book is exclusively devoted.

THE MEASUREMENT OF SENSITIVITY

Measurement is the first necessity of any kind of successful training. Without measures, we cannot select those who need training, design programs to meet the need, give trainees knowledge of the progress they are making, or evaluate the effectiveness of the training they have had. It is, therefore, to the hard questions involved in the measurement of sensitivity that we now turn: How should a person be presented to the predictors? What kinds of predictions should they be asked to make? How should they record their predictions? Most important of all, how is the goodness of the measure to be determined?

The development of The Test of Sensitivity (Table 1-1) required concrete answers to these questions. These answers are discussed below along with the alternative answers of other investigators. To begin with, the test does differentiate between those with low and high sensitivity. The mean score in a group of college students is about 51, but a tenth of them score less than 42 (36 is a chance score) while a tenth score above 59.

TABLE 1-1
The Test of Sensitivity

DIRECTIONS: How well can you predict the feelings and behavior of people? In each of the following actual cases some information is given about a person. Study the facts, then pick the answer to each statement that you think is correct. Circle "T" on the answer sheet if you think the statement is true; "F" if you think it is false. The correct answers are known from more complete information about the individuals.

Amos

Amos is the traffic manager for a Milwaukee brewery. He was promoted from the driver ranks and possesses a fourth-grade educational background. He is very loyal to the company and has high moral standards. When working in the ranks, he gained the reputation of being the hardest-working driver. He is a big man and says, "Hard work never hurt anyone."

T* F 1. He works ten to twelve hours a day and six to seven days a week.

T* F 2. He believes his employees should be paid on a commission basis.

T F* 3. He feels that the union's seniority rule is as good a basis as any for promoting helpers to drivers.

T* F 4. He tries to promote his product at all times, even to the point of losing friends.

Betty

Betty is the tall and slender receptionist of a university dean. Thirty-nine years old, she has top seniority among the seven girls in the office. The job requires that she meet the large number of students who have been asked to see the dean or who come to him for advice. She refers to students as "dumbbells," openly blames them for their errors, and swears when she is angry, which she often is.

T F* 5. She consults the other girls about the regulation of the heat and ventilation in the office.

T F* 6. She compliments the other girls when they do a good job.

T* F 7. She was an only child.

T F* 8. She is dependable about passing along phone messages she receives for the other girls.

Christopher

Christopher's parents live in a small western town where his father teaches school and his mother is a librarian. Both parents are shy and quiet, fond of reading and natural history. His brother, five years older, is now a lawyer. Christopher has always been thin

*Indicates correct answer.

TABLE 1-1, continued

and frail but seldom ill. He began to talk early, but did not walk early. He seldom cried and required little discipline as a child. His intelligence test scores are considerably above those of the average college student.

T   F*   9.   Christopher seldom daydreamed.

T   F*   10.   He enjoyed his school gang.

T*   F   11.   He feels that he is not a true participant in life.

T   F*   12.   While in college he went to many movies.

T*   F   13.   He creates imaginary friends.

T   F*   14.   He enjoyed high school activities.

T*   F   15.   Occasionally, when excited, he loses his voice.

T   F*   16.   His college grades are lower than the grades of other students of his intelligence.

Dorian

When he first came to Harvard Dorian was a tall, narrow-shouldered, twenty-four-year-old graduate student in engineering. He was born on a farm in Wisconsin, the youngest of a large family. He received most of his education at country schools until he entered engineering college. Recalling his family and childhood Dorian said, "My earliest impressions of life that I can remember now were to a large extent miserable. As a baby I was constantly ailing, apparently having one childhood disease after another, starting off with measles at the age of six weeks. Mother was an intelligent, gentle, loving woman, and was much thought of by friends and neighbors. My father was at times a brutal man and inclined, when drinking, to be unpleasant to me. At such times he would make fun of me, call me all sorts of unpleasant names and say that I probably wouldn't live the year out, and that it would be better if I didn't. My father had become an invalid, I forgot to mention before, shortly after mother died. He was in acute need of a job, for he had no money and was living on what he could borrow from a brother. He was earning his meals by working in a restaurant."

Dorian was one of fifty college students hired for an intensive study of personality at Harvard in the 1930s.

T*   F   17.   In an experiment involving a mild electric shock, Dorian was unusually disturbed.

T*   F   18.   He had some difficulty in recalling the names and ages of his brother and sisters.

T   F*   19.   Dorian was a good conversationalist.

T*   F   20.   He had recently become a Christian Scientist.

Edgar

Edgar is sixteen years old. A bit slight for his age, he is a medium-brown Negro boy, the oldest of four children in a middle-class New Orleans family. His mother is a physically powerful woman, religious, dominant, and thrifty. She has been the head of the family since the father deserted seven years ago. She insists on well-mannered and obedient children. Edgar's father was a semiskilled worker. Before he deserted the

*Indicates correct answers.

TABLE 1-1, continued

family the mother had decided that Edgar would be a doctor. Now she works to keep up appearances and to keep the children in school. Edgar was not to bring "lower-class" children home or to play with them. He had to stay in the yard after 4 P.M. His mother frequently used beatings in disciplining her children. In spite of money problems his mother arranged for Edgar to attend a private Negro prep school. He was above average intelligence and maintained good academic and athletic records throughout school.

T* F   21. He is severely punished by his mother when he exhibits curiosity about sex.

T F*   22. He shows few signs of anxiety or worry.

T* F   23. He saves his money to buy good clothes.

T F*   24. He feels strongly that lower-class Negroes are unfairly persecuted.

T* F   25. He says, "I'm as good as anybody in the world."

T* F   26. He is boastful.

T* F   27. He is verbally but not physically aggressive.

T F*   28. He is proud of his mother.

Frank

Frank entered Dartmouth College from a private school and graduated as an economics major. He was of slight build, average height, good health, a very superior intelligence. An observer who had known him and his family for a long time commented, "The only child of very admiring and doting parents, during his precollege life he was brought up to be a perfect gentleman; so much so, in fact, that he failed to reveal the usual boyish traits as completely as he should have. As he grew older, he veered from the exemplary behavior and developed a reputation of being a great ladies' man, driving somewhat recklessly, and being indifferent to the serious aspects of living. At times, his appearance is very smooth, and then again he is quite neglectful and looks extremely seedy. The mother has been a semi-invalid during all of the boy's life and has dominated him, and I believe imposed upon him beyond reason."

T* F   29. When asked what superpoliteness expressed, he replied, "contempt!"

T* F   30. Fellow students think of him as a "snob."

T F*   31. Frank received high grades in college.

T F*   32. Frank has few artistic interests.

George

George was the second son of Irish immigrant parents who had grade school educations. His father's earnings were meager at first but improved when encouraged by his wife. He invested a small inheritance in a flower shop. George's mother felt that education was less important than religion, but necessary for getting ahead socially. She was very affectionate, but dominating. George's parents decided he should be a doctor. His father was rather passive, but capable of outbursts. Punishment of the children was severe. It included shaming, denying of affection, spanking, and denying

*Indicates correct answer.

TABLE 1-1, continued

of pleasure. As a child George was his parents' favorite, and was often the center of attraction. He was good-looking, and was considerably above average intelligence. Later, however, he lost favor when his brothers made more social progress.

T   F*   33. He found it easy to make decisions.

T*   F   34. He had very strong guilt feelings about masturbation.

T*   F   35. He acted childish in high school.

T*   F   36. He was a "show-off" in kindergarten.

T*   F   37. He bragged about his sexual conquests.

T*   F   38. He bragged about being so young in high school.

T   F*   39. He was very studious.

T   F*   40. He found it much easier to get along with boys than girls.

Mrs. Harrison

Margaret Harrison is the owner and manager of an independent woman's ready-to-wear shop in a suburb of Cleveland. She also does all the buying, which means leaving the shop in charge of a saleswoman twice a year while she is in New York. She is married to a man who is lame. Because of this he has refused to work for quite some time. He does odd jobs around the store and gives orders to the employees. He drinks heavily. Mrs. Harrison is about fifty-five years old. She is large, sturdy, and extremely intelligent. She has had a great deal of experience in the retail field. She is in the upper middle class. She is industrious and ambitious, but has a quick temper and never admits a mistake.

There are five saleswomen, two maids, and ten alteration women working for her. They receive excellent pay and work from 9:00 A.M. to 5:30 P.M. with an hour off for lunch. The merchandise in the shop is extremely high-priced, and consequently the customers are very wealthy, high-society people.

T   F*   41. Mrs. Harrison is liked by her employees.

T*   F   42. She is constantly enlarging her shop.

T   F*   43. She let her employees take a ten-minute break in the afternoon.

T*   F   44. She doesn't hesitate to state her opinion if she disagrees with a customer's taste in clothes.

John

John at fifteen was five feet four and weighed 105 pounds. He had a childhood record of ill health. John was usually reserved but sometimes expressed himself forcefully. He was not at home in social gatherings, though he often attended. He enjoyed talking about books, art, politics, and movie stars. He got good marks in literature and language, but poor ones in math. John grew up in a middle-class suburban area. His father provides a modest income as a plumber. He is patient and friendly with John. John's mother, the dominant figure in the household, is often apprehensive about his safety and demands much of his time.

T*   F   45. John is unusually fearful of his emotional impulses.

*Indicates correct answer.

TABLE 1-1, continued

T* F 46. John stated, "I wish my mother could be happier."

T F* 47. John saw himself as seldom worrying about things which he had done, but never told to anyone.

T F* 48. John felt that radical agitators should not be allowed to make public speeches.

Karl

Karl, a Dartmouth student, was a cheery, sociable, and conventional young man of average intelligence who was earnest and diligent in his college work. He graduated, however, in the lowest tenth of his class. He had considerable feelings of inferiority and has a fear of making independent judgments. His completions of incomplete sentences ("artificial as *the ice cream in a soda fountain window*," "exciting as *a battle between a mongoose and a cobra*," "idealistic as *the life of a nun*," etc.) indicated that Karl had a creative capacity that had not been used in his academic work. Both of his parents were talented musicians but he could not carry a tune or play an instrument.

T* F 49. In his autobiography he wrote that he was "the most even-tempered cuss that has ever walked on two feet."

T* F 50. About the same number of friends described him as "even-tempered" as described him as "quick-tempered".

T* F 51. Karl was unable to organize and present ideas clearly.

T F* 52. He clearly distinguished between what he thought from what others expected him to think.

The Lawrences

William Lawrence, twenty-four, and Laura, twenty-three, have been married for a year and a half. Both his and her parents had approved of their marriage. Their parents were foreign-born, were similar in social and economic backgrounds, and lived in the same community. At the time of their marriage, William had had only irregular employment since his graduation from high school. William is proud of his dead mother. She had run her husband's affairs, planned her seven children's vocational and social activities, and faced death with an unsagging spirit. The youngest of his three sisters, all of whom were much like their mother, took care of him when their mother died. Laura, although she wanted to teach kindergarten, had worked as a store clerk for two years before her marriage and continued to work at the same job afterward. Her father had been a successful merchant. However, he developed an interest in gambling and had given up several good positions impulsively. He often gave Laura and her mother tongue lashings. Her mother was patient and long suffering. The Lawrences had few friends and belonged to no social organizations.

T* F 53. William expected his wife to do many things for him.

T* F 54. His mother was also named Laura.

T* F 55. He feels that his childhood was happy.

T F* 56. He knows that he wants to depend on his wife as he used to depend upon his mother and sisters.

T* F 57. William commenting on getting married, said, "With superhuman

*Indicates correct answer.

TABLE 1-1, continued

effort I forced myself to go to the courthouse and say, 'I want a license.'"

T   F*   58. Laura continued to respect her father even after he had ceased to support the family.

T*   F   59. William considers his marriage a mistake.

T   F*   60. William still greatly admires his wife's appearance and personality.

The Medford Twins

Earl and Frank, identical twins, were born in a Midwestern city, of uneducated and unmarried parents. When the boys were six months old, they were turned over to their mother's sister. She kept Frank but placed Earl with a family who had advertised their wish to board a baby. This family soon assumed full responsibility for Earl and took him to a city in the Northwest without consulting the aunt of the two boys. Earl's foster father was a college graduate and a successful salesman; Frank's a streetcar conductor. Earl graduated from college; Frank attended high school only six months, though later he attended night school. Earl was raised in comfort; Frank was brought up by his fond aunt with little economic security in the neighborhood where he was born. Both twins had happy homes with only moderate discipline.

They were both interviewed and tested by psychologists in 1941 when they were thirty-seven years old. The twins were remarkably similar in many respects: same height, same color hair, same fingerprints, same good health, same poor spelling, same ratings on many personality traits, very similar vocational interest scores, etc. In some respects, however, they were different. For each of the statements indicate the name of the twin to whom you think the statement applies.

Mark "1" for Earl and "2" for Frank.

1   2*   61. Was less pompous and affected.

1   2*   62. Said that what he wished for most was the happiness of his family.

1*   2   63. Was more eager to impress people.

1*   2   64. Said that what he wanted most in life was a good business with men working for him.

1   2*   65. Was more emotional.

1*   2   66. Was more timid and self-conscious.

1*   2   67. Was more disturbed by his failure to achieve his ambitions.

1   2*   68. Was more friendly in his personal relations.

The Nelson Twins

Fred and John, identical twins, had very similar backgrounds and personality. Their father, an unsuccessful and alcoholic son of a well-to-do father, had gone to Cuba to make his fortune. He failed there as a farmer and also failed in Florida where the family had moved when the boys were four years old. He eventually returned to New England to live with the twins' grandmother. The mother of the twins was industrious and long-suffering. Though she was, for the most part, responsible for rearing the children, their father was sporadically a demanding and cruel disciplinarian. The twins left

*Indicates correct answer.

TABLE 1-1, continued

school after the eighth grade and went to work in the same factory on semiskilled jobs. They are working at identical jobs today. They have the same eye and hair color, and look very much alike. Both have type O and RH positive blood. Both are shy, dependent, passive, and anxious.

The twins came to the attention of physicians at the age of forty-six because John had developed a severe duodenal ulcer while Fred remained in good health. For each of the statements below indicate the name of the twin to whom you think the statement applies.

Mark "1" for Fred and "2" for John.

1* 2   69. Had better understanding of himself and of other people.

1* 2   70. Was more optimistic.

1   2*   71. Showed greater hatred of his father.

1* 2   72. Described his wife as a good cook and mother.

1   2*   73. While the level of gastric secretion was much higher than normal in both twins, his level was higher than his brother's.

1   2*   74. Was more resentful that their mother had not given them more from the $100,000 she inherited about ten years ago.

1* 2   75. Was a warmer and more tender person.

1* 2   76. Was readier to accept blame.

*Indicates correct answer.

Before discussing these answers, the reader needs to be alerted to the fact that this book will have much to do with tables. These tables are numerous, many are long, some (like Table 1-1) are tests, others are scales, and still others give details of training procedures. The fundamental reason for their inclusion is our conviction that the reader will get more out of generalizations related to specifics than he would from generalizations alone. The specifics can give him a more concrete appreciation of the problems being discussed as well as an embarrassingly quick grasp of the limitations of our present knowledge about many of them. The tables also give the researcher and the trainer tools that he can immediately and conveniently utilize. The reader, however, will need to adapt his review of these materials to his own immediate purpose. If this purpose is to understand the text, in most tables it will only be necessary to read the introduction and a few examples. In Table 1-1, for example, he need only read through Amos.

How Should the Person Be Presented?

The answer of the test: by thumbnail sketches. Investigators have more frequently used such sketches than filmed interviews, photographs, or taped interviews. However, face-to-face interactions have been more often used than all other methods combined. They have the virtue of being closest to everyday reality. From a measurement point of view, however, the method presents almost insurmountable obstacles: The same person is not presented to different judges in the same way; the method is time-consuming; and experiments using the method cannot be duplicated because a person appears in a face-to-face study and then disappears, seldom being available again.

Photographs, while quite practical, are so limited in the amount of information they give judges that they are useful for only limited purposes. Tests based on written records can be made quite reliable, are easy to develop, and are flexible in use. They have less face validity than the taped interview and much less than the filmed interview. The development of film tests, on the other hand, is expensive; once developed, however, they are simple and convenient to use.

The measure of sensitivity with the greatest generality would expose judges to a large and heterogeneous sample of people by different methods: personal interaction, written records, taped interview, sound film, etc. Making such measurements, however, is severely restricted by the small number of suitable tests available as well by the limited time that a group of perceivers has available to complete them. For this reason, few experimenters have used more than one method of presentation. Some have used only one person to be judged, most have used several, and practically none have used more than ten.

What Kind of Predictions Should the Predictor Make?

The Sensitivity Test required predictions of all the following types except those of the first person:

First Person   What does he think of *me*?
Examples: He thinks I am a snob. He doesn't like me.

Second Person   What does he think of *himself*?
Examples: He feels that he is not a true participant in life. John saw himself as seldom worrying about things which he had done, but never told to anyone.

Third Person   What do other people think of him?
Examples: Fellow students think of him as a snob. He shows few signs of anxiety or worry.

Nonpersonal   How does he behave?
Examples: He works ten to twelve hours a day and six to seven days a week. His college grades are lower than the grades of other students of his intelligence.

First-person predictions are omitted because we cannot sensibly ask a judge to predict what a person described in a written case thinks of the judge.

First-person prediction measures are limited to personal interactions. Such measures are awkward to plan and time-consuming to make. Yet self-insight, a highly prized human trait, is measured through determining the accuracy of first-person predictions. Furthermore, what we think a person thinks of us has a decisive influence on what we think of him.

A convincing case can be made for the importance of second- and third-person sensitivity, at least in certain situations. It is, for example, vital for the psychotherapist to understand what the client thinks of himself (second person). In most human relations situations it is equally vital to know what others think—rightly or wrongly—of a person.

The most convincing test of the reality of a person is what he actually *does.* It is difficult to construct a good measure based on predicting actual behavior, although with increasing frequency investigators are developing such measures (Cline and Richards, 1960; Soskin, 1959; Weiss, 1963). The ideal measure would include subscores for each type of prediction.

How Is the Accuracy of the Prediction to Be Determined?

In everyday life, our answer to this question is commonly the rationalistic one: By whether his prediction agrees with ours. Psychologists and other professionals seem to be particularly susceptible to this kind of answer. Mahoney (1960), for example, developed a sensitivity test that consisted of four selections from fiction portraying markedly different personalities. Those taking the test are instructed to read the selection, to get a "feel" for the individual portrayed, and then to complete twenty multiple-choice incomplete statements as they think the individual in the selection would have completed them. Mahoney gave the test to twenty-three psychologists who had been picked as being particularly sensitive people. The answer they gave most often was taken as the correct one. The internal consistencies and stabilities of scores on the test were quite high: a respondent who agreed with the experts on one question at one time agreed with the experts on other questions at other times. So the test was reliable, but was it valid, i.e., did the answers of the experts agree with the answers that the fictional personalities would have given? There is no empirical way of knowing.

How can I empirically test my predictions about what another person thinks of me? By asking him. How can I test my predictions about what another person thinks of himself? By asking him. How can I test my predictions about what other people think of him? By asking them. How can I test my predictions about how he will behave? By comparing them with his actual behavior. The empirical approach to correct answers is being used with increasing frequency.

How Should Predictions Be Recorded?

Ratings are by far the most frequent way that investigators have asked judges to record their predictions. A method using objective questions, either of the multiple-choice or the true-false type, is also common and is the one used in the Sensitivity Test. The matching method, which requires the judge to match some data about a person with some other data about a person, has also sometimes been used. The matching method has substantial merits: it is flexible, it generally seems realistic to the judges, and it seems close to the global way in which we naturally form impressions of people.

In general, the recording method, which may seem to be an unimportant matter, has a profound influence on the accuracy of predictions. Analysis of this influence, for example, leads to the conclusion that ratings provide too much freedom for individual differences in rationalistic understanding to operate. Consequently, they should be avoided, not only in the construction of sensitivity tests but also in any situation where empirical understanding is the goal.

How Reliable Is the Test?

In developing the test it was assumed that the wider the range of people presented and the wider the range of facts provided about them, the better the measure would be. The test, therefore, involves sixteen people: men and women, young and old, educated and uneducated. Most of them are described in detailed case studies by psychologists. Amos, however, was described by his son, Betty by a neighbor, and Mrs. Harrison by an employee.

Internal consistency is the degree to which different parts of a measure agree with each other. A ruler on which the distance from two to three inches is not the same as the distance from three to four inches would lack internal consistency. A sensitivity test on which those who did well on the first half of the test did not do well on the second half would lack internal consistency. A common way of measuring the internal consistency of a test is to obtain two subscores: the first, by adding the odd-numbered items; the second, by adding the even-numbered items. The higher the correlation between these two parts of the test, the higher its internal consistency.

The most common reason for the low reliability of sensitivity tests is that the predictive tasks are so hard that the respondents can only guess. Sometimes items are ambiguously worded. Whatever the reason, if scores on parts of the test are not related to each other, scores on the whole test are extremely unlikely to be related to anything else. The Sensitivity Test does have adequate reliability, for the scores on the odd and even items have a correlation of about .70.

The internal consistency of the test was achieved with the aid of item analysis. In applying this technique, a group first made a large number of predictions about each case. For Amos, for example, forty predictions were made. The individual answers of the fourth of the group that made the most accurate predictions overall were then compared with the fourth of the group that made the least accurate ones. The percentage of these two groups getting each of the forty items correct was compared. If the poor group got it right more often, it was discarded. If both groups got it right about equally often, it was also discarded. Those items that best discriminated between the poor and the good group were retained. This process eliminates items that are too easy, too hard, or too ambiguous. The cases of Betty, Christopher, and so on were treated in the same way. Finally, all the revised cases were answered by another large group and the item-analysis process repeated. As a result, each item in each of the cases is consistent with the whole. That is, the group that does well on the test as a whole does well on each of the individual items.

How Stable Is the Test?

Stability, or repeat reliability, is the degree of agreement between scores on the same measure taken at two different times. The stability of scores is important, for it is almost useless to know that a person is highly sensitive today if he is going to be insensitive tomorrow. The repeat reliability of the Sensitivity Test was determined by having groups of the same students take the test on two different occasions several months apart. It is possible, but not likely, for a test to have high internal consistency and low repeat reliability. In the case of the present test, the median correlations of scores for people retaking the test was also about .70.

How Practical Is the Test?

The test is easily completed in three-quarters of an hour and can be machine-scored. These practical advantages increase the likelihood that the test will be validated. A test never has only one possible validity; it has many. A test of sensitivity may be assumed to measure many things: knowledge of psychology, range of experiences with people, leadership competence, success as a psychotherapist, personal maturity, performance as a school teacher, etc. The easier it is to determine the truth of these assumptions, the better.

How Valid Is the Test?

Validity is the degree to which a measure is actually measuring what it is supposed to measure. Now a sensitivity test that violates common sense, lacks internal consistency, and lacks repeat reliability cannot be valid. The more realistic it seems and the higher internal consistency and repeat reliability it has, the more likely it is to be valid. However, a test can have all of these qualities and still lack validity. The most convincing index of the validity of a measure is a high correlation with an independent measure of what it is supposed to be measuring.

But where is one to obtain such an independent measure of sensitivity? The test was developed in the first place because there were no adequate measures available. One way around this dilemma is to compare the scores of groups one would expect to differ in their sensitivity. Thus one might compare those who had had no psychology courses with those who had had a great many. However, as we shall see in the next chapter, these groups actually do not differ in their sensitivity. Perhaps the best possibility would be to compare sensitive and insensitive groups made up by obtaining nominations from intimates. Thus far, this method has not been tried.

The validity of the test may be seriously challenged from a quite different quarter. It assumes that sensitivity is a general ability. It stresses, therefore, what is *common* to making true or false predictions about different people in different situations. If we assume, however, that sensitivity is not a general ability but is made up of unrelated components, we would follow a quite different path. We would then look not for what different predictions about different people have in common but what they have that is different.

COMPONENTS OF SENSITIVITY

Is sensitivity one ability or many? Is a person's degree of empirical understanding best viewed as determined by a single ability or as determined by many relatively independent components? A "component" is a separable part of a whole that fits with other parts to determine the functioning of the whole. Thus the engine, wheels, and chassis are independent parts of a car that fit together to determine the mechanical functioning of the whole. The head, heart, and lungs are body components that fit together to determine physiological functioning. Verbal comprehension, rote memory, and reasoning are components of intelligence that determine intellectual functioning.

Until 1938, it was assumed that intelligence was a general ability. In this year, Thurstone published his analysis of intelligence tests. The analysis revealed that intelligence tests were widely varying mixtures of such primary mental abilities as verbal comprehension, word fluency, numerical ability, space ability, memory ability, perceptual ability, and reasoning ability. These abilities are so loosely related that it is quite possible to be high on one and low on others. Thus a person may have a high verbal comprehension and low rote memory, high space ability and low word fluency.

The fight between the generalists and the particularists over intelligence has subsided. It is still with us in the measurement of sensitivity. Cronbach (1955), after a mathematically sophisticated and involved analysis of ratings made by judges of others, concludes:

> Social perception research has been dominated by simple, operationally defined measures. Our analysis has shown that any such measure may combine and thereby conceal important variables, or may depend heavily on unwanted components. Only by careful subdivision of global measures can an investigator hope to know what he is dealing with.

Crow and Hammond (1957) reached a particularistic conclusion as a result of their study of fifteen different kinds of predictions made by sixty-five medical students of patients they saw on sound films:

> Failure to find support for the hypothesis of a general ability of interpersonal perceptiveness in this study makes the assumption of generality untenable. Consequently, comparison of the results of interpersonal studies based on different measuring techniques can be justified only when the comparability of such results has been empirically demonstrated.

Cline and Richards (1960), however, tend to side with the generalists. Their conclusion was based upon an analysis of a wide range of predictions about people also presented on sound films:

> The results of this study, in other words, indicate that there is a general ability to perceive others accurately. This general ability, however, consists of two (at least) independent parts: Sensitivity to the Generalized Other and Interpersonal Sensitivity. . . . It may appear paradoxical (or inappropriate) to conclude that at the same time the ability to perceive others accurately is general and that it consists of two independent components. The authors are of the opinion, however, that these seemingly conflicting conclusions mean that the ability to perceive others accurately is factorially complex and that the independent components reflect this complexity.

Should we take a general or a component view of sensitivity? The answer depends, in part, on whether the purpose is to select sensitive people or to train them. If selection is the aim, then the general answer is to be favored. What we wish in selection is to place individuals on a single scale that ranges from the least to the most sensitive. If training is the aim, however, then a component view is extremely helpful. Viewing sensitivity as a general ability gives us no clues as to where to begin training, what to train for, or how to train.

Figure 2 summarizes the four components that form the framework for the present book. They grow from studies of sensitivity components by others and from the author's efforts to translate their results into effective training programs.

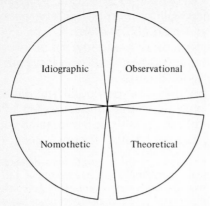

Figure 2   Components of sensitivity

Observational Sensitivity

"Observation" has both abstract and specific meanings. Abstractly, it is the act of noticing or perceiving. Specifically, it is "a game in which players examine an assortment of articles for a short time and then write down the names of as many of the objects as they can remember." We define and shall use observational sensitivity in a specific way as *the ability to look at and listen to another person and remember what he looked like and said.*

Observation is sometimes pictured as a quite passive affair: the eye is a motion-picture camera; the ear, a tape recorder. What we see a person do and hear him say is transcribed on the slate of our awareness. The records are then sorted, edited, and evaluated. No picture could be further from the truth, for we do not observe people; we perceive them. And we perceive what we want to perceive, what we expect to perceive, and what we have learned to perceive.

Perceivers differ widely in their ability to discriminate what they see and hear from what they feel and infer about a person. It is an important task of training to develop the ability to make such discriminations.

Theoretical Sensitivity

Theoretical sensitivity is *the ability to select and use theories to make more accurate predictions about others.* A theory is a set of concepts with assumptions regarding the relationships between them. Innumerable explicit, dynamic, and interpersonal theories are available as aids to improve our understanding of sensitivity and to improve sensitivity. At the moment, for instance, we are describing a component theory of sensitivity that involves four concepts and assumes that these components are relatively independent of each other.

While trainees resist using observation, they use theories with alacrity. Shapiro (1964), for example, has reported on his six years of experience in the teaching of observational skills in child psychiatry to fourth-year medical students. It consists of six two-hour sessions. The first three are based on twenty-minute edited tapes of family interactions, the fourth consists of observing a child in play therapy through a one-way screen, and the last two consist of observing the instructor interviewing members of a family. In commenting on the course, the instructor says:

> The students tend to interpret the observed facts in terms of such theoretical concepts as Oedipus complex, penis envy, or castration anxiety. It is the instructor's task to hold them to an accurate description of behavior first, before they try to account for it. They soon discover that sharp disagreement often develops over simple behavioral terms. It is not easy to notice that a father uses words his son does not understand.

The critical problem in theoretical training is not that of learning a theory; it is selecting and learning to use one in a way that actually improves sensitivity.

Nomothetic Sensitivity

Nomothetic sensitivity is *the ability to learn about the typical member of a group and to use this knowledge in making more accurate predictions about individuals in that group.* Allport (1937) first introduced the word to American psychologists (p. 22):

> The philosopher Windelband proposed to separate the nomothetic from the idiographic disciplines. The former, he held, seek only general laws and employ only those procedures admitted by the exact sciences. Psychology in the main has been striving to make itself a completely nomothetic discipline. The idiographic sciences such as history, biography, and literature, on the other hand, endeavor to understand some particular event in nature or in society. A psychology of individuality would be essentially idiographic.
>
> The dichotomy, however, is too sharp: it requires a psychology divided against itself. . . . It is more helpful to regard the two methods as overlapping and as contributing to one another. In the field of medicine, diagnosis and therapy are idiographic procedures, but both rest intimately upon a knowledge of the common factors in disease, determined by the nomothetic sciences of bacteriology and biochemistry. Likewise, biography is clearly idiographic, and yet in the best biographies one finds an artful blend of generalization with individual portraiture. A complete study of the individual will embrace both approaches.

Our predictions about a particular woman are influenced by our nomothetic knowledge of women in general; of a particular Catholic, by our nomothetic knowledge of Catholics; and of a particular Russian, by our nomothetic knowledge of Russians. A person's nomothetic sensitivity is determined by both the amount of knowledge he has about a group and by his ability to apply it.

Nomothetic sensitivity is firmly established as a component. It is almost identical with what the analytical studies of Cronbach (1955) and Cline and Richards (1960) refer to as "Sensitivity to the Generalized Other". One reason for the confident establishment of the component is that its influence on predictions is often overwhelming. A group of student judges, as a typical example, was told only the general category of a series of students: undergraduate male education major, graduate female art student, etc. They then filled out an interest inventory as they thought each student had filled it out. Next the judges observed each student as he described the room he was in, made a drawing at the blackboard, and engaged in several other expressive acts. After seeing each student, the judges again filled out the interest inventory as they thought the student had filled it out. The predictions were *more* accurate based on the nomothetic information alone (Stone, Leavitt, and Gage, 1957).

Stereotypes are standardized mental pictures, often erroneous, of groups. The following incident suggests the power that stereotypes have to resist formal training (Lamming, 1960):

> *I would recall an episode on a ship which had brought a number of West Indians to Britain. I was talking to a Trinidadian civil servant who had come "to take something called a Devonshire course." A man about forty to forty-five, intelligent enough to be in the senior grade of the Trinidad Civil Service, which is by no means backward, a man of some substance among his own class of people. We were talking in a general way about life among the emigrants. The ship was now steady; the tugs were coming along side. Suddenly there was consternation in the Trinidadian's expression.*
>
> *"But . . . but," he said, "look down there."*
>
> *I looked, and since I had lived six years in England I failed to see anything of particular significance. I asked him what he had seen: and then I realized what was happening.*
>
> *"They* do *that kind of work, too?" he asked. He meant the white hands and faces on the tug. In spite of films, in spite of reading Dickens—for he would have had to at the school which trained him for the Civil Service—in spite of all this received information, this man had never really felt, as a possibility and a fact, the existence of the English worker. This sudden bewilderment had sprung from his idea of England; and one element in that idea was that he had never seen an Englishman working with his hands in the streets of Port of Spain.*

Idiographic Sensitivity

Here are some of the major differences between the defenders of an idiographic against a nomothetic approach to understanding (Sarbin, Taft, and Bailey, 1960):

1 The defenders of uniqueness aim at an artistic "understanding" of a person rather than the construction of statistical-general laws.

2 They are interested in the "whole" personality rather than part of it.

3   They focus on the person as an individual rather than as a member of the class.

4   They favor intuition rather than logical analysis as a method.

5   They stress combining impressions into patterns rather than adding them.

To use idiographic sensitivity as a component, however, it is vital that it be defined and measured in a way that sharply differentiates it from observational, theoretical, and nomothetic sensitivity. Cronbach (1955), Crow and Hammond (1957), and Cline and Richards (1960) define and measure nomothetic sensitivity as predictive accuracy arising from knowing what the typical member of a group is like and using this knowledge in making accurate predictions about individual members of the group. Idiographic sensitivity they then define as accuracy arising from knowing in what ways the individual member is *different* from his group. However, such a definition does not discriminate idiographic sensitivity from either observational or theoretical sensitivity.

For this reason, we define idiographic sensitivity as the *ability to use increasing exposure to and information about a person in making increasingly accurate predictions about him.* The definition assumes that people who are equal in their observational, theoretical, and nomothetic sensitivity and make equally accurate predictions about a person after a brief acquaintance with him may differ a great deal after long acquaintance. Thus couples who were equally sensitive to each other at marriage may differ a great deal after twenty years of marriage.

Less is known about idiographic sensitivity than any of the other components. The vast majority of studies of sensitivity, for reasons of experimental convenience, have exposed the person to be predicted to the predictors for less than an hour; many, for only a few minutes. A few studies have concerned themselves with the sensitivity of married couples but none of these have traced the development of sensitivity over the relationship. Teachers have occasionally determined improvements in the sensitivity of their students to them over the period of a course and counselors have occasionally determined improvements in their sensitivity to their clients over the period of the psychotherapy.

The four components divide the book: Part Two, Observational Sensitivity; Part Three, Theoretical Sensitivity; Part Four, Nomothetic Sensitivity; and Part Five, Idiographic Sensitivity. Within each part, the first chapter seeks to understand the component and how it works; the second chapter explores new methods of applying this understanding to the improvement of sensitivity training. The next chapter describes present methods of training to develop sensitivity and attempts to account for their failure to do so.

CHAPTER 2

TRAINING METHODS

SCIENTISTS in many disciplines aspire to improve man's understanding of his fellow men. Anthropologists strive to improve his understanding of men in different cultures; sociologists, of men from different social backgrounds; economists, of men playing different occupational roles; political scientists, of men in different governments. It is to psychologists, however, that students turn to increase their understanding of the individuals they meet in their daily lives.

A wave of educational effort with mounting enrollments reflect this trend. The number of college students being graduated annually with a major in psychology is now approaching 10,000 and the total far exceeds 100,000. In 1949, 4 percent of those who were granted a Ph.D. received it in psychology; by 1959, the percentage had doubled, largely because of the increasing demand for clinical psychologists. T-group training, a dot on the horizon a decade ago, is now high in the skies.

T-group participation, course instruction, and clinical training are the general methods that psychologists are using to improve sensitivity. Table 2-1 shows these methods and suggests the component goals of sensitivity that they do and do not aim to reach. This chapter describes briefly each of these methods, presents evidence of their ineffectiveness, and offers guidelines for the development of more effective programs.

TABLE 2-1
Types of Training and Their Goals

Goals of Training	T-Group Participation	Psychology Instruction	Clinical Training
Observational Sensitivity	Yes	No	Yes
Theoretical Sensitivity	No	Yes	Yes
Nomothetic Sensitivity	No	Yes	Yes
Idiographic Sensitivity	Yes	No	Yes

T-GROUP PARTICIPATION

In 1946 psychologists at the Massachusetts Institute of Technology discovered the T-group idea while running a two-week workshop aimed at reducing tensions in Connecticut communities. Some of the members attending overheard the staff listening to and discussing tapes of the sessions in which they had participated. They thought it was the most valuable part of the workshop. Thus was born the basic T(training)-group idea—to have participants discuss themselves and the ways they see themselves relating to each other in a small, unstructured, face-to-face group.

The idea is flexible and is called by a variety of other names, including sensitivity-, laboratory-, and encounter-group training. The activities of these groups are never planned in advance. The role of the leader varies but never includes forceful direction of the group's activities. The T group stresses "emotional learning" rather than intellectual learning. It stresses the "here and now" rather than the there and then.

The following description of one part of one training session suggests how the groups function (Tannenbaum, Weschler, and Massarik, 1961, p. 123):

> At the fifth meeting the group's feelings about its own progress became the initial focus of discussion. The "talkers" participated as usual, conversation shifting rapidly from one point to another. Dissatisfaction was mounting, expressed through loud, snide remarks by some and through apathy by others.
>
> George Franklin appeared particularly disturbed. Finally pounding the table, he exclaimed, "I don't know what is going on here! I should be paid for listening to this drivel? I'm getting just a bit sick of wasting my time here. If the profs don't put out—I quit!" George was pleased; he was angry, and he had said so. As he sat back in his chair, he felt he had the group behind him. He felt he had the guts to say what most of the others were thinking! Some members of the group applauded loudly, but others showed obvious disapproval. They wondered why George was excited over so insignificant an issue, why he hadn't done something constructive rather than just sounding off as usual. Why, they wondered, did he say their comments were "drivel"?
>
> George Franklin became the focus of discussion. "What do you mean, George, by saying this is nonsense?" "What do you expect, a neat set of rules to meet all your problems?" George was getting uncomfortable. These were questions difficult for him to answer. Gradually he began to realize that a large part of the group disagreed with him; then he began to wonder why. He was learning something about people he hadn't known before. " . . . How does it feel, George, to have people disagree with you when you thought you had them behind you? . . . "
>
> Bob White was first annoyed with George and now with the discussion. He was getting tense, a bit shaky perhaps. Bob didn't like anybody to get a raw deal, and he felt that George was getting it. At first Bob tried to minimize George's outburst, and then he suggested that the group get on to the real issues; but the group continued to focus on George. Finally Bob said, "Why don't you leave George alone and stop picking on him? We're not getting anywhere this way."
>
> With the help of the leaders, the group focused on Bob. "What do you mean, 'picking' on him?" "Why, Bob, have you tried to change the discussion?" "Why are you so protective of George?" Bob began to realize that the group wanted to

focus on George; he also saw that George didn't think he was being picked on, but felt he was learning something about himself and how others reacted to him. "Why do I always get upset," Bob began to wonder, "when people start to look at each other? Why do I feel sort of sick when people get angry at each other?" . . . Now Bob was learning something about how people saw him, while gaining some insight into his own behavior.

The development of sensitivity is only one goal of the training. Others include the development of self-insight, awareness of group processes, and skill in intervening constructively in group activities. Behind these goals are less explicit but more comprehensive ones: The development of a spirit of inquiry about one's role in the world, of an expanded "interpersonal consciousness," and of "authenticity" in interpersonal relationships. In general, it is unclear what outcomes are expected from any specific T-group effort: Increased awareness? Increased knowledge? Changes in values? Changes in attitudes? Changes in motivation? Changes in behavior? Changes in job performance? Increases in sensitivity?

Our concern is with sensitivity: Do T-group experiences increase the predictive accuracy of trainees? The following four studies used objective measures to determine whether T-group training improved the ability of participants to predict the behavior of (1) their leader, (2) individual members of the group, (3) the group as a whole, and (4) individuals outside of the group.

Three T groups with about twenty college students in each group met for several hours each week for sixteen weeks (Lohmann, Zenger, and Weschler, 1959). At the beginning, the three trainers completed the Gordon Personality Profile. It provides measures of ascendancy, responsibility, emotional stability, sociability, and general adjustment. The students took the same test. They also twice completed the test as they thought their own leader had filled it out, first at the beginning and then at the end of the training. There was only a slight gain in accuracy. Even this gain resulted from an artifact. The trainees judged their trainer more favorably at the beginning than they did at the end. The trainers actually had a modest view of themselves. The final and less favorable judgments of the students of him, therefore, were closer to his own estimate of himself. One might expect the members of any group to learn that much about their leader in sixteen weeks.

A T group composed of nine college men and three women met for several hours a week for four months (Bennis et al., 1957). They were given a list of descriptions of how they might behave in a group ("energizer," "changer," "help-seeker," "compromiser," etc.) and asked to sort them into one of two categories: "like me in a group" or "not like me in a group." Each member also sorted the descriptions as they thought each of the other members would sort them, first at the beginning of training and then at the end. The accuracy of initial and final predictions were compared. Result: no improvement.

Gage and Exline (1953) had two National Training Laboratory groups of fifteen and eighteen persons respond to a fifty-item questionnaire before and after a three-week session. The items were opinion statements concerning group processes, leadership styles, and the scientific study of human relations. Each trainee also filled out the questionnaire as he thought the average member in the group would, first before and then after the training. Result: no improvement.

These results indicate that T-group training does not improve the sensitivity of trainees to their leader, to each other, or to their group. One would not expect, therefore, that it would improve their sensitivity to people outside the group. Crow (1957) verified the expectation. Medical students in Colorado were shown sound motion pictures of physicians interviewing patients. They made predictions about them. They then took a training course that extended over a year to increase their sensitivity to patients as individuals. At the end of the training, they saw the filmed interviews again, and again made predictions. Result: "Contrary to expectations, a training program in interpersonal relations for medical students *decreased* the trainees' accuracy in judging others."

Questioning the adequacy of previous sensitivity measures, Danish and Kagan (1971) have developed a sophisticated measure of "affective sensitivity." The measure uses a videotape situational test containing forty-one scenes involving eleven different counselors taken from actual counseling sessions. After seeing a videotape sequence, a subject chooses from several multiple-choice alternatives the one that he thinks describes the affective state that the client is "really" experiencing. The test has internal consistencies and repeat reliabilities in the .70s.

The Affective Sensitivity Scale was given to fifty-one members in six T groups before and after their training. Result: the average member in two groups improved significantly; in two groups, insignificantly; and in two groups, declined slightly. In the face of these discouraging results the authors concluded, "If affective sensitivity is a trait like that of intelligence, then both hereditary potential and environmental conditions may be influential and large gains by groups should probably not be expected to occur. This raises a question about whether or not people can be "taught" to improve their affective sensitivity . . . . "

These pessimistic conclusions are based on objective measures of sensitivity. Subjective measures give totally different results. Trainees almost invariably are enthusiastic about the training. They report that their self-perceptions, sensitivity, and interpersonal effectiveness were changed in highly beneficial ways. Some argue that the feelings of the trainees at the end of the training are *the* criterion. The use of empirical measures interferes with the training, is dehumanizing, and is irrelevant to its central purpose.

Is the ultimate measure of success to be subjective or objective? Is it to be by estimates of the trainees of how much they feel they have improved, or by measures that are independent of whether the trainees feel they have improved? As we tried to make clear in the last chapter, the answer depends upon whether the actual goal of the training and the trainees is the development of rationalistic understanding ("the degree to which a person feels close to, sympathetic with, and understanding of another person") or empirical understanding ("the degree to which one person can predict another person's feelings, thoughts, and behavior").

Dunnette (1969) concludes from his extensive review of T-group research that the desire for rationalistic understanding dominates the T group as well as many related activities in our society:

> I intend something close to the early Christian concept of agape, *a sense of spontaneous giving of the self, the free expression of self in interaction with others, without calculation of cost of gain to either the giver or the receiver, and a deep commitment to the worth and humanity of man.*
> I refer to the many current social revolts—the New Morality, the Hippies, and in particular to the explosive growth of group training programs . . . Intimacy Training . . . Sensitivity Training, T-grouping, or Awareness Training.

In a similar vein but considering religious rites rather than T groups, Cassirer (1946) concludes:

> What appears here is a fundamental feeling of mankind, a feeling that is common to the most primitive rites and to the most sublime spiritualized mystic religions. It is the deep desire of the individual to be freed from the fetters of its individuality, to immerse itself in the stream of universal life, to lose its identity, to be absorbed in the whole of nature.

T groups do develop rationalistic understanding; they do not seem to develop empirical understanding. The concern of this book is with the latter. This concern, however, does not blind us to the obvious fact that rationalistic understanding seems more real to us, is more deeply desired, and is probably more important to our personal survival and well-being than is empirical understanding. Our only plea is that the reader not confuse the two kinds of understanding and not try to reduce one to the other.

THE TEACHING OF PSYCHOLOGY

Psychology aims to give man a power of predicting human behavior and experience beyond that which he can achieve through his own unaided common sense. With increasing frequency, students take psychology courses. Typically, one course is enough, for at any given time more students are enrolled in the first course than in all the other courses combined. Yet more than 10,000 students graduate each year with a major in psychology. More than a third of them go on to graduate school. About one in ten students who receive a doctorate degree get it in psychology. Does the training make them more sensitive?

Table 2-2 summarizes ten studies dealing with the question. Their answers to the question are clear-cut. Are undergraduates who had psychology courses more sensitive than those who have not? No. Are professional psychologists more sensitive than graduate students in psychology? No. Are clinical psychologists more sensitive than experimental psychologists? No. Are professional psychologists more sensitive than physical scientists, actors, personnel managers, and members of other professional groups? No. Indeed, more than one of these studies shows that the less well-trained groups do significantly *better.*

Why does the training fail? To begin with, it is largely limited to theoretical and nomothetic sensitivity. No effective attention is paid to either observation or idiographic understanding. Students are given neither practice nor feedback on their ability to apply what they have learned to specific persons. Rather, they are trained to use objective measures. They learn what such measures are and the results that have accumulated from using them. They learn to develop them, to administer them, and to interpret them. On the whole, they are warned against rather than trained to use their subjective impressions.

What impact does instruction have? The instructed have a better understanding of what psychology is, know more about what psychologists do, and have a more favorable attitude toward psychology. Many are influenced to go to graduate school and to become psychologists. Course offerings in the past twenty years has been increasingly in the direction of developing curriculum for graduate school preparation (APA Monitor, March, 1971). What is the teacher's purpose in teaching? MacLeod (1971) rejects as unworthy such answers as: "I want to build the enrollment in our courses, to enlist more majors, to send more students to good graduate schools" and "I like the comfort and freedom of the academic world, and to achieve this sort of life I must do a minimum of teaching." His view is that

> . . . any psychology worth teaching is a psychology centered on problems that have persisted since the beginning of recorded history, problems connected with man's conception of himself and of his relation to the world about him. Ultimately these are problems of philosophy, but psychology's contribution has been to bring them within the range of empirical inquiry.

The development of sensitivity is one of these persistent problems.

TABLE 2-2
The Influence of Psychology Instruction on Sensitivity

Experimenter	Method	Did Training Increase Sensitivity?
1 Estes (1938)	Two-minute silent movies of each of six subjects were shown to fifty-six judges (including nine psychologists) who were then asked to match a subject to one of six personality sketches.	No. Psychologists did worse than musicians, painters, actors, and personnel managers.
2 Luft (1950)	After reading the verbatim record of an hour's interview with a subject, twenty-eight psychologists and twenty-eight physical scientists predicted the answers that the subject had made to a variety of personality tests.	No. In some comparisons, physical scientists were superior.
3 Wedell and Smith (1951)	Two hundred employees were each interviewed by three psychologists with advanced degrees and three without advanced degrees. The interviewers then tried to answer fifty-five questions on a job satisfaction questionnaire as the employees themselves had answered them.	No. Those with advanced degrees showed more frequent and serious discrepancies than those without.
4 Kelly and Fiske (1951)	Experienced psychologists and trainees predicted the eventual professional success of graduate students by means of a wide variety of materials in various combinations.	No. Trainees "utilized the materials as effectively as the more mature."
5 Soskin (1954)	Graduate students and experienced clinical psychologists answered a personality inventory as they thought a twenty-six-year-old mother had answered it. They were given her responses to projective tests.	No. The graduate students were as accurate in their predictions as the clinicians.
6 Trumbo (1955)	The sensitivity scores of forty-four students who had just completed the introductory course were compared with the scores of forty-four students of the same intelligence who had completed five courses in psychology.	No. The advanced students did no better than the beginning students.

TABLE 2-2, continued

Experimenter	Method	Did Training Increase Sensitivity?
7 Taft (1955)	Psychologists and graduate students in and out of psychology made trait ratings and predicted inventory responses of subjects in a large assessment program.	No. The small differences found were largely due to the superiority of experimental over clinical psychologists.
8 Grossman (1963)	The scores of 130 undergraduates on a variety of written and film tests of sensitivity were correlated with the number of credits they had had in psychology.	No. There were no significant correlations between credits, and the median correlation was approximately zero.
9 Weiss (1963)	Sixty clinical psychologists and sixty physical scientists predicted the behavior of three undergraduates, sometimes with only identifying information and sometimes with the typescript of a half-hour taped interview.	No. "Physical scientists perform more accurately than psychologists when a greater amount of information is available."
10 Levy and Ulman (1967)	Twenty-six professional mental health workers (psychologists, psychiatrists, social workers, art therapists), thirty student health workers, and twenty-eight untrained artists and students predicted which of ninety-six paintings had been painted by schizophrenics and which by normals.	No. "Mental health workers, including art therapists, do not have greater ability than others for the diagnostic task required in this study."

CLINICAL TRAINING

Since 1920, the number of professional psychologists in the United States has increased from less than 1,000 to more than 30,000. About half of them work in colleges and universities, a quarter in government agencies, and the rest in private organizations. Wherever they work, sensitivity is their business. Some are concerned with predicting the behavior of children, others with predicting the behavior of workers and leaders, and still others with predicting the performance of groups and organizations.

Half of these psychologists have had some clinical training. Clinical programs vary a great deal and are changing rapidly. In general, however, the training involves not only instruction but also supervised practice. With the aid of validated intelligence tests, personality tests, inventories, and scales, the psychologist can often predict quite accurately how a person feels and what he will do. Without their aid, however, the clinically trained are no better predictors than those without such training.

THE NECESSITY OF FEEDBACK

Feedback (knowledge of results, reinforcement, reward) is necessary in order to learn anything. To become more sensitive, a person must know when he is insensitive. The trainee is certainly more likely to learn if he is provided with knowledge of his predictive successes and failures. T groups, psychology classes, and clinical training rarely provide such feedback.

The typical psychology class, no matter what its stated aims, gives students feedback on their knowledge of the vocabulary and principles of psychology. Consequently, they become more fluent in their use of such words as "repression," "reaction formation," and "projection." But they do not become more accurate in their predictions about persons. To become more sensitive, they need feedback on their sensitivity.

Clinical training provides some feedback. Supervisors, for example, listen to taped interviews between an intern and his client in order to give the intern information on when and why he has been insensitive. Interns seek feedback from their clients by asking them for it. This kind of feedback, however, is infrequent, imprecise, and subjective.

T-group training has made the greatest effort to meet the need for adequate feedback. Sometimes, for example, a participant is not allowed to express his own ideas until he has first repeated what was said by the person who spoke before him. Here is a typical comment of a participant after trying this technique: "For the first time in my life I find that I am really listening to what others say." Feedback is also one of the few T-group elements that has been examined empirically. Campbell and Dunnette (1968) conclude from their survey of the research that even in the T-group situation feedback is inadequate.

Trainees cannot learn without feedback; they may not even learn with it. Goldberg (1965), for example, gave intensive feedback to three clinical psychologists, ten psychology graduate students, and ten nonpsychologists in an effort to improve their ability to discriminate the Minnesota Multiphasic Personality Inventory (MMPI) profile of psychotic patient from a neurotic one. Result: the trainees did not improve even after thousands of feedback occasions and a number of different training procedures.

If feedback does not lead trainees to set new goals for themselves, it does not work. Locke and Bryan (1969) have shown how goals work in a laboratory setting. They paid forty students to work on simple addition problems for an hour. They set ten of them an easy goal and gave them feedback; another ten were given the same goal as during a practice period with feedback; the third ten were given a hard goal and feedback; and the final ten were given a hard goal but no feedback. The ingenious experiment was designed so that those who got feedback could not use it in setting their personal goals. Under these conditions, feedback had no effect on performance. The authors concluded: "More attention should be paid to the goals and intentions which S develops in response in the incentives E provides."

The more feedback reveals a discrepancy between where a trainee is and where he wants to be, the more successful the feedback is likely to be. Watley (1968) trained educational counselors in predicting the college achievement of freshmen. The counselors who were initially informed that they were in the bottom third in their predictive accuracy improved. Those counselors who knew they were initially average or superior did not improve. Spier (1969) fed back percentile scores to trainees on their performance on a sensitivity test taken at the beginning of training. Those who knew they were in the bottom third improved significantly during training; those in the middle third, slightly; and those in the top third, not at all.

The more the feedback situation encourages trainees to set hard goals for themselves, the more successful the feedback is likely to be. Mietus (1969) gave students in a large college class their scores on a test of sensitivity at the beginning of training. They were then asked to set and report improvement goals for themselves. At the end of training, they took the sensitivity test again. The gains of fifty-six students who had set hard goals for themselves were compared with the gains of fifty-six matched students who had the same initial scores but had set easy goals for themselves. The hard goal setters improved more than the easy goal setters.

GUIDES TO PROGRAM DEVELOPMENT

Training must give trainees feedback. The better this feedback motivates the trainee to improve his sensitivity and the better it informs him of his progress in doing so, the more successful the training will be. How can more effective feedback patterns be developed? This book makes strenuous efforts to apply these general principles: (1) formulate more realistic goals, (2) sequence the goals, (3) reduce defensiveness, (4) fit the method to the goal, and (5) evaluate the success of training. The difficulty in applying them is amply testified by the general failure of T groups, psychology instruction, or clinical training to do so. Here, the significance of these guides are briefly discussed.

Formulate More Realistic Goals

The goals of the typical college course are content-centered: "The aim of this course is to cover the theories, methods, facts, and principles of abnormal psychology." The question of whether changes in the sensitivity of students occur as a result of mastering the content is ignored. In T groups the goals are more trainee-centered but also more vague. As a consequence, the trainer does not know exactly what he is supposed to be doing or the trainee what he is supposed to be learning.

The component approach permits the differentiation of more specific observational, theoretical, nomothetic, and idiographic goals. It is part of the task of the following chapters to make explicit critical and realistic goals in each of these areas.

Sequence the Goals

In the process of becoming more sensitive, the trainee must learn many different things. Which of these things is it most efficient to learn first? Second? Third? Finding the best order for learning is the problem of *sequencing.*

The relationship between didactic and practicum training is a central and unsolved sequencing problem in the education of clinical psychologists. Should didactic training precede, follow, or be intermingled with the practicum work? Some experts are quite sure that a mastery of general psychology, personality theory, and experimental methods must precede actual clinical experience. They hold that such knowledge is essential if the trainee is to be ready to observe adequately what goes on in the clinical situation, to interpret properly what he sees and hears, and to understand fully the professional setting and its requirements. Other experts are just as sure that some clinical experience should precede most, if not all, of the academic training. They believe that the student should first encounter clinical phenomena, should be puzzled by them, and should then raise questions which give his academic study more meaning and direction. Still other experts feel that the two types of training should run along together: as the classroom training proceeds from general to specific, practicum experience proceeds from the simple to the complex. As there are no decisive facts that bear on this question, the controversy continues. As far as the development of sensitivity is concerned, the component view suggests that all the experts are right: Attempts to improve sensitivity without an adequate theory are ineffective; the mastery of abstract theory apart from concrete people is ineffective; and, therefore, the simultaneous exposure to both theory and people is the most effective way of increasing sensitivity. The unanswered question is: How can this be done?

Part of the answer is to concentrate on the components one at a time. Within the framework of a particular component, the training can then focus on unified wholes, facilitate the shift from less to more adequate theories, and provide the trainee with knowledge of his progress in mastering the component. Within such a framework, the student can be exposed to a wide variety of persons, traits, and situations.

How should the components themselves be sequenced? An argument can be advanced for various sequences. Improvements in observation may be produced more quickly; improvements in theoretical sensitivity may have the most pervasive and enduring influence; and improvements in nomothetic and idiographic sensitivity may be of greatest immediate value and practical importance. We shall proceed on the guess that the sequence as given in the following chapters is most efficient: observational, theoretical, nomothetic, and idiographic. Any sequence is preferable to an attempt to deal with all of the components simultaneously.

Reduce Defensiveness

To increase his sensitivity, the trainee must change some of his beliefs about people. As the evidence of both psychology and sensitivity training amply testifies, the process of changing one's beliefs can be very stressful. In fact, it is widely assumed that such stress is both inevitable and necessary. It seems to be a dubious assumption, for as stress increases, resistance to change increases. At any rate, the component approach provides several ways of reducing stress and the consequent rigidity.

Sequencing goals reduces stress. The more important a goal is to a trainee and the more uncertain he is about his achievement of it, the more stressful the situation is likely to be. Since general sensitivity is both more important and more uncertain than any of its components, stress can be reduced by considering the components one at a time rather than all at once. The components also vary in the importance that trainees attach to them. People are likely to be less concerned about the accuracy of their observations than about their sensitivity to groups. In general, then, stress can be reduced by taking up the goals one at a time, beginning with the one least likely to generate stress. Stress can also be controlled by varying the training methods. Who is judged? What kind of predictions are to be made? And how are the predictions to be recorded? A person is unlikely to be disturbed when he finds out about his errors in rating a person he has read about. He is more likely to be disturbed when he finds out that others do not think he has as much sense of humor as he thinks he has. Generally, the situation becomes more stressful for us the closer we feel to the person we are judging, the more relevant the predictions are to our opinions of ourselves, and the more we are compelled to discriminate the good people from the not-so-good. Ranking forces people to discriminate; rating does not, since all people can be given the same rating. The popularity of rating over ranking is largely due to the distaste for making the discriminations required by ranking. Stress also varies with the social desirability of the quality being considered: less stress is generated by judgments about the neatness of our handwriting than about our self-insight and sense of humor. The trainee is more likely to develop skill in dealing constructively with stress if the level of stress is raised gradually.

However approached, the reduction of defensiveness in training is critical. Feedback frequently confronts the trainee not just with information that contradicts his opinion but contradicts his perceptions of what a particular person "really" is.

Fit the Method to the Goal

Many methods are used in sensitivity training: lectures, group discussions, case studies, role playing, T groups, etc. Training methods are ways of reaching training goals. A particular method, therefore, should be one adapted to achieving a particular goal. In practically all training, however, it is the method that dominates. For example, Sensitivity Training as evolved by the National Training Laboratory does not stress its goals but its T-group method.

Stress upon a method leads to fuzziness about aims. Thus the goals of different NTL-type programs vary a great deal depending upon who sets them up, who pays for them, who conducts them, and where they are held. Tannenbaum, Weschler, and Massarik (1961, p. 232) complain:

> The trainers may value greater insights into defenses, more realistic perception of others, understanding of communication processes, or newly found awareness of the forces operating in a group. Fellow participants may stress willingness to understand and listen to others, effectiveness in role playing, recognition of the trainee's impact on a discussion, or his efforts to help the group achieve its goals. The trainee himself may most wish to develop feelings of confidence and security, to improve his ability to handle tough situations, to gain skills in interviewing and listening, and to experience relief from some of the tensions and anxieties with which he feels himself saddled.

It may be that most methods are good for nothing and one is good for everything. More likely, the critical question is not what is *the* best method but what is the best use for any particular method. Such time-consuming methods as role playing and T-group sessions are often used when forms of the written case study would be more effective. Combinations of methods would probably be still more effective. Thus learning programs utilizing written case-study material might eventually prove to be the best way of teaching the elements of sensitivity; the more time-consuming methods could then be limited to advanced training. In general, though, what we are trying to do comes before how we are going to do it.

Evaluate the Success of Training

Whether a method works and how it can be improved can only be confidently answered by evaluating it. In the typical program in our educational system, there is no evaluation that can, by the most generous scientific standards, be called adequate. What is true of training in general is even more true of sensitivity training.

A good evaluation must use valid criteria, as was stressed in the last chapter. It must also use an experimental design which ensures that any apparent improvement is due to the training and not to something else. Our concern here is with the problem of experimental design.

Four general types of designs have been used to evaluate training:

1 Measures after training without a control group

2 Measures before and after training without a control group

3 Measures after training with a control group

4 Measures before and after training with a control group

The first of these designs is the most often used but the poorest; the last is the least often used but the best.

Measurements are widely used after training without a control group. For example, students attend a course in human relations. At the end, they take a test covering their knowledge of the facts and principles of human relations. From their test scores, what can be confidently concluded about the effectiveness of the training? While the test scores report how much different students know about the course content, they tell nothing for certain about when, where, and how they learned it. Measures taken after training without a control group are better than nothing—but not much better.

The use of before-and-after measures does show whether changes did take place during the training period. To this extent, it represents an improvement. Thus if the same test that was given at the end of a human relations course had also been given at the beginning, the *difference* in knowledge would measure the changes that had taken place. Its weakness is that it does not establish with certainty that the change was due to the training. Thus it is generally true that just taking the same test a *second* time results in improvement. It may be that the students learned what they learned outside of the training situation.

After-training measures with a control group can give quite trustworthy evidence about both the impact of training and the reasons for the results. Its remedial weakness is that it is hard to make sure that the experimental and control groups were the same at the beginning of training. This difficulty can be overcome by matching the experimental and control groups before training begins.

The design that uses measures before and after training with a control group has these advantages:

1 Matching experimental and control groups on the before-training measures avoids the danger that the groups may not be comparable at the beginning.

2 Taking the difference between before-and-after measures in the trained group indicates what changes took place during the training period.

3 Comparing these changes with the changes that took place in the untrained control group during the training period isolates the changes caused by the training itself.

The exactness of the design has the advantage, among others, that conifdent conclusions can be drawn from a study based on a small number of trainees.

The use of different designs permits us to answer with varying confidence the question: How effective has the training been? The answer determines whether the training program is worth repeating. Even more important, it helps answer the question: How can the training be improved?

The following chapters take a component view of sensitivity. They assume that the most effective sequence of training involves first the development of observational sensitivity and then, in turn, theoretical, nomothetic, and idiographic sensitivity. The reader is first asked to look at each goal in terms of the processes that retard or advance its achievement. This examination provides the basis for defining the critical obstacles to progress as well as for suggesting methods of overcoming them. As a beginning, however, each training chapter considers ways of measuring the component ability, for it is only through the use of such measures that it becomes possible to measure the success of training and, therefore, to improve its effectiveness.

OBSERVATIONAL SENSITIVITY

CHAPTER 3
PERSON PERCEPTION

THE sensitive person is a good observer—he looks at and listens to people and remembers what he sees and hears. However, most of us do not observe a person; we perceive an instant and integrated whole person. Thus the better we understand the process of person perception and the more effectively observational training takes these processes into account, the more successful it is likely to be.

THE FORMATION OF IMPRESSIONS

Here is an impression formed by a summer school student of her instructor which she began writing during her first class (Allport, 1937, pp. 502–504):

> *Entrance: late-quiet and firm; passes out papers; fixes cuffs and coat; does not face class in speaking. Slightly condescending feeling toward class as "under-graduate." Some shyness—much more composed with back to class.*
>
> *Self-indulgent: indifferent to dress—coat too short, trousers unpressed. Standard of personal neatness not high; skin of face clear but not hands. Moderately well-kept, but he does not have a sense of cleanliness about him; uses pomade. One feels that he likes his gray hair and thinks it a distinction.*
>
> *Witty but acid—remarks not really funny. Would be best company when slightly drunk—inhibitions removed. Fond of satiric remarks toward world in general, especially women, but possibly not unfair or unjust in general reaction.*
>
> *Type more feminine in some ways than masculine. Nervous fussiness—scratches himself—sits like a woman. Probably likes to play around with women, but very conscious underneath of essential superiority. Could be conventionally attached to wife—or might leave her for a temporary attachment that he would rationalize as "cerebral affinity."*
>
> *No large expressive moments; may be due to dislike of teaching—certainly some conflict. Rather subtle and complex, not sensitive to class, cynical, even satiric toward whole business. He is a type found at times in faculties of women's colleges . . . . Not a type I like.*

From the beginning, her impression is not a series of unrelated facts but conveys a *whole* impression ("firm," "condescending," "shy"). As she writes, the vague whole becomes more detailed, more *differentiated*. But, like a portrait by an artist, the later details are *integrated* into the whole. The whole is dominated by an emotional tone, a perceptual character, an *expressive quality*.

The Instant Whole

An impression forms rapidly and as a whole. Asch (1946) gave students instructions like these:

> I shall read to you a number of characteristics that belong to a particular person. Please listen to them carefully and try to form an impression of the kind of person described. You will later be asked to give a brief characterization of the person in just a few sentences. I will read the list slowly and will repeat it once.

One such list was: *energetic, assured, talkative, cold, ironical, inquisitive, persuasive.* None of the hundreds of students in the many experiments ever merely repeated a list of traits as a description; all perceived a unified picture of the man behind the traits. Here are two typical impressions from the list:

> He is the type of person you meet all too often; sure of himself, talks too much, always trying to bring you around to his way of thinking and with not much feeling for the other fellow.

> He seems to be the kind of person who would make a great impression upon others at first meeting. However, as time went by, his acquaintances would easily come to see through the mask. Underneath would be revealed his arrogance and selfishness.

The power of the drive toward unified impressions is indicated by a study in which seventy-nine college students saw in a film five scenes of a young woman (Gollin, 1954). Two scenes suggested that she was "bad": (1) being picked up in front of a run-down hotel and (2) entering a glass-fronted store that might have been a bar and coming out with a man. The middle scene was neutral: (3) walking along and talking to a female companion. The other two scenes suggested that she was "good": (4) giving money to a beggar and (5) helping a woman who had fallen on a public stairway. Afterward, the students were asked to:

> Write down on paper given to you the impression you have formed of the person who appears in all the scenes. Please be as detailed as you can, that is, write your impression as if you were telling someone about this individual's personality.

About half of the students described the girl as bad *or* good. They described the girl as pictured in scenes 1 and 2 ignoring the other scenes, or they described the girl as pictured in scenes 4 and 5, ignoring the other scenes. That is, they ignored most of what they saw in order to form a unified impression of the girl.

Differentiation and Integration

From beginning to end, our impression of a person forms a whole. As the impression develops, this whole becomes more and more differentiated, i.e., we use more and more traits to describe him. He is no longer just a "good guy" but he is also "sincere," "honest," "understanding," "loyal," and "trustworthy." He is no longer just a bad guy he is also "malicious," "cruel," "conceited," and "greedy." To begin with, the summer school student saw her instructor as "condescending." He soon also became "self-indulgent," "acid," "satiric," and "feminine."

As an impression develops it becomes more elaborate and complex. It does not, however, fall apart. It remains *integrated,* i.e., the traits are related to each other. The "good guy" is also "honest," "understanding," and "loyal" and is almost certain not to be "malicious," "cruel," or "conceited."

The Centrality of Expressive Experience

The summer school student's impression of her instructor started as a unified whole, then gradually differentiated. From the beginning, however, this differentiating whole was dominated by an emotional tone, a perceptual character, an expressive quality, i.e., the instructor was perceived as "condescending," "self-indulgent," "acid," "cynical," and "satiric." Such words reflect the most influential and most confusing aspect of impression formation. The expressive quality that a person has for us is not simply determined by what we hear him say and see him do. Rather, how we feel about the person determines what we hear and see and, even more, how we interpret what we hear and see. The issue of sensory versus expressive qualities is so fundamental and so difficult that we shall return to it again and again. Here we present in a brief and dogmatic way some hypotheses about the issue.

Expressiveness, we assume, is the primary and indivisible unit of perception. A blush, a smile, or a menacing look cannot be dissected. The words we use to report our impressions of a person primarily reflect and intensify the expressive quality that we originally perceive. The quality is not a subjective appendage that is subsequently added to the objective content of our impression. On the contrary, it *is* the impression. These expressive qualities are as valid and as "real" as the sensory ones. "Self-indulgent" reflects reality as much as does "red hair." Dewey (1925, p. 96) stressed this point:

> Empirically, things are poignant, tragic, beautiful, humorous, settled, disturbed, comfortable, annoying, barren, harsh, consoling, splendid, fearful . . . . These traits stand in themselves on precisely the same level as colors, sounds, qualities of contact, taste and smell. Any criterion that finds the latter to be ultimate and "hard" data will, impartially applied, come to the same conclusion about the former. Any quality as such is final.

The theory of the primacy of expressive experience contradicts the sensationalist theory which has dominated perceptual psychology for centuries. In support of the primacy of expressive qualities, Cassirer (1957, p. 66-67) states:

. . . to dissolve the world of perception into a sum of particular impressions is to underestimate the part played in it not only by the "higher" intellectual functions, but also by the strong, instinctive substrate on which it rests. The sensationalist theory of perception retains, as it were, only the bare trunk of the tree of knowledge—it sees neither its crown, which rises free into the air, into the ether of pure thought, nor its roots, which sink into the earth. These roots do not lie in the simple ideas of sensation and reflection, which empiricist psychology and epistemology regard as the ultimate foundation of all knowledge of reality. They consist not in the "elements" of sensation but in original and immediate characters of expression. Concrete perception does not wholly detach itself from these characters even where it resolutely and consciously takes the road of pure objectivization. It never dissolves into a mere complex of sensuous qualities— such as light or dark, cold or warm—but is always attuned to a specific expressive tone: it is never directed exclusively toward the "what" of the object but encompasses the mode of its total manifestation—the character of the luring or menacing, the familiar or uncanny, the soothing or frightening, which lies in this phenomenon purely as such and independently of its objective interpretation.

A theory should serve the dual functions of unifying or making congruent known empirical findings and suggesting new empirical relations to be explored or verified. In the area of person perception, the expressive theory seems to fill these functions in a much more satisfactory way than the sensationalist theory.

The primacy and primitiveness of expressive experience, for example, fits the facts about animal and infant perceptions. Thus chimpanzees recognize the expressive quality of their fellows and respond to them in terms of the quality they perceive. Koffka (Cassirer, 1957, p. 64) reports of infants:

The stimuli which most influence the behavior of the child are not those which seem particularly simple to the psychologist because simple sensations correspond to them. The first differentiated sound reactions respond to the human voice, hence to highly complex stimuli (and "sensations"). The infant is not interested in simple colors, but in human faces . . . . by the middle of the first year of life the effect of the parents' facial expression on the child can be established . . . . to explain this by experience, to assume that these phenomena arose by combination of simple optical sensations with each other and with pleasant or unpleasant consequences from the original chaos of sensation, seems impossible . . . . We are left with the opinion that phenomena such as "friendliness" or "unfriendliness" are extremely primitive—even more primitive, for example, than that of a blue spot.

As we shall see throughout the present book, the theory of the centrality of expressive qualities harmonizes many of the confusing facts and suggests solutions to many of the puzzling problems in the area of person perception.

Expressive qualities dominate person perceptions. However, these qualities are not consistent across individuals. Different people looking at the same person often perceive widely different qualities. Toch and Schulte (1961), for example, showed police and students a scene of violence (murder, suicide, etc.) to the left eye, and simultaneously, by the use of a modified stereoscope, a scene of peace (a farmer plowing, a worker drilling, etc.) to the right eye for half a second. They then asked subjects to report what they saw. Practically all saw only one of the two scenes. The police, however, saw more than twice as many of the violent scenes as the students.

Furthermore, expressive qualities are not stable within individuals. That is, the same perceiver may see the same individual with quite different qualities at two different times. Thus a person may perceive another as unfriendly at one moment but then as having a quite different expressive quality the next.

Psychologists try to eliminate these personal, emotional, and inconsistent expressive qualities in their task of contributing to the stabilization and consolidation of our ideas about human behavior and experience. The methodologically ascetic behaviorist eliminates these qualities in his work by concentrating on behavior and ignoring experience. In the area of person perception, less ascetic researchers are inclined to concentrate on such sensory qualities as the loudness of the voice or physical appearance. But at home or at play, as well as at work, the person perceptions of the psychologist, like everyone else's, are ruled by expressive qualities. The problems of sensitivity cannot be solved by ignoring the primacy of expressive experience. They can only be solved by striving to understand how this fundamental law of perception leads to our understanding and misunderstanding of others.

THE GOODNESS OF IMPRESSIONS

The words we use to describe our impression of a person both reflect and intensify the expressive quality that we perceive. Analysis of these words reveal that the central difference we perceive between people is that some are "bad" and some are "good." Every word has both a denotative and a connotative meaning. The denotative meaning identifies and describes an objective and observable aspect of a person. The connotative meaning describes an emotional and expressive quality. Semantic differential analysis is a tool for studying these connotative or emotional meanings.

In the form in which it is usually administered, the semantic differential contains a set of scales that measure possible dimensions of emotional meaning: "false-true," "sharp-dull," "delicate-rugged," "worthless-valuable," etc. At the top of a page is a word like "loud" whose emotional meaning is analyzed by having respondents check where they would rate the word on each of the dimensions of emotional meaning. Thus "loud" would be rated on a six-point scale from false to true, from sharp to dull, etc.

The numerous scales of the semantic differential are measures of *assumed* dimensions of the emotional meanings of words. But how many actual dimensions are there? Factor analysis, a complex statistical procedure, answers this question. The first step in a factor analysis of the semantic scales is to determine the ratings of a large number of words on each of the scales. The next step is to correlate the scores of each word on each scale with the scores of other words on each scale. If all the correlations are zero, then each scale would be measuring an independent dimension of emotional meaning. If all the correlations are perfect, then all the assumed dimensions measured would, in fact, be only one dimension. The usual case in factor analysis is that the assumed dimensions are neither entirely independent or dependent. Instead, they cluster in groups of related dimensions that are independent of each other.

Factor-analytic studies of semantic differential data have been numerous (Warr and Knapper, 1968). Three factors consistently emerge: evaluation, potency, and activity. Of these the evaluative factor dominates, often accounting for three-fourths of the variance. It is so dominating that strenuous efforts to prevent subjects from making this type of response have been unsuccessful. Scales loaded on the evaluative factor are the following: like-dislike, approach-avoid, and good-bad. In brief, the many words we may use in reporting an impression are largely many ways of describing one expressive quality.

What are the good and bad words we use? Anderson (1968) had 100 college students rate 555 personality-trait words. They were told to think of a person who could be described by each word and to rate the word from "1," least favorable or desirable, to "7," most favorable or desirable. On most of the words, the students were in very close agreement in their ratings. The average rating of each word was determined. The words were then ranked from "1," the most desirable word, to "555," the least desirable word. The top ten were: sincere, honest, understanding, loyal, truthful, trustworthy, intelligent, dependable, open-minded, and thoughtful; the bottom ten: deceitful, dishonorable, malicious, obnoxious, untruthful, dishonest, cruel, mean, phony, and liar. Few words were in the middle; most were definitely good or bad. The students were also asked to rate the meaningfulness of the words from "I have almost no idea of the meaning" to "I have a very clear and definite understanding of the meaning." The good and bad words were more meaningful than the neutral words. "Liar" was judged the most meaningful of all.

Children also reveal the dominance of goodness in their perceptions of others. Yarrow and Campbell (1963) asked each of 267 boys and girls in a summer camp to choose one child whom he felt he knew the most about. Each was asked to "tell all about him, as if you were telling a friend back home." A content analysis of their descriptions "showed two very strong tendencies: (a) broad positive or negative judgments were given by 85 per cent, and (b) these judgments were elaborated primarily in terms of peer actions having direct interpersonal consequences."

The Perceiver of Good

Some people generally take a dark view of others while some take a very bright view. Psychologists, like everybody else, differ in the badness or goodness they perceive in the typical man. Freud (1961, pp. 58–59), it seems, was impressed by the general badness of men:

> . . . men are not gentle creatures who want to be loved, and who at the most can defend themselves if they are attacked; they are, on the contrary, creatures among whose instinctual endowments is to be reckoned a powerful share of aggressiveness. As a result, their neighbor is for them not only a potential helper or sexual object, but also someone who tempts them to satisfy their aggressiveness on him, to exploit his capacity for work without compensation, to use him sexually without consent, to seize his possessions, to humiliate him, to cause him pain, to torture and to kill him . . . . Who, in the face of all his experience of life and of history, will have the courage to dispute this assertion? . . . Anyone who calls to mind the atrocities committed during the racial migrations or the invasions of the Huns, or by the people known as Mongols under Genghiz Khan or Tamerlane, or at the capture of Jerusalem by the pious Crusaders, or even, indeed, the horrors of the recent World War—anyone who calls these things to mind will have to bow humbly before the truth of this view.

Allport (1954, p. 14) perceived more goodness in men:

> Normal men everywhere reject, in principle and by preference, the path of war and destruction. They like to live in peace and friendship with their neighbors; they prefer to love and be loved rather than to hate and be hated . . . . While wars rage, yet our desire is for peace, and while animosity prevails, the weight of mankind's approval is on the side of affiliation.

The Employee Rating Scale (Table 3-1) provides one convenient measure of a person's tendency to take a favorable view of others (Grossman, 1963). The information given about Jim Nelson and the other two men is deliberately ambiguous so that the ratings will more fully reflect the bias of the rater. The thirty items were selected from an original group of ninety items on the basis of their ability to discriminate low from high raters. Since all the items are favorable, the higher the total score of the rater, the more favorable his impressions of the three men.

Results from using the scale document two important trends. First, persons differ in the general level of goodness that they perceive in others. While the mean rating on the scale is favorable (4.0), the ratings range from extremely unfavorable to extremely favorable. In the second place, some people are narrow spreaders and some are wide spreaders. That is, some people vary little from their mean

TABLE 3-1
The Employee Rating Scale

GENERAL DIRECTIONS: This is a study of how people rate other people. You are given a brief sketch of three employees: George Drake, Harry Maynard, and Jim Nelson. On the basis of this sketch rate them on the personality traits, give your evaluation of their worth as employees, and answer the inventory statements as you think they did.

I George Drake—Electrical Appliance Inspector

George Drake works as an inspector on the assembly line in a company manufacturing electrical appliances. He likes his work fairly well and has been promoted regularly. George is the kind of fellow who likes to study things. At one time he had wanted to study to be an engineer. This was impossible because at that time he had to support his mother. This doesn't seem to have affected him, however, except that he sometimes feels a little uncomfortable around college-trained men. George has lots of friends both at work and away from work.

Personality Ratings

On the basis of the information given, do you think George has the following qualities? Mark each one as follows: (1) Quite unlike him (2) A little unlike him (3) A little like him (4) Rather like him (5) Quite like him.

1　2　3　4　5　　　1. Ambitious

1　2　3　4　5　　　2. Careful

1　2　3　4　5　　　3. Flexible

Evaluation

Assume that you are George's supervisor and must give him a merit rating on the following qualities. Mark each quality as follows: (1) Poor (2) Fair (3) Average (4) Good (5) Superior.

1　2　3　4　5　　　4. Safety

1　2　3　4　5　　　5. Dependability

1　2　3　4　5　　　6. Initiative

1　2　3　4　5　　　7. Job knowledge

1　2　3　4　5　　　8. Suggestiveness

1　2　3　4　5　　　9. Industriousness

1　2　3　4　5　　10. Enthusiasm

II Harry Maynard—Accountant

Harry Maynard is a senior accountant for a large paper company. He is forty-two years old, married, and has two children of school age. His favorite recreation is fishing.

Harry started as a messenger, learned accounting on his own, and worked his way up. He has only a high school education, although most of the other accountants are college-trained. Nevertheless, he gets along with the others very well and he is well liked by them. Harry is a good accountant and he likes his work very much.

TABLE 3-1, continued

Personality Ratings

On the basis of the information given, do you think Harry has the following qualities? Mark each one as follows: (1) Quite unlike him (2) A little unlike him (3) A little like him (4) Rather like him (5) Quite like him.

1 2 3 4 5   11. Friendly

1 2 3 4 5   12. Honest

1 2 3 4 5   13. Stable

1 2 3 4 5   14. Flexible

1 2 3 4 5   15. Practical

Evaluation

Assume that you are Harry's supervisor and must give him a merit rating on the following qualities. Mark each quality as follows: (1) Poor (2) Fair (3) Average (4) Good (5) Superior.

1 2 3 4 5   16. Safety

1 2 3 4 5   17. Punctuality

Inventory

Harry filled out an anonymous personality inventory when he was hired. He responded to each of the statements below by marking them: (1) Strongly disagree (2) Disagree (3) Neither agree nor disagree (4) Agree (5) Strongly agree. Answer the following statements as you think Harry answered them.

1 2 3 4 5   18. I am guided in my conduct by firm principles.

1 2 3 4 5   19. I assert myself with energy on any occasion.

1 2 3 4 5   20. I never neglect serious things in order to have a good time.

III *Jim Nelson—Foreman*

For the last ten years Jim Nelson has been the foreman in the shipping department of an automobile parts manufacturing company. When Jim was appointed foreman, several others with more seniority were also considered for the job. Jim got the job because he had had more education than the others. Some of the men resented this and made Jim's task as supervisor a pretty tough one at first. However, this has been forgotten now and Jim gets along with the men very well. Jim's greatest handicap as a supervisor is the fact that he is somewhat shy. Also, he occasionally has difficulty expressing himself. His strongest quality is his sincere interest in his job.

Personality Ratings

On the basis of the information given, do you think Jim has the following qualities? Mark each one as follows: (1) Quite unlike him (2) A little unlike him (3) A little like him (4) Rather like him (5) Quite like him.

1 2 3 4 5   21. Realistic

1 2 3 4 5   22. Ambitious

TABLE 3-1, continued

1 2 3 4 5   23. Flexible

1 2 3 4 5   24. Practical

Evaluation

Assume that you are Jim's supervisor and must give him a merit rating on the following qualities. Mark each quality as follows: (1) Poor (2) Fair (3) Average (4) Good (5) Superior.

1 2 3 4 5   25. Initiative

1 2 3 4 5   26. Potentiality

1 2 3 4 5   27. Industriousness

Inventory

Jim filled out an anonymous personality inventory when he was hired. He responded to each of the statements below by marking them: (1) Strongly disagree (2) Disagree (3) Neither agree nor disagree (4) Agree (5) Strongly agree. Answer the following three statements as you think Jim answered them.

1 2 3 4 5   28. I like reading about business trends.

1 2 3 4 5   29. I am systematic in caring for my personal property.

1 2 3 4 5   30. I never neglect serious things in order to have a good time.

rating regardless of whether it is low or high while other people vary a great deal on their ratings from one trait to another and from one person to another. Grossman (1963) found the level and the spread of ratings to be both internally consistent and stable. So did Gross (1961) and Crow and Hammond (1957), who used quite different measures. The latter found the internal consistency of the spread scores of medical students to be .60 six months apart. With remarkable consistency, then, the lower spreaders at the beginning of training were low spreaders at the end; high spreaders at the beginning were high spreaders at the end.

What kind of person tends to form good impressions of others? The author selected seventeen students from a large class who had high ratings on the Employee Rating Scale as well as high ratings on two other measures of high rating tendencies. They were matched for age and intelligence with seventeen students who made consistently low ratings on the three measures. Both groups also completed a forty-item inventory measuring boldness (Table 5-1). On thirty-eight of the forty items, the high raters more often answered in the bold direction. They were more optimistic, dominating, energetic, and self-confident. Fey (1957), among many others, found that those who were high in self-acceptance were high in their acceptance of others. In general, then, those who have a good impression of themselves tend to form good impressions of others. The tendency has a cradle-to-the-grave aspect, for self-confidence is among the most stable of personality traits (Kelly, 1955).

Who are the wide spreaders, the people who see others as either very good *or* very bad? Gollin (1954) showed college students films of a woman engaged in both good and bad activities. They were then asked to write their impressions. About half gave simplified impressions by ignoring either the desirable *or* the undesirable behavior. About a fourth gave aggregate impressions in which they mentioned both the good and bad activities but did not try to relate them. Another fourth attempted to relate the good and bad activities. The wide spreaders, then, were not relational but simple thinkers.

The ability to think relationally about people develops slowly with age. Gollin (1958) tested more than seven hundred elementary and secondary school students in Minnesota. A five-scene silent motion picture was used to present the behavior of an eleven-year-old boy. The first scene was a close-up of the boy. Two of the following scenes showed the boy engaged in socially approved behavior. One of these showed two other small boys playing catch when a larger boy breaks up their game by shoving them aside and taking their ball. The eleven-year-old enters and recovers the ball, drives the larger boy off, and returns the ball to the smaller boys. In the other good scene a small boy riding a tricycle falls into a heap of dry leaves and appears to have hurt himself. The eleven-year-old comes along, helps him up, rights his tricycle, brushes him off, and gets him started again. Two of the scenes show the boy engaged in socially undesirable behavior. In one, two boys are engaged in building a "soap-box" car. The eleven-year-old pushes over the boy who is sawing, snatches the paint brush from the other boy, and smears the number and the side of the car with the paint. In the other, the eleven-year-old grabs comic books from younger boys, tears some of them up, and scatters the others by kicking.

At the end of the film, the judges were asked "to write as much about the boy as you can, that is, pretend you are telling someone about him. Give your opinion of the boy, write what you think about him." The statements were then classified as trying or not trying to account for the good and bad behavior of the boy by using relational concepts. To be classified as relational it was only necessary that the student had tried; it was not necessary that the attempt had been either satisfactory or complete. Relational thinking increased with age: 2 percent at ten; 15 percent at fourteen; 51 percent at seventeen.

EMPATHY WITH PEOPLE

"Empathy" is a potent word in the field of person perception (Marwell, 1964). It is used as a basic concept in rationalistic, artistic, and empirical approaches to understanding others. From the rationalistic view it is the intellectual identification with or vicariously experiencing of the feelings, thoughts, or attitudes of a person. From the artistic view, the attribution of feelings aroused by an object in nature or art to the object itself, as when one speaks of a painting full of love. From the empirical view, it also covers sensitivity as we are using it.

The result is confusion. Thus Kurtz and Grummon (1971) used six different measures of the empathy of thirty-one counselors. Two were measures of rationalistic empathy (the counselor rated himself on statements like "I try to see things through his eyes" and the client rated him on statements like "He tries to see things through my eyes"). Two were measures of empirical empathy, i.e., the counselor predicted the responses of his client to an adjective check list and to the Role Concept Repertory Test. And two were measures involving the estimates of independent judges of the empathy of the therapist with his client. *None* of the measures had any positive relationship to any other one. In fact, some of the correlations were negative. For example, counselors who rated themselves higher in empathy were rated lower in empathy by the independent judges.

Consequently, we will use "empathy" in a more limited and specific way as *the degree of similarity that one person assumes between himself and another person.* Empathy, thus defined, is not an outcome but a process. It is not *any* kind of understanding; it is a powerful influence on the process of person perception that may decrease as well as increase sensitivity. How can differences in empathy, then, be measured? How do low and high empathizers differ? What is the relationship between empathy with a person and impressions of his goodness? Between empathy and observational sensitivity?

The Empathic Perceiver

The Empathy Test (Table 3-2) measures differences in the tendency to assume similarity between oneself and others. It includes both individuals and groups, men and women. Adding the total number of "1" (true-true) and "2" (false-false) responses gives the empathy scores. The mean score for several hundred college students was 44, with scores ranging from 25 to 62. The internal consistencies of the scale center around .70.

It is also possible to obtain actual similarity and sensitivity scores from the test. The actual answers of the typical man, the typical woman, Naomi, and Harold are included in parentheses. For machine scoring, an actual similarity key can be made by counting the items on which a respondent's answers for himself agree with the actual answers. Thus items 1, 2, and 3 would be keyed as 2 + 4, item 4 as 1 + 3; item 5 as 2 + 4, etc. The sensitivity key can be made by counting the number of items on which the respondent's assumptions of similarity or dissimilarity agreed with his actual similarity or dissimilarity. Thus items 1, 2, and 3 would be keyed as 2 + 3; item 4 as 1 + 4; item 5 as 2 + 3, etc.

The test is the outcome of studies with a variety of approaches to the problem of measurement. Earlier forms asked the respondent to first answer questions as he would answer them and then to answer as he thought the people in the test would answer them. Scoring these earlier forms required computer assistance. A critical simplification was later made by asking respondents themselves to indicate the similarities they would assume.

TABLE 3-2
The Empathy Test

Your "empathy" is your tendency to assume similarity between yourself and others. That is, when you empathize, you assume that another person's feelings are similar to your own. Without empathy we could not understand others. With empathy, however, we still sometimes misunderstand others because we incorrectly assume similarity.

This is a test of your empathic accuracy, the correctness of your assumptions of similarity and dissimilarity to others. The test has four parts: (1) empathy with the typical man, (2) empathy with the typical woman, (3) empathy with Naomi Warren, a particular woman, and (4) empathy with Harold Warren, a particular man.

Part I   You and the Typical Man

The replies of thousands of American men to each of the interests below have been analyzed. In making their replies they were asked to disregard as much as they could considerations of salary, social status, and possibilities of future advancement. They were asked to consider only whether they would like or dislike the interest, regardless of any necessary skills, abilities or training.

Ask yourself these two questions about each of the interests below:

A.   Do I like the interest more than I dislike it or do I dislike it more than I like it?

B.   Would the majority of American men say that they liked the interest more than they disliked it or would they say they disliked it more than they liked it?

Mark "1" (like-like)	If you *like* the interest and also think that the typical man would *like* it.
Mark "2" (dislike-dislike)	If you *dislike* the interest and also think the typical man would *dislike* it.
Mark "3" (like-dislike)	If you *like* the interest but think the typical man would *dislike* it.

TABLE 3-2, continued

Mark "4" (dislike-like)   If you *dislike* the interest but think the typical man would *like* it.

1. Auto salesman (D)*	7. Jeweler (D)
2. Talkative people (D)	8. Life insurance salesman (D)
3. Civil Service employee (D)	9. Pharmacist (D)
4. Algebra (L)	10. Real estate salesman (D)
5. Dentist (D)	11. Printer (D)
6. Factory worker (D)	12. Politician (D)

Part II   You and the Typical Woman

Proceed in this part exactly as in Part I, except this time you will compare your interests with those of the majority of *women.*

Mark "1" (like-like)   If you *like* the interest and also think the typical woman would *like* it.

Mark "2" (dislike-dislike)   If you *dislike* the interest and think the typical woman would also *dislike* it.

Mark "3" (like-dislike)   If you *like* the interest but think the typical woman would *dislike* it.

Mark "4" (dislike-like)   If you *dislike* the interest but think the typical woman would *like* it.

13. Proofreader (D)	19. *True Story* magazine (D)
14. Companion to elderly person (D)	20. Stenographer (D)
15. Accountant (D)	21. Statistician (D)
16. Bank teller (D)	22. Teacher, commercial (D)
17. Beauty specialist (D)	23. Discussions of economic affairs (L)
18. Artist's model (D)	24. Governor of a state (D)

Part III   You and Naomi Warren

In the preceding section you assessed the similarity between yourself and the typical woman. Here you are to assess the similarity between yourself and a particular woman, Naomi Warren.

She is the forty-year-old wife of a social science professor and the mother of three children who are now in college. Naomi is the eldest of four sisters, all of whom like to write. Naomi has published several children's books, another sister has published a novel, another sister is a newspaper reporter, and the other sister writes poetry. Naomi's daughter is planning to be a writer also. Naomi plays tennis, skates, skis, and generally enjoys the outdoors. She enjoys cooking but is casual about her housekeeping. She is a member of several civic groups but dislikes speaking before a group.

Naomi answered "true" or "false" to all of the following items.

Mark "1"   If you think the statement is *true* or more true than false of yourself, and also think that Naomi answered *true.*

Mark "2"   If you think the statement is *false* for yourself, and also think that Naomi answered *false.*

---

*Letters in parentheses indicate the correct answer, i.e., that given by the typical man. (D) indicates "dislike"; (L) indicates "like."

TABLE 3-2, continued

Mark "3"   If you think the statement is *true* of yourself and think Naomi answered *false*.

Mark "4"   If you think the statement is *false* for yourself and think Naomi answered *true*.

25. I like to make a very careful plan before starting in to do anything. (2)
26. I like to be with people who don't take life too seriously. (1)
27. I always keep control of myself in an emergency situation. (1)
28. I trust in God to support the right and condemn the wrong. (2)
29. In matters of conduct I conform very closely to custom. (2)
30. It is as important for a person to be reverent as it is for him to be sympathetic. (2)
31. The idea of God means more to me than any other idea. (2)
32. Women should have as much right to propose dates to men as men to women. (2)
33. I tend to judge people in terms of their concrete accomplishments. (2)
34. I like to have people around me practically all the time. (2)
35. Quite a few things make me emotional. (2)
36. I am moderate in my tastes and sentiments. (1)
37. I like to discuss my emotions with others. (2)
38. In the long run, science provides the best hope for solving the world's problems. (1)
39. I am really only interested in what is useful. (2)
40. Most of the time I am extremely carefree and relaxed. (2)
41. I have frequently assumed the leadership of groups. (2)
42. I never complain about my sufferings and hardships. (2)
43. I have very strong likes and dislikes. (1)
44. I spend a lot of time philosophizing with myself. (2)
45. I am almost never extremely excited or thrilled. (1)
46. I think that cremation is the best method of burial. (1)
47. There are few things I enjoy more than being a leader of people. (2)
48. Radical agitators should be allowed to make public speeches. (1)

Part IV   You and Harold Warren

Here you are to assess the similarity between yourself and Harold Warren, the fifty-year-old husband of Naomi.

Harold comes from a large family, and his mother died when he was a young boy. Harold and his brothers were raised by an ambitious maiden aunt who was a schoolteacher and who insisted on his regular church attendance. However, he has not been to church for several decades. Politically, he is a Democrat, but he has never been active in politics. Like his wife, he is an enthusiastic participant in amateur sports and has never been seriously ill. He has also written several books and is a wide reader not only in his own field but also in the fields of literature and philosophy.

Harold also completed the following items.

Mark "1"   If you think the statement is *true* or more true than false of yourself, and you also think that Harold answered *true*.

Mark "2"   If you think the statement is *false* of yourself, and also think that Harold answered *false*.

Mark "3"   If you think the statement is *true* of yourself, but think that Harold answered *false*.

Mark "4"   If you think the statement is *false* of yourself but think that Harold answered *true*.

TABLE 3-2, continued

49. I think there are few more important things in life than money. (2)
50. I am guided in all my conduct by firm principles. (2)
51. Whenever I have to undertake a job I make out a careful plan of procedure. (2)
52. Quite a few things make me emotional. (2)
53. I tend to judge people in terms of their concrete accomplishments. (2)
54. The European attitude toward mistresses is more sensible than ours. (1)
55. In matters of conduct I conform very closely to custom. (2)
56. I haven't yet reached any final opinion about the nature of God. (1)
57. It is as important for a person to be reverent as it is for him to be sympathetic. (2)
58. In the long run, science provides the best hope for solving the world's problems. (1)
59. Radical agitators should be allowed to make public speeches. (1)
60. Women should have as much right to propose dates to men as men to women. (1)
61. I tend to accept the world as it is and not worry about how it might be. (1)
62. I always keep my feet solidly on the ground. (2)
63. I am really only interested in what is useful. (2)
64. I prefer friends who have well-developed artistic tastes. (1)
65. I like to have people around me practically all the time. (2)
66. I am cautious about undertaking anything which may lead to humiliating experiences. (2)
67. There are few things I enjoy more than being a leader of people. (2)
68. I am a rather carefree person. (1)
69. I never complain about my sufferings and hardships. (1)
70. I have sometimes corrected others, not because they were wrong, but only because they irritated me. (2)
71. I have occasional difficulty getting the temperature of my bath the way I like it. (2)
72. I have very strong likes and dislikes. (2)

The scale approaches empathy from a trait point of view, i.e., differences in empathy that are due to the personality of the empathizer. Personality is neither the only or the strongest determiner of empathy. Whether we assume similarity also depends upon whether we recognize actual similarities. It depends upon whether he is the same age, sex, race, and educational status as ourselves. It particularly depends upon whether we perceive him as a member of the same social group to which we belong.

The Empathic Personality

What is the person who generally assumes a great deal of similarity like? The author gave several tests of empathy, all constructed like the one in Table 3-2, to a large lecture class. From this group, twenty-five who consistently assumed a high degree of similarity were matched for sex and intelligence with a group who consistently did not assume much similarity. Members of both of these groups answered the 200 statements in a personality inventory (see Table 5-1). The answers of these two groups to each statement were contrasted. In this process, forty-eight statements that one group answered "true" much more often than the other were isolated.

These forty-eight statements were then answered by groups with low and high empathy in another large class. The twenty-four statements in Table 3-3 are those that both high empathizers in this second group and high empathizers in the original group answered in the same way.

TABLE 3-3
The Empathic Personality

Cautious vs. Bold

T*	1.	I like having people around me practically all of the time.
T	2.	I always prefer to work with others.
T	3.	I would rather listen to a story than tell one.
T	4.	I am cautious about undertaking anything which may lead to humiliating experiences.
F	5.	I am almost never embarrassed.

Unemotional vs. Emotional

T	6.	I am fairly easily moved to laughter or tears.
T	7.	I am moderate in my tastes and sentiments.
T	8.	I think much and speak little.
F	9.	I have strong likes and dislikes.
F	10.	I become emotional fairly easily.
F	11.	It takes a great deal to make me emotional.
F	12.	I have sometimes corrected others, not because they were wrong, but only because they irritated me.

Present-minded vs. Future-minded

T	13.	I generally seek whatever makes me happy here and now.
F	14.	I always keep control of myself in an emergency situation.
F	15.	I find it rather hard to keep a rigid routine.

Artistic vs. Practical

T	16.	I am mainly interested in ideas that are very practical.
F	17.	I get an intense pleasure from just looking at a beautiful building.

Rationalistic vs. Empirical

T	18.	It is necessary to retain the belief that God exists as a personal being.
T	19.	In matters of conduct I conform very closely to custom.
T	20.	The thought of God gives me a complete sense of security.
T	21.	I control my sexual impulses by instituting prohibitions and restrictions.
F	22.	Some of my friends think my ideas are a bit wild and impractical.
F	23.	I am temperamentally more a skeptic than a believer.
F	24.	The European attitude toward mistresses is more sensible than ours.

*The letters in this column indicate the answers of the high empathizer.

These most discriminating items are arranged under the trait scale from which they were drawn. An inspection of the answers of high empathizers to these items indicates that they see themselves as conservative, conforming, and religious. They are emotional but inhibited. They are gregarious but quiet and acquiescent. They are more practical than artistic. They are present-minded but orderly.

Why does the empathizer empathize? Perhaps he is less able to see the real differences between himself and others. Perhaps he is afraid to recognize the differences he does see. Perhaps, considering the prominence of his rationalistic tendencies, he ignores empirical differences because he wants so much to like, to feel close to, and to sympathize with others. At any rate, these empathic differences are probably hard to alter, and exert a powerful influence on the formation of impressions.

GOODNESS AND EMPATHY

Empathy determines goodness. Byrne and Clore (1967) had forty men and forty women at the University of Texas fill out an attitude survey consisting of twelve six-point items dealing with a variety of issues such as political parties, birth control, and careers for women. They were each then given the responses of an anonymous stranger and asked to estimate his intelligence, knowledge of current events, morality, adjustment, and the degree to which the student would probably like the person and enjoy working with him. The scales of the "strangers" were actually prepared by the experimenters so that each student was judging a person who was either similar to himself on ten items and dissimilar on two or similar on two and dissimilar on ten. The mean attraction scores of similar and dissimilar strangers were then calculated. The similar strangers were rated as much more attractive.

Newcomb (1956) studied the relationship between empathy and goodness in a more lifelike setting at the University of Michigan. The seventeen students involved were all transfer students, all strangers to each other, and all residents of the same cooperative house. In return for spending five hours a week being interviewed and filling out questionnaires, they were given free room and board for the semester. The men were given no voice in the selection of room-mates, but (within the limits of the university regulations) were given freedom to conduct the house, including the cooking and eating arrangements, as they chose. Before their arrival, each of the seventeen men filled out a questionnaire covering attitudes toward a wide range of issues: classical music, immortality, sexual morality, house rules, university regulations about driving, etc. During the semester, the men completed a variety of personality inventories, and rated themselves and each other on numerous rating scales. They also reported whom they liked and disliked. From these data, both an index of each man's liking for each of the other men and an index of his assumed similarity to each of them were calculated. Result: The greater the empathy, the greater the attraction ($r = .69$). Based upon this and later studies, Newcomb (1963) painted the following picture of the acquaintance process:

> Each acquaintance is characterized by a continuing process of reciprocal scanning: What kinds of things does this person view as important? Whatever they are, how does he feel about them, and also about the things I regard as important (including myself)? If the discrepancy seems not too glaring, explorative communication continues, and with it comes the possibility of changes in the scale of importance. In the long run (four months, in my own investigation), attraction and association come to be relatively concentrated upon those who are perceived, usually with a considerable accuracy, as having notions similar to one's own of what is important and as having attitudes similar to one's own toward important things.

Berger (1969) verified the strong relationship between empathy and goodness in realistic detail. He first had more than a hundred college men and women fill out a questionnaire measuring their attitudes toward unions. They indicated the favorableness of their attitude by checking statements like the following on a scale from (1) strongly disagree to (5) strongly agree: "Unions are detrimental to society," "unions are necessary to our society as it is organized," etc. The students were then divided into two groups.

At a later meeting both groups separately saw a videotape of a man giving the same informative speech on unions. However, for the "pro" group the tape began with the statement "Frankly, I am very much in favor of unions," and for the "con" group with the statement "Frankly, I am very much opposed to unions." The goodness perceived in the speaker by the students was then measured by having them rate him on both "bad" traits such as narrow-minded, annoying, and incompetent, and on such "good" traits as interesting, intelligent, and honest. Finally, student empathy with the speaker (as measured by the union attitude scale) was correlated with the goodness the students perceived in him. In the pro group, the more favorable a student's attitude toward unions, the more attractive he found the speaker. In the con group, the more favorable his attitude toward unions, the less attractive the speaker. In general, the more a student thought the speaker agreed with him about unions, the better he perceived the speaker to be.

Empathy creates goodness: The more we think a person is like us, the better we perceive him to be. The individual with an empathic personality, however, does not perceive people as better than others do. The author has frequently correlated the number of assumptions of similarity to a particular person with the number of desirable qualities ascribed to him. In general, those who assume more similarities do not ascribe more desirable traits. The good personality and the empathic personality are in some conflict. Those who ascribe many desirable traits to others are those who ascribe many desirable traits to themselves—they are self-confident, optimistic, and energetic. On the other hand, those who assume that others are much like themselves tend to be more cautious than bold.

EMPATHY AND OBSERVATION

What is the relationship between empathy and our tendency to look at, listen to, and remember what a person says? The research evidence gives a clear but, thus far, not an emphatic answer: We look at and listen to people whom we assume are like us; we do not look at or listen to people whom we assume are not like us.

Bakan and Leckart (1966) showed extroverts introverted pictures like a man reading a book. They also showed them extroverted pictures like a group of people at a party. They were asked to look at the pictures one at a time, viewing each one as long as they wanted. The extroverts spent more time looking at the extroverted pictures. Kagan (1967) had a group of "academic" students and a group of "social" students listen to a studious girl and a gregarious girl reciting poems. The two groups of students were later asked to recall as much of the poems as they could. Result: "Recall was best when a girl listened to a communicator with whom she shared personality traits." Waly and Cook (1966) taught segregationists and antisegregationists to learn verbatim six segregationist and six antisegregationist opinions. By the fifth learning trial, the segregationist had learned better the segregationist statements and vice versa.

Finally, what is the relationship between our empathy with a person and our observational sensitivity to him? Between our tendency to assume that he is like or different from us and our tendency to look at, listen to, and remember what he said? The answer seems to be that we observe people who we think are like us and agree with us and turn off those who are not like us or that disagree with us.

Forsythe (1970) gave 150 college students these instructions:

> This is an exercise in empathy, i.e., your ability to assess your general similarity to other people. You will see five-minute interviews with Mrs. D, Mrs. N, and Mrs. P.
> Put your name and student number on the answer sheet. Then, in the lower half of the answer sheet write the names of the women as follows with a space after each:

```
                    RANK
             Mrs. D _____
             Mrs. N _____
             Mrs. P _____
```

After you have seen the film, put a "1" beside the woman whom you think would
be *most like* you in her personality traits and in her religious, social, and political
behavior and attitudes. Put "2" beside the women who would be next most like
you. Put "3" beside the woman who you think would be *least* like you.

Immediately afterward, the students were unexpectedly given a
test of the accuracy with which they had observed the three women.
The test consisted of sixteen true-false items for each woman like the
following: "She had on a black coat," "She wore earrings," "She had
gloves on," "She stuttered at times," etc. The accuracy of their
observation of a woman was then related to their empathy with her.
Conclusion: "A person observes more accurately those people with
whom he has more empathy."

Berger (1969) also related empathy to observation, i.e., how well a
student remembered facts about unions that were incorporated into
a speech. The greater the empathy, the better the memory for the
facts.

Women are better observers of people than men. Witryol and
Kaess (1957) found women superior to men on three different
observational tasks. The more difficult the task was, the greater was
their superiority. Two tasks required the recall of names associated
with photographs. In the third and most difficult task, five men and
five women were individually given aliases and assigned to a group
in which the experimenter conducted a one-minute "sidewalk interview" with each of them. In every interview the interviewee spoke
his alias at least once. Later, in the test situation, the ten aliases were
written on a blackboard, the participants were asked to stand up one
at a time, and the members of the group tried to match the person
with the correct alias. The women were not superior because of their
superior intelligence, for the men and women had the same average
intelligence. The women were not superior because of their superior
rote memory, for their performance on a test of number memory was
the same as the men's. The authors conclude, "Our tentative explanation for the consistent female superiority . . . is found in the
emphasis upon greater social facility for the female sex role with the
concomitant development of better skills." Another, but not conflicting, explanation is that women assume more similarity between
themselves and others than men do and, consequently, tend to look
at, listen to, and remember what others say more efficiently.

CHAPTER 4

OBSERVATIONAL TRAINING

WE DO NOT observe a shell and infer its kernel; we perceive a nut. Neither do we observe a person and infer his traits; we perceive a person. People do not come shelled; we learn to shell them, to separate what a person looks like and says from what we infer about him, to discriminate his sensory from his expressive qualities. The first task of observational training, therefore, is not to teach trainees what to look at and listen to; it is to train them *to* look and listen. The goal is a perceptual one: to discriminate sensory from expressive qualities, to see shells and kernels, not nuts.

Measures of observational sensitivity are essential for the development of successful programs. They clarify the specific training goals, make them more realistic, and permit an evaluation of training success. But trainees differ a great deal in their initial ability to discriminate sensory from expressive qualities. Consequently, we first need ways of diagnosing such differences in order to identify trainees most in need of observational training. However, the ability to discriminate is just a step toward maintaining the observer role under stress. At the end of the chapter, we turn to the problems of what and how to observe.

THE MEASUREMENT OF OBSERVATIONAL SENSITIVITY

Table 4-1 is a measure of deliberate observation, i.e., the respondents are initially instructed to observe as well as they can. Bruni (1963) developed the test from sound-color interviews filmed and distributed by Cline (1955). The twelve-item test provides separate subscores for accuracy in observing both men and women as well as for accuracy in what was seen and heard. The mean scores for 100 college students on the men test was 36 with a range from 16 to 49; on the women test, 39 with a range from 17 to 54; on the appearance test, 34 with a range from 19 to 51; and on the conversation test, 40 with a range from 15 to 41. The mean total score was 74 and with a range from 43 to 102. The entire test is included here not for the reader to examine in detail, but for the convenience of those who might wish to use it in observational research.

TABLE 4-1
Test of Observation
(Bruni, 1963)

GENERAL DIRECTIONS: This is a test of your ability to observe people. You are going to see five-minute filmed interviews. You will be asked to answer questions about what they looked like, said, and did. The test is divided into two parts:

Part I. Observation of Men
Part II. Observation of Women

Instructions for Part I

This part of the test is concerned with the appearance, actions, and conversation of the three men. The statements in the test are of the following kinds:

He had a red hat
He smiled frequently
He said he liked to play chess

Answer the questions by using spaces 1, 2, 3, and 4 on the separate answer sheet.

Mark "1" if you think the correct answer is Mr. G (the man in the first interview).

Mark "2" if you think the correct answer is Mr. W (the man in the second interview).

Mark "3" if you think the correct answer is Mr. Z (the man in the third interview).

Mark "4" if you think the statement applies to *none* of the three men.

Do all the items and try not to leave any blank.

DO NOT TURN THIS PAGE UNTIL THE FILM IS FINISHED
INSTRUCTIONS FOR PART II FOLLOW PART I

Part I Appearance and Actions

The first thirty statements refer to the appearance and actions of the men. REMEMBER to use "1" for Mr. G, "2" for Mr. W, "3" for Mr. Z, and "4" for statements that refer to *none* of the men.

Answers

(3)　　1. He smiled frequently.
(4)　　2. He kept wringing his hands.
(1)　　3. His shirt and jacket were the same color.
(2)　　4. He left quickly.
(4)　　5. He shook the interviewer's hand when he entered.
(3)　　6. He wore a knit white pullover shirt.
(4)　　7. He wore a wedding ring.
(3)　　8. He sat far back from the table.
(2)　　9. He gave a quick smile upon leaving.
(2)　　10. He put his left hand to his chin.
(1)　　11. He had a rather high forehead.
(1)　　12. He did not change his facial expression.
(3)　　13. His eyes appeared to be red.
(4)　　14. He had a nervous stutter.
(2)　　15. His elbows were on the table.
(1)　　16. He folded a piece of paper.

TABLE 4-1, continued

(3)	17.	He had a very soft voice.
(4)	18.	He moved his chair forward.
(3)	19.	His hands were in his lap most of the time.
(3)	20.	He sat sideways to the interviewer.
(3)	21.	He was wearing a shiny belt.
(2)	22.	There was a birthmark on his upper lip.
(3)	23.	He wore a tan sport jacket.
(2)	24.	He needed to shave.
(2)	25.	He covered his mouth.
(2)	26.	There was a pen or pencil in his hand.
(4)	27.	He had a pen clipped to his shirt.
(4)	28.	His hair was parted on the right.
(4)	29.	He wore a turtle-neck sweater.
(1)	30.	He did not shift his body at all during the interview.

Conversation

The following statements refer to what the interviewees *said*. Remember to use "1" for Mr. G, "2" for Mr. W, "3" for Mr. Z, and "4" for *none* of them.

He said that

(2)	31.	He did not want to talk about himself.
(1)	32.	He would sometimes go to a person who lied about him.
(4)	33.	Being in movies makes him nervous.
(2)	34.	He is not very athletic.
(4)	35.	People don't need religion.
(1)	36.	He has been in home movies.
(2)	37.	He keeps his emotions in check.
(4)	38.	He never attends church.
(1)	39.	He likes dancing.
(4)	40.	He likes being married.
(2)	41.	Moral teachings are important to most people.
(3)	42.	He would get "sore" if someone lied about him.
(1)	43.	People need a basic belief.
(1)	44.	It is good to get along with people.
(2)	45.	He likes music.
(1)	46.	He is an average person.
(1)	47.	He likes to "play around."
(3)	48.	He wouldn't like it if his brother took his car.
(1)	49.	Religion is not a major issue to him.
(3)	50.	People have a big conscience.
(3)	51.	Religion keeps him from things he feels like doing.
(4)	52.	He never goes to parties.
(2)	53.	He has few friends.
(3)	54.	Only a mean or big thing makes him lose his temper.
(2)	55.	He gets along well with intimate friends.
(3)	56.	Religion is important to him.
(3)	57.	He doesn't mind being in movies.
(4)	58.	It is important to have a hobby.
(4)	59.	He likes summer sports.
(3)	60.	He is disturbed at the way people get after parties.

TABLE 4-1, continued

Instructions for Part II

This part of the test is concerned with the appearance, actions, and conversation of the three women. The statements in the test are of the following kinds:

She had a red hat
She smiled frequently
She said she liked to play tennis

Answer the questions by using spaces 1, 2, 3, and 4 on the separate answer sheet.

Mark "1" if you think the correct answer is Mrs. D (the woman in the first interview).

Mark "2" if you think the correct answer is Mrs. N (the woman in the second interview).

Mark "3" if you think the correct answer is Mrs. P (the woman in the third interview).

Mark "4" if you think the statement applies to *none* of the three women.

Please answer all the statements, leaving none blank.

DO NOT TURN THIS PAGE UNTIL THE FILM IS FINISHED

Part II   Appearance and Actions

The first thirty statements refer to the appearance and actions of the women. REMEMBER to use "1" for Mrs. D, "2" for Mrs. N, "3" for Mrs. P, and "4" for statements that refer to *none* of the women.

Answers

(1)	61.	She wore short sleeves.
(4)	62.	She wore a necklace.
(1)	63.	She faced the camera directly.
(1)	64.	Her hair was messy and uncombed.
(2)	65.	She wore a ring on her right hand.
(2)	66.	She smiled very infrequently.
(3)	67.	Her hands were below the table.
(1)	68.	She clenched her fingers.
(3)	69.	She had very thin eyebrows.
(4)	70.	She straightened her glasses.
(1)	71.	She leaned back in her chair.
(3)	72.	Her hair was turned under at the ends.
(1)	73.	She had a long, thin neck.
(4)	74.	She had to clear her throat.
(2)	75.	She spoke slowly and softly.
(3)	76.	Her coat had a button undone.
(3)	77.	She looked down as she left.
(4)	78.	She nervously tugged at her collar.
(3)	79.	She wore shiny silver earrings.
(2)	80.	Her ring had a dark-colored stone.
(4)	81.	Her watch had a gold strap on it.
(4)	82.	She wore no lipstick.
(2)	83.	She had waves in her hair.
(3)	84.	She used no hand gestures at all.

TABLE 4-1, continued

(2)	85.	She took something from the table as she left.
(1)	86.	She gestured with both hands.
(3)	87.	She carried no purse.
(1)	88.	She wore no earrings.
(4)	89.	She put her gloves on the table.
(2)	90.	She sat sideways to the interviewer.

Conversation

The remaining statements refer to what the interviewees *said*. Remember to use "1" for Mrs. D, "2" for Mrs. N, "3" for Mrs. P, and "4" for *none* of them.

She said that

(2)	91.	She wished she had more patience.
(4)	92.	She reads a great deal.
(1)	93.	She expects people to be inconsiderate.
(4)	94.	She has few friends.
(2)	95.	Religion makes people better.
(4)	96.	In her spare time she works in her home.
(2)	97.	It is a problem for her to put up with ten other employees.
(1)	98.	Religion is something to cling to and depend on.
(3)	99.	She loses her temper when she's tired and nervous.
(4)	100.	She thinks religious persons don't lose their temper.
(3)	101.	Religion should be the greatest thing in the home.
(4)	102.	She has no time for hobbies.
(3)	103.	She would give money for mentally disturbed people.
(1)	104.	She never gets finished with housework.
(3)	105.	She thinks she is quite a hard worker.
(2)	106.	She loses her temper often.
(3)	107.	She would laugh off a lie told about her.
(2)	108.	Religion should be "over 50 percent of one's life."
(2)	109.	One of her handicaps is lack of time to do what she wants to do.
(4)	110.	She thinks there is good in everyone.
(1)	111.	She tends to control her temper too much.
(2)	112.	Her work is in the field of religion.
(3)	113.	Remembering names is her greatest problem.
(4)	114.	She can't control her temper.
(1)	115.	The inconsiderateness of people makes her lose her temper.
(1)	116.	A lie would make her mad.
(4)	117.	Her greatest problem is neglecting her family.
(1)	118.	She likes to do things that are creative.
(2)	119.	She agreed that she is "very busy."
(3)	120.	Religion is important in her home.

Better observers of men tended to be better observers of women, but not much better ($r = .38$). Better lookers tended to be better listeners, but not much better ($r = .32$). In spite of these somewhat independent elements, the overall internal consistency was moderately good ($r = .74$). The scores were also stable; the correlation between scores of the same students taking the test eight weeks apart was .69. Thus even among intelligent college students there are large differences in the ability to observe people accurately. Furthermore, the good observers were good predicters: The higher a student's score in observing the men and women, the more accurate were his predictions about them.

What are the characteristics of the good observer? Bruni related scores on his test to nearly a hundred physiological, intellectual, and personality measures. The search was almost fruitless. The only significant relationship found was with goodness, i.e., the higher a student's score on the Employee Rating Scale (Table 3-1), the higher his observation score. There was a strong suggestion that good observers might be better in picking out embedded figures, and a weak suggestion that they had higher pulse rates.

Perhaps it is incidental rather than deliberate observation that is significant. Forsythe (1970) measured incidental observation by giving a misleading set of instructions before the films were shown: "This is an exercise in empathy designed to assess your general similarity to other people . . . " This kind of measure only works once on the same group. The second time, regardless of instructions, the respondents would set themselves to observe. At any rate, those who are good incidental observers seem to benefit more from training. Mietus (1969) paired forty-four low scorers on the test of incidental observation with forty-four high scorers who had similar sensitivity scores prior to training. The high scorers improved more as a result of training.

Incredible as it may seem to the reader, these are the only efforts known to the author to develop general tests of either deliberate or incidental observation. A few tests of observational sensitivity have been developed for a specific research and have no general usefulness. Harvard students, for example, with varying degrees of prejudice against Jews, were shown photographs of Jews and non-Jews to determine how accurately they could identify the two groups (Lindzey and Rogolsky, 1950). The purpose was to determine whether the prejudiced were more accurate at this particular kind of observation. They were: "The bigot . . . is particularly sensitive or *vigilant* to stimuli that will permit the correct identification of the Jew and non-Jew." Standard listening comprehension tests have been developed that follow the format of reading comprehension tests. Hartlage (1963), for example, tested the listening comprehension of blind and sighted high school students by playing recorded prose selections to them. Intelligence-test scores were highly related to listening scores. There was no difference, however, between blind and sighted students in listening ability. Brown (1962) used the Educational Testing Service Test of Listening to verify the hunch that good listeners would imitate the breathing pattern of the speaker. They did not.

However, people did have different breathing patterns when they were listening.

Why have psychologists neglected the oldest, most used, and most important element in interpersonal communication? It is not because of the inherent difficulty of measuring observation, for, as Bruni's test illustrates, the process is relatively simple. It is not its triviality, for common sense suggests that observation is a highly significant component of sensitivity. We seem to have here indirect but strong evidence of the centrality of expressive qualities in perception. Like everyone else, psychologists perceive a person as dominated by an expressive quality. They, too, see nuts, not shells and kernels.

THE DIAGNOSIS OF PERCEPTUAL STYLE

Our perception of a person is dominated by his expressive quality rather than by his sensory qualities. People seem to differ a great deal, however, in the grip that expressive qualities have upon their perceptions. Satisfactory measurement of these differences would have the multiple merits of defining the discrimination goal concretely for the trainees, of informing them where they stand in relationship to it, and of providing a framework for specific training exercises. Ehrlich and Lipsey (1968) and Mullin (1962) have provided practical solutions to the measurement problem.

Ehrlich and Lipsey had persons estimate their own perceptual style. Among the items in their revised self-rating scale were the following:

When I meet people for the first time, I immediately have a strong reaction to them.

I find that certain new people turn me on—almost immediately.

Even when I talk to a person for just a few minutes, I am likely to have a strong reaction to him.

When I meet people for the first time, I know immediately if I like or dislike them.

I do not make judgments about people until I am sure of the facts.

It takes me quite a while to make up my mind about how I feel about a person.

My reactions to new people are very neutral.

I feel that one needs to know a person for a long time before he has a good idea of what a person is really like.

The rating scale permitted the respondents to indicate their degree of agreement or disagreement with each statement. There were wide and consistent differences in these self-estimates. The authors also report some evidence that strong reactors were more cautious, more concerned about making a good first impression, more likely to make predictions based on little information, and less likely to change their first impressions on the basis of later information.

Mullin (1962) earlier developed a film test of affective style. He first had students in a pilot study look at five-minute silent films of six different people being interviewed. At the end of each film he asked the students to write "as lifelike a picture of the person as you can." He then classified each sentence of each student's description into one of three categories: (1) physical ("is wearing a coat," "has dark features," "is wearing glasses," etc.); (2) sociological ("is unmarried," "is looking for work," "could be retired school teacher," etc.); (3) affective ("is unsure of himself," "loves to gossip," "does not trust the interviewer," "worries a lot," etc.). The students varied widely and consistently: the correlation between the average number of affective sentences they used in describing one person and the average number they used in describing another person was .79.

Based on the responses given in the pilot study, Mullin then developed an objective test consisting of ninety statements, thirty for each of three film subjects. The three alternatives were selected from statements made by the students in the pilot study, the underlined ones being those classified as psychological. The test is reliable, correlations for different college groups ranging from .82 to .86. That is, the tendency of students to choose the "affective" statements remains remarkably constant from statement to statement and from person to person.

The Test of Perceptual Style (Table 4-2) is an abbreviation of Mullin's original test. It concerns two instead of three people, has twenty-four instead of ninety items, and presents the subject with two instead of three alternatives. However, the internal consistency is still about .70. The mean score on the test is 13 and the range from 1 to 23 among 150 college students. Women are significantly stronger reactors than men. As in Ehrlich and Lipsey's study, Mullin found higher scorers were more cautious, i.e., less confident, less optimistic, and less dominating. They were also younger and felt more distant from people. They were poorer in their observations and in their predictions about people.

THE DISCRIMINATION OF SENSORY FROM EXPRESSIVE QUALITIES

The failure to differentiate sharply between sensory and expressive perceptions seems to account for considerable fuzziness and confusion in many observational training programs. Schlessinger, Muslin, and Baittle (1968) had resident psychiatrists view the filming of a diagnostic interview conducted by the teacher. Their spontaneous

TABLE 4-2
Test of Perceptual Style
(Adapted from Mullin, 1962)

DIRECTIONS: You will see two people in silent movies: *Try to form as life-like an impression of each as you can.* The first will be of Mrs. P and the second of Mr. W. As each film is finished the camera will be stopped. Then, in each of the pairs of statements numbered below, *pick the one that is more like your impression of the person* on the separate answer sheet.

The Case of Mrs. P

1.   (1) is sincere* (2) is wearing a coat.
2.   (1) is about forty years old (2) is self-satisfied.*
3.   (1) did most of the talking (2) is one who makes a good impression.*
4.   (1) moistens her lips (2) is experienced with small groups.*
5.   (1) considers the interview serious* (2) shows signs of amusement.
6.   (1) is a modest dresser (2) is uncertain of her answers.*
7.   (1) enjoys her family* (2) has dark features.
8.   (1) is amusing* (2) is a modest dresser.
9.   (1) wants to make an impression on interviewer* (2) has good posture.
10.   (1) feels self-conscious* (2) is dressed in red.
11.   (1) is verbal (2) is feeling under pressure.*
12.   (1) laughs often (2) is indecisive.*

The Case of Mr. W

13.   (1) is unsure of himself* (2) is wearing a striped sweater.
14.   (1) is wearing glasses (2) is somewhat perplexed.*
15.   (1) often grasps his chin (2) is on guard most of the time.*
16.   (1) leaves smiling (2) is uncertain of the future.*
17.   (1) does not trust the interviewer* (2) smiles little.
18.   (1) is confident in his opinions* (2) is of medium height.
19.   (1) was eager to leave* (2) left quickly.
20.   (1) hopes he has put his story over* (2) has black hair.
21.   (1) has curly hair (2) is earnestly interested in the situation.*
22.   (1) knows what's going on* (2) needs a shave.
23.   (1) feels a bit insecure* (2) is in his early twenties.
24.   (1) is self-concerned* (2) changes his facial expression little.

*Indicates correct answer.

impressions were recorded in brief reports they were asked to write. A teaching session followed in which the videotape was used with interruptions and segmental replays. At weekly intervals thereafter, for twelve weeks, the residents were filmed performing diagnostic interviews. Some conclusions:

> Our experience demonstrated that anxiety was a critically important factor influencing observation . . . a tendency toward premature closures such as a diagnosis of psychosis early in the interview accompanied by stereotyped observations . . . a diagnosis of a lesser pathological condition was made early in the interview and the resident was thereafter not readily influenced by conflicting evidence in what he observed . . . tendency to discuss dynamics divorced from

observations as an intellectual exercise . . . repetition in the form of rote learning. For example, the significance of hand movements as a nonverbal cue had been emphasized by the instructor in one case. In their effort to apply this knowledge in the following session, the residents focused on the hand movements of another patient for whom they were of no particular significance.

Muslin, et al. (1967) had judges compare the tape-recorded interviews of therapist-client sessions with tapes of the supervisor and the therapist discussing the same sessions. Conclusion: "Judges were unable to formulate the nature of the patient's current difficulties from the material offered during supervision."

Both the psychiatrists and the interns in these training programs seem to be like everybody else. They formed instant whole impressions, resisted modifying them, and made only a vague and fluctuating differentiation between what a patient said and did and what expressive quality he seemed to have. It is apparently not enough for trainees to understand the difference between observation and inference or even to be able to discriminate the difference in practice. They need to be *drilled* in making the discrimination, for even the best observers are poor observers. For example, a lecturer took out a cigarette, traced eight circles with it in the air, moved it horizontally several times, and then placed it in his mouth and lit. A few minutes later he asked members of the large group to describe what he had done with the cigarette. No one could give even a roughly accurate report.

Having trainees rate and discuss their own perceptual styles is a natural place for discrimination training to begin. The results of such ratings can be pooled, the differences in the group identified, and the value of observation as a goal discussed. Trainees might then be asked to recall and discuss occasions on which expressive qualities or sensory qualities dominated:

Expressive Impression: Describe a person whom you very much liked or disliked. Describe the emotional situation, the person, and your feelings about him.

Sensory Impression: Describe a person such as a teacher, an entertainer, or a television performer that you did not particularly like or dislike but to whom you paid close attention. Report only what he looked like, said, and did.

Finally, they might be asked to describe only their sensory perceptions of a person seen in a film, speaking before the group, or interacting with them. These descriptions would then be discussed and criticized for the direct or indirect intrusion of expressive qualities.

Trainees learn fast to become temporarily good observers. Kepes (1965) gave the observational test (Table 4-1) before and after an observational training program. During the program, trainees in the experimental group were given practice and feedback in observing fellow students. They made large gains on every part of the test. However, students in a control group who were given no practice or feedback made equally large gains. The clarification of the goal seems enough to promote an effective observational set.

To develop permanently good observers is much more time-consuming. The goal of one program, for example, was to improve the trainee's skill as a good listener and his ability to get people to "open up" (Maier, Hoffman, and Lansky, 1960). To achieve these aims students participated in weekly role-playing sessions and had practice in reflecting feeling. The criterion of success was the quality of performance in a role-playing scene at the end of training. Results: a modest improvement in listening; no improvement in the ability to get people to talk. Conclusion:

> For the amount and type of training received by supervisors and executives in the typical industrial course in human relations the implication of these results is obvious. Training is a slow process of reorientation and of the accumulation of new concepts, attitudes, and skills . . . we can conclude that where management is seriously interested in training supervisory personnel in effective human relations, they might expect to invest considerably more time than is presently customary.

The development of the ability to discriminate between expressive and sensory qualities is not merely a matter of learning to pay attention to sensory qualities. It is primarily a matter of learning to play the observer role.

THE OBSERVER ROLE

The role we are playing influences the dominance as well as the kind of expressive qualities we perceive in the person to whom we are relating. For example, General Electric managers attending a series of small conferences were divided into a John Group and a Manager group (Kellogg, 1962). Both groups were given the following information:

John:
John Jones is a young man in his thirties, with a liberal arts degree, and a law degree. He was in the top fifth of his class in arts, but only in the top half in law. He was originally hired on a relations rotating program and was placed in union relations for his first job. After about a year there, he went into salary and wage administration and has been in this field for about three years. He is bright, quick, outgoing; he is quite a leader; he is persuasive both orally and in writing. He is not very detail-minded, dislikes routine and records very much. He wants to be eventually at least a relations manager and possibly a general manager. He had had some assignments in manufacturing and he liked them very much, so that he is torn between relations and manufacturing and really would welcome advice on this point.

Manager:
John's manager is about fifty years old. He has been in the salary and wage field all his life. He would like to be promoted but has been passed over twice, so that he feels it is

not very likely. He is personally very methodical, detail-minded, and a little withdrawn and reserved. He feels that John's records are not as accurate as they could be and that John does not spend enough time at his desk doing his paper work. He does recognize some excellent results—John has won the confidence of managers, his advice on pay levels and rates is frequently asked, and better understanding about pay administration has been achieved.

The Manager group was asked to pretend that it was the evening before a discussion with John to help him make a plan for his development. In addition to the above descriptions, the group was given details about his education, work history, past performance appraisals (average or better), and a few test results. The members of the John group were asked to pretend that they were John, faced the next day with a discussion of his development needs and plans. After the two groups had discussed the situation and made their plans, a chairman of each group presented them to the class.

In eleven different conferences, the Manager and John groups invariably saw the situation in quite different ways. The managers saw John as a below-average employee even though they knew he had received above-average ratings from his former supervisors. The Johns saw the manager as a person impossible to work for who blocked his advancement and failed to give rewards for good work. The managers and Johns set widely different aims for their discussion. The managers planned to get John to be more exact, keep his records better, and develop more self-discipline. The Johns planned to get out from under the manager without making him an enemy.

As the John and Manager experiences suggest, it is relatively easy for us to shift temporarily from one role to another. Naval Air Cadets heard a recorded interview between a psychologist and a former prisoner of war who had signed several communistic statements (Jones and deCharms, 1957). Cadets in one group were asked to imagine whether they would like the prisoner as a friend; in another group, they were to imagine they were members of a judicial board of inquiry empowered to study the case and to decide what the formal charges should be; and in a third group, they were to imagine they were members of a medical-psychological board of review empowered to find out why the prisoner did what he did. The varying sets produced strikingly different pictures of the prisoner.

The need for counselors to stress the observer role is an old story. Thus one outcome of the Western Electric Company (1938) studies at the Hawthorne plant was the recognition that supervisors should pay more attention to their employees. The training program contained these directives:

1 Listen—don't talk.

2 Give full interest and attention.

3 Never argue.

4 Do not listen exclusively to the manifest content of the expression.

5 Listen for:
   What he wants to say
   What he does not want to say
   What he cannot say without help

6 As you listen, plot out tentatively and for subsequent correction the pattern that is being set before you. To test, summarize what he has said and present for comment. Always do this with caution—that is, clarify but do not add or twist.

Exhorting a trainee, however, has never been an effective way of changing his roles or teaching him anything else.

To become a good observer, the trainee must learn to shift his attention from the subjective to objective, from himself to the other person. The shift has considerable consequences for the development of sensitivity. Lundy (1956) had students fill out the Allport-Vernon scale of values. Two weeks later each student met with two other students and discussed a topic for five minutes with each of them. Before and after each discussion the students filled out the scale as they thought their partners had filled it out. With one partner the student was instructed to focus his attention upon himself; with the other, to focus attention upon his partner. Results: When the student focused upon himself his tendency to assume similarity increased and his sensitivity decreased; when he focused upon the other student his empathy decreased and his sensitivity increased. Conclusion:

> Therapists who, by their training, concentrate upon themselves and what they have to say may succeed only in projecting their own ideas upon the patient. Therapists trained to pay attention to their patients may be better able to understand the particular patient being treated.
>
> Patients, by the same token, may become more accurate and less projective in their perceptions of other people if they can be brought around to paying attention to other people instead of to themselves.

The longer the trainee can maintain the observer set, the more sensitive he tends to become. Dailey (1952) gave two groups of perceivers a little information about a person. The first group was asked to make predictions on the basis of trivial information and the second group was not asked to make such predictions. Both groups were then given more complete information and again asked to make predictions. The second group, which had *not* made initial predictions, made more accurate final predictions. The result was not due to the first group's sticking rigidly to its earlier specific predictions, for the perceivers made more serious errors in new predictions about the person: "The effect appears to be on the observer's understanding of the *person* rather than of the person's traits or behavior." In fact, the result seemed to be due primarily to being given time to form an impression. In one part of the study, perceivers who were given some information about a person and a waiting period before they received the rest made less accurate predictions than perceivers who did not have the waiting period.

The problem of observational training is to teach trainees to maintain the observer role in tense interpersonal situations. It is then that the perception of sensory qualities fade and expressive qualities intensify. Kagan and Schauble (1969) have developed a series of film materials that seem eminently suitable for this purpose. The person in each film clip is addressing the viewer with feeling.

The *Rejection* sequence, for example, portrays varying degrees of rejection toward the viewer. In the first vignette the actor communicates subtle negative feelings to the listener:

> I don't suppose we'd be too unhappy if you decide you'd like to stay with us. You could probably fit in, I imagine. I don't know that—no, I don't suppose that would be too much of an objection. You know, I think we've decided by now—figured out pretty much that you and we wouldn't be too awfully unhappy with that. You seem to be the sort of person I think we could get along with so—I think you'd be pretty welcome here.

More rejection and hostility are added with each vignette. In the next to the last vignette the actor loudly and angrily tells the listener:

> Well, I've listened and I don't like your ideas one damn bit; as a matter of fact they just about make me sick. It's you and people like you who cause most of the stink and misery around us and I'm just not fond of it and I hate to see it and if it weren't for some of the proprieties in life I'd climb right over this table and punch you right in the mouth. As far as I'm concerned you can just pick up your ideas and your notions and get right the hell out of here. I hope that's quite clear.

The films produce strong reactions. Danish and Brodsky (1970) showed them to thirty policemen attending a Basic Police Training School. Even the early vignettes produced a strong response:

> Some trainees become so agitated that they were unable to stay seated during the discussions between segments. They leaped up and down in their seats calling for the attention of the other trainees, raising and lowering their hands for recognition, and speaking out although three or four others were speaking simultaneously. . . . They repeatedly indicated that they would not permit anyone to talk to them in that manner and that they would probably strike or mace the individual. In fact, it seemed that it was the wish of the trainee for the actor to break the law so that he would be able to strike out physically at the actor. During the last vignette the trainees were instructed to respond aloud to the actor's comments. Very little verbal aggression appeared, but rather a chorus of sounds simulating physical aggression ("pow"; "bang") toward the actor was displayed.

The task of trainees is to continue to report accurately what the person in the film looked like, said, and did as the emotional stress is increased. Later, the stress could be further increased by having persons speak before the group in ways designed to provoke an emotional response. The stress could be continually increased by moving gradually from simulated to actual life situations. The direc-

tive throughout is: "Do not say what you feel about what he said—
say what he said."

THE SEQUENCING OF CUES

In the theater, a "cue" is a word or a bit of stage business in a play
that signals to an actor that it is time for him to begin. In psychology,
it is a sensory indicator of the nature of the person perceived. When
we observe, we observe different types of cues: written, auditory,
visual, kinetic, olfactory, or tactile. Observation is necessarily selective, for we cannot possibly attend to all the cues that we are
receiving about a person.

Our concern is with the observation of cues that lead to more
accurate predictions about people. In the following chapters, therefore, we will be concerned with specific ones that lead to more
accurate predictions of the traits of individuals and groups as well as
those cues that lead to more accurate predictions about relationships
between one person and another. Here our interest is in the types of
cues and, especially, in training observers to observe them in the best
sequence.

The Power of Unobserved Cues

When we observe, we observe cues. Normally, however, we do not
observe but perceive. And it is the expressive qualities that dominate
this perception. The cues that lead to perceiving a person as familiar,
friendly, and helpful or strange, hostile, and threatening are numerous and powerful. The review of Duncan (1969) of nonverbal communication stresses the subtle but powerful influence that kinetic,
paralinguistic, proxemic, olfactory, tactile, and artifactual cues have
upon the goodness of our impressions of others. Mehrabian (1969)
stresses that facial cues more than vocal ones determine impressions
but that vocal ones are more influential than verbal ones. In general,
these cues tell us not what the other person is, but how he is relating
to us. For example, we seem to like people who look at us when we
are saying good things about ourselves and look away when we are
saying bad things (Ellsworth and Carlsmith, 1968). Style of dress has
a marked influence on the traits we ascribe to people (Hamid, 1968).

Evidence of the power that visual cues of which we are unaware
have over our perceptions is extensive. For example, persons seen
on videotape for a few seconds were perceived as being more
intelligent when they wore glasses than when they did not (Argyle
and McHenry, 1971). Girls without lipstick were perceived as more
conscientious, serious, and talkative but less interested in men than
when they wore lipstick (McKeachie, 1952). Men with dark complex-

ions, tense faces, square jaws, and rough-textured skins are perceived as cold and ruthless.

We are often more sensitive to a person when we do not see him than when we do. A group of student judges, for example, were told only the general category of a series of students: undergraduate male education major, graduate female art student, etc. They then filled out an interest inventory as they thought each student had filled it out. Next the judges observed each student as he described the room he was in, made a drawing at the blackboard, and engaged in several other expressive acts. After seeing each student, the judges again filled out the interest inventory as they thought the student had filled it out. The accuracy of the before-and-after predictions was compared. They were *more* accurate before than after. The judges made better predictions without seeing the person than they did with seeing him (Stone, Leavitt, and Gage, 1957).

What is the best sequence for the different types of cues? In commenting on this question, Cline (1968) says:

> Many times seeing the person you are interviewing can actually interfere with or reduce the accuracy of one's judgment. This might be illustrated in an anecdotal way by telling of one film which showed a very attractive young blond woman who had a considerable impact on all audiences who saw her. She tended to project the image of a very sexy blonde with a great deal of animal vitality. It was found that most judges rarely ever listened to what she had to say and responded primarily to her visual impact which was considerable. Most judges did quite poorly in judging her. If, however, they merely read a transcript of what she said or even just heard what she said without ever seeing her, they almost invariably did far better in their judgments because they focused primarily on the content of her verbal communication which was quite revealing, direct, open and could be taken for the most part at face value. Or as this woman said to our interviewer, "Nobody ever listens to what I have to say."

Cline's comments are supported by the results of his elaborate manipulation of kinds of cues presented to eleven different groups with twenty-five adults in each group. The task for all groups was to pre̅c̅ t the personality traits and behavior of six men and women. Each group received a different set of cues: group 1 saw and heard the standard set of six judging films; group 2 was given only the age and sex of each interviewee; group 3 read the occupation, education, sex, marital status, race, and seven similar facts about each interviewee; group 4 saw the visual content of the film but heard nothing; group 5 heard the sound track but saw nothing; group 6 heard the sound track for thirty seconds; group 7 saw the visual content of the film but heard the sound track for only thirty seconds; group 8 read a printed transcript of each interview; group 9 read only a personality sketch about each interviewee; group 10 read a personality sketch and a printed transcript of each interview; group 11 read the sketch and predicted and then read the printed transcript and predicted again. Result: "The most accurate groups of all were those groups who read the personality sketch and/or read the printed transcript of the interview."

1. Written Cues

We may be more interested in reading about a person after, rather than before, we meet him. The evidence shows, however, that we form a more accurate impression if we read all there is to know before we have met him. The explanation also seems clear: The impression formed from written cues is weaker but less influenced by the static of deceptive visual cues. The perceiver who does his homework is a better predicter.

Is it better to read what is good about a person before reading what is bad? Miller and Rowe (1967) gave students written descriptions of prospective roommates and then asked them to rate each prospect from (1) definitely would consider as a roommate to (6) definitely would not consider. The descriptions gave four traits for each prospect. The traits ranged from three favorable and one unfavorable to one favorable and three unfavorable. Conclusion: ". . . when an individual must evaluate another individual on the basis of limited information . . . the evaluation will be influenced more by the unfavorable evidence than by the favorable evidence."

The bad drives out the good. But does it drive it further out when it comes first? Briscoe, Woodyard, and Shaw (1967) made a thorough investigation of this question by giving some subjects unfavorable before favorable information and others favorable information before unfavorable. Conclusion: "The results clearly demonstrated that the unfavorable first impression changed less when discrepant information was given than did the favorable first impression." The authors offer the following explanation: "When a person exhibits favorable attributes or behaviors, he is merely doing what is expected of him and thus merits no special approbation . . . . Negative behaviors, on the other hand, cannot readily be attributed to social forces, and hence unfavorable information provides more unambiguous evidence about the individual's personality."

The bad evidence may be less ambiguous than the good. Both, however, must be taken into account in forming an accurate impression of a person. Maugham (1938, p. 10) has commented on this necessity:

Rousseau in the course of his Confessions *narrates incidents that have profoundly shocked the sensibility of mankind. By describing them so frankly he falsified his values and so gave them in his book a greater importance than they had in his life. There were events among a multitude of others, virtuous or at least neutral, that he omitted because they were too ordinary to seem worth recording. There is a sort of man who pays no attention to his good actions, but is tormented by his bad ones. This is the type that most often writes about himself. He leaves out his redeeming qualities and so appears only weak, unprincipled and vicious.*

The trainee should be taught not only to read about a person before he sees him and to take the good with the bad. He should be taught to take the good *before* the bad.

2. Auditory Cues

Should we listen to what a person says before we see him saying it? Giedt (1955, 1958) recorded interviews with four patients in order "to study the sorts of observations that aid the clinician in making accurate judgments of a patient's personality." The interviews were presented as silent films, written transcripts, sound recordings, or complete sound films to forty-eight psychiatrists, social workers, and psychologists. These professionals made ratings of the personality characteristics and predicted the responses to incomplete sentences of the interviewed patients.

The experts were able to predict as accurately from reading a transcript of the interview as from seeing a film of the interview. In fact, at least some of the judges were misled by seeing the dress, appearance, and facial expressions of the patients. It was hard for the observers to pick up appropriate expressive movements and correctly interpret their meaning—noting that a person had a "rigid face" led to overestimates of a patient's rigidity; noting that a person had "an intent look" was a poor indicator of anxiety. Furthermore, impressions from appearances seem to dominate impressions from more objective sources. For example, observers often listed the right cues for making a correct judgment but would then say things like "But he didn't seem anxious," and shift to a wrong prediction. In general, visual cues seem to dominate written and auditory ones.

Giedt (1955) concludes that written and auditory cues should have a higher priority than visual ones:

> *Often at considerable expense and inconvenience to both applicant and employer, a personal interview is arranged. If the results obtained in this study hold for the assessment of employees, then it might be possible for an applicant to be interviewed by telephone or for him to submit either a sound recording or a written protocol of an interview conducted by some recognized local interviewer.*

3. Visual Cues

The longer we delay our visual exposure to a person, the more accurate our impressions of him are likely to be. The optimum sequence seems to be: Read about the person and then write an impression of him, giving priority to the favorable facts about him;

hear him speak and then revise the impression; and, finally, see him and again revise the impression.

This sequence moderates the dominating influence of expressive qualities that seem to be largely conveyed by visual cues. But we do not normally wish to avoid these qualities. We seek them, we want to see and be seen. Face-to-face interaction with a person does expose us to the maximum number of cues about him. Unfortunately, we miss, distort, or forget most of them in favor of a simple, emotional, and global impression.

The immediate recording of visual cues can overcome most of these difficulties, for the sooner we record cues, the more we remember. Three groups of four persons recorded their observations of people they had interviewed (Symonds and Dietrich, 1941). The first group recorded their impressions immediately; the second, after two days; and the third, after seven days. The interviews recorded immediately were far more complete.

If we fail to record, we forget many cues that would be valuable aids in predicting the person's future behavior. Thus work supervisors are interested in present behavior of their subordinates that will help them in predicting their future behavior. Supervisors readily forget such behaviors. Supervisors of the Delco-Remy Division of General Motors recorded incidents of effective performances among their men after different intervals: twenty-five recorded them daily; twenty-five recorded them every two days, and twenty-five recorded them each week (Flanagan and Burns, 1962). The following incident is typical:

> I observed an employee looking through the scrap tub. Shortly after, he came to me stating that someone had thrown a large piece of cast-iron piston into the scrap tub. We salvaged this piston and a short time later used the piece to make a pulley for a very urgently needed job.

The supervisors who kept daily records reported twice as many incidents as those who kept biweekly ones. Electric recordings provide a complete record. A comparison of written reports with electric recordings showed that the former omitted over half of the facts (Covner, 1942). Of the facts that were written, the most common error was to change the order in which things were said so that the implication was given that one statement lead to another when actually it did not. Unfortunately, making recordings is sometimes impossible and making typescripts of recordings is always burdensome.

Jottings are a good solution for the recording problem in many situations. They take little time, they keep ideas and acts in sequence, and they serve as a useful reminder of details. The supervisors at Delco-Remy were trained to jot down incidents of effective and ineffective behavior like these for John Henry: "Needed ladder" and "Good decision on bolts." Later these jottings recalled to the supervisor that "Henry had to get ladder to reach raw stock near machine so that time was wasted getting and returning the ladder" and "Henry quickly decided on the best size of bolts to use on new part." In this study, the average supervisor spent only five minutes each day making such jottings.

Finally, a reservation. The written, auditory, and visual sequencing of cues fits both the theoretical framework of this book and the few facts that bear upon this problem. No one, however, has presented the same cues in these different modalities in varying sequences to test incisively their influence on predictive accuracy.

In summarizing the little we know about observational training, it seems clear that trainees can learn quickly to discriminate sensory from expressive qualities although those with generally strong emotional reactions to others have greater difficulties. The major problem, however, is that human beings are expressers rather than observers and, consequently lose their ability to observe in tense interpersonal situations. One solution to this problem is to control the sequence of cues that the observer receives—written before auditory, auditory before visual. The difficulty with *this* solution is that people would generally rather interact with a person than look at him, rather see him than hear him, and rather hear him than read about him. Above all, they would rather talk than listen, rather express themselves than receive expressions. Daniel and Otis (1950) recorded a sample of sixty employment interviews from eight companies. The average interview lasted ten minutes, the interviewee talking for one-third of the time and the interviewer talking for two-thirds. The cartoon of the bored patient listening to the childhood experiences of his therapist suggests that interviewers are not the only professional listeners who prefer to talk.

THEORETICAL SENSITIVITY

CHAPTER 5

MYTHIC VERSUS SCIENTIFIC THINKING

THE world is so complex that we are easily dazzled by the vast array of things to feel, describe, and predict. Scientists have developed a variety of ways of dealing with the problem of complexity. Mechanical devices provide one: the telescope limits the astronomer's attention to one part of the heavens; the microscope focuses the attention of the biologist upon one part of the environment. Theories provide an even more powerful way, for a theory tells us not only what to look for but also what *not* to look for or worry about. A theory defines a set of terms and assumes relationships between the terms. Freudian theory, for example, defines the id, ego, and superego and assumes relationships between them.

The primary business of psychology is scientific thinking: The development of theories that give man a power of prediction beyond that which he can achieve through his own unaided common sense. The business is successful in that the predictions the psychologist can make from his measures have steadily grown in their range and accuracy. The business is a failure, however, in that the psychologist, unaided by his measures, generally cannot make predictions that are more accurate than the common-sense judgments of those who are not psychologists. Nor can he make more accurate predictions than his own measures. The next section presents some of the evidence that supports these statements.

Why is the psychologist no better than anyone else in the accuracy of his intuitive predictions? What can be done to improve the situation? This chapter offers answers to these questions. The answers, however, are so abstract and so speculative that it may help the reader to have a brief idea of what they are at the beginning. The psychologist is no better than nonpsychologists, we suggest, because his intuitive predictions, like theirs, are based on mythic rather than scientific thinking. The solution we recommend is that he develop and use empirically derived theories.

CLINICAL VERSUS ACTUARIAL PREDICTIONS

Chapter 2 reviewed the evidence that neither T-group participation nor psychology instruction nor clinical training seems to increase sensitivity. Here we are concerned with the related problem that the psychologist cannot seem to use information gained from his own measures to make more accurate predictions than can be made from the measures alone. For several decades, psychologists have referred to this dilemma as the problem of clinical versus actuarial prediction.

Here is an example of the problem. Ten students in a graduate course in interviewing took a long objective examination on the text they had been studying. The instructor scored the papers but did not give the students the results. Instead, he first asked them to develop a statistical formula for predicting how each one would rank on the test—who would be highest, who would be next highest, etc. The students based the formula on the average grades obtained by each student as an undergraduate, the number of courses in psychology he had taken, and his years as a graduate student in psychology. They gathered this information from each student, put it in the formula developed, and predicted the rank each student would obtain by the mechanical application of the formula.

The students were then asked to try "to beat the formula." They were given all the information that went into the formula, the formula itself, and the success of the formula in predicting test scores. In addition, they were permitted to interview each other to obtain any information they thought would be helpful. Each student then ranked the other students and himself as he thought they had performed on the test. Each student's rankings were then related to the examination scores actually obtained. No student's subjective rankings were as accurate as the rankings done by the statistical formula. The predictions arrived at mechanically were more accurate than the subjective judgments.

In an early effort to solve this problem, 1,000 criminals paroled from Illinois state prisons were studied (Burgess, 1928). An objective measure of the probable success of a prisoner's parole was developed by using twenty-one facts gathered from the case histories of the criminals: the nature of the crime, length of sentence, nationality of the father, county of indictment, size of the community, type of residence, chronological age, and so on. A prisoner was given + or − on each factor. Thus, if he were below a certain age he would be given +; above, −. If he obtained less than a set number of pluses out of the twenty-one, he was predicted to be a failure; above, a success. Accuracy was measured by comparing the actual failure or success of the paroles with that predicted by the formula. Two prison psychiatrists studied the same twenty-one facts and made their own predictions. Result: the objective measure was more sensitive than the psychiatrists'.

Meehl (1954) compared the predictions of counselors with objective predictions. The task was to predict the college grades of 500 entering freshmen. The objective prediction used a formula involving their scholastic aptitude scores and high school grade point averages. In making their subjective predictions, the counselors not only had the aptitude scores and ranking of the students but an hour interview with each as well. Still, the objective predictions were more accurate than the subjective ones. Of twenty-seven similar studies found by Meehl (1957), subjective predictions were never superior to objective ones and sometimes were inferior.

People, in general, seem unable to successfully combine empirical with intuitive predictions. Reviews of studies in other fields show a "distressing" lack of accuracy. Hoffman, Slovic, and Rorer (1968), for example, showed nine radiologists seven commonly used symptoms of malignant gastric ulcer in various patterns. Each radiologist rated each of ninety-six patterns from 1 (definitely benign) to 7 (definitely malignant). Each also rated the same patterns in the same patients a second time. Each radiologist was in high agreement with himself, making much the same predictions on the cases the second time. However, they were in very little agreement with each other (the median correlation was .38). Even if they had been in agreement, they might well have been wrong in their diagnoses. However, if a radiologist did not agree with other radiologists, it is highly unlikely that he would agree with the correct diagnosis. Conclusion: "The most striking result of the present study was the lack of agreement among diagnosticians who are presumably experts at the task to which they were assigned."

The conclusions of the scientists, then, are incompatible with the conclusions from empirical measures. The theorist cannot integrate his thinking processes with the processes of his theories. The incompatibility seems to arise from conflicting ways of thinking. The theorist normally thinks in a mythic way; his theory, in a scientific way.

MYTHIC VERSUS SCIENTIFIC ORIENTATIONS

What is mythic thinking and how does it differ from scientific thinking? Mythic thinking is not a weak and diseased type of scientific thinking. It is a totally different *kind* of thinking. Mythic thinking is motivated by quite different human needs; it is based on quite different ways of perceiving the world; and it operates by quite different processes than scientific thinking. In scientific thinking, the whole consists of its parts and results from them. In mythic thinking, the whole does not *have* parts. The part *is* the whole.

The dictionary says that a myth is a legendary story that is usually concerned with deities and the creation of the world and its inhabitants. Thus there is an old Greek myth that human beings were originally shaped in circular fashion with four arms and four legs. Their great strength and vigor led them to conspire against the gods. In order to subdue and punish them, Zeus sliced every one in two. However, they became so apathetic and sad that Zeus eventually allowed the separated parts of the whole person to occasionally and briefly rejoin each other. Now, the common focus of interest in the study of myths is upon their content. The focus of our interest is not upon the content of myths but upon the motivational, perceptual, and cognitive processes that lead to the development of a myth and to the belief that the myth reflects objective reality. In this sense, *our* myths are our beliefs about what is real. Our interest is in how these beliefs arise. More specifically, we are concerned with the problem of how our beliefs about what another person "really" is can arise on the basis of little evidence and can remain unaltered in the face of mounting conflicting facts.

Mythic thinking, we are saying, is a different kind of thinking that is so pervasive and powerful that it overwhelms the delicate processes of scientific thinking. Some eminent authorities do not agree. Levi-Strauss (1963), for example, states that the same logical processes operate in myth as in science and that man has always been thinking in the same equally logical way. The improvement in thinking lies not in the alleged progress of man's mind. It lies in the discovery of new areas to which he can more successfully apply his "unchanged and unchanging powers." Briefly, Levi-Strauss holds that man has shifted his attention from the effort to solve unsolvable internal conflicts to the effort to solve problems concerned with his relationship to the external world.

Our antithetical view is derived from the classic three-volume work on symbolic forms by the philosophical anthropologist Ernst Cassirer. On the question of mythic versus scientific thinking he says, in small part (1955, vol. 2, pp. 34–36):

> What distinguishes empirical reality, the constant core of objective being, from the mere world of representation or imagination, is that in it the permanent is more and more clearly differentiated from the fluid, the constant from the variable. . . . Myth lives entirely by the presence of its object—by the intensity with which it seizes and takes possession of consciousness in a specific moment. Myth lacks any means of extending the moment beyond itself, of looking ahead of it or behind it, of relating it as a particular to the elements of reality as a whole. . . . It lacks any fixed dividing line between mere "representation" and "real" perception, between wish and fulfillment, between image and thing. This is most clearly revealed by the crucial significance of dream experience in the genesis and growth of the mythical. . . . It possesses neither the impulsion or the means to correct or criticize what is given here and now, to limit its objectivity by measuring it against something not given, something past or future.

Our purpose here is not to present a general exposition of Cassirer's views. It is to use his distinction between mythic and scientific thinking to clarify basic problems in sensitivity training. In working toward this end, we will focus upon the totally different roles that theory plays in mythic and scientific thinking. A theory, we have said, is a set of concepts with assumed relationships between them. Both mythic and scientific thinking utilize theories, for they both use concepts and assume relationships between them. However, they use different kinds of concepts, assume different kinds of relationships between these concepts, and have totally different approaches to the verification of these assumed relationships. In a nutshell, what we will be asserting is that we all engage in both mythic and scientific thinking, that we sometimes use scientific theories in our mythic thinking, and that some types of personality theories are more likely to be used in this way than others.

In the next three sections we will be concerned with the different kinds of concepts, relationships, and verification processes used in mythic and scientific thinking. In order to make these differences more concrete, we will use a simple five-trait theory as an example of a scientific theory. The development, correlates, and interpretation of this theory are discussed in more detail elsewhere (Smith, 1968). Table 5-1 defines these independent traits and provides forty-item scales for measuring each.

At this point, the reader will find it sufficient to read the definitions at the beginning of each trait scale. However, the scales also provide a more complete background for discussion in earlier chapters in which these traits were used. They are also used extensively in the training procedures presented in the chapters that follow.

TABLE 5-1
Five Trait Scales

A definition of each of the five traits is given below with forty statements that measure the trait. The statements are grouped under subordinate traits in the cluster and the answer for the "high" end of the scale indicated. Norms for 100 college men and 100 college women in 1970 are given after the statements. The two most discriminating items in each scale are indicated with an asterisk.

The Cautious vs. the Bold

The cautious person is physically inactive, quiet, and aloof individual who avoids leadership positions, lacks confidence in himself, and takes a pessimistic view of the world. The bold person is an energetic, talkative, and gregarious individual who is self-confident and optimistic and who seeks and enjoys positions of leadership and responsibility.

Nonleader vs. Leader

T   1.*   I am generally regarded by others as a leader.
T   2.   I enjoy speaking in public.
T   3.   There are few things I enjoy more than being a leader of people.
T   4.   I have frequently assumed the leadership of groups.

TABLE 5-1, continued

T	5.	I enjoy taking full responsibility for introducing people at a party.
T	6.	I am always taking on added social responsibility.
T	7.	I am generally the leader of the people I know.
T	8.	I am often called upon to settle arguments between people.
F	9.	I am seldom the center of attention in a group.
F	10.	I would rather listen to a story than tell one.
F	11.	I sometimes find it hard to lead people and maintain them in order.
F	12.*	I generally keep in the background at social functions.

Low vs. High Self-Confidence

T	13.	I am very self-confident.
T	14.	I am almost never embarrassed.
F	15.	I am often lacking in self-confidence.
F	16.	I am cautious about undertaking anything which may lead to humiliating experiences.
F	17.	I feel somewhat inferior as a person to a few of my friends.
F	18.	I am frequently discouraged by my own inadequacies.
F	19.	When I meet a stranger, I sometimes think he is a better person than I am.
F	20.	I am somewhat more shy than the average person.
F	21.	I generally feel self-conscious in the presence of important superiors.

Pessimistic vs. Optimistic

T	22.	Most of the time, I am extremely carefree and relaxed.
T	23.	I am a rather carefree person.
T	24.	I am very optimistic.
F	25.	Some people I know can look forward to a happier life than I can.
F	26.	I have quite a few fears about my future.
F	27.	I am at least as much of a pessimist as an optimist.
F	28.	I sometimes become melancholy without very good reasons.
F	29.	I have some feelings of inferiority.

Inactive vs. Active

T	30.	I am generally active in my everyday life.
T	31.	I spend myself freely as I have plenty of energy.
T	32.	I frequently become involved in too many activities.
T	33.	I am a very adventurous person.
F	34.	I prefer quiet games to extremely active ones.
F	35.	I generally talk very quietly.

Socially Aloof vs. Gregarious

T	36.	I like to have people around me practically all the time.
T	37.	I always like to be with people rather than be alone.
T	38.	I always prefer to work with others.
F	39.	I am inclined to limit my friends to a few people.
F	40.	I dislike it when I am with people constantly.

Percentiles

	Cautious 0	10	20	30	40	50	60	70	80	90	Bold 99
Men	3	9	15	16	18	20	23	25	27	30	34
Women	4	8	10	12	15	18	20	22	25	28	38

TABLE 5-1, continued

The Unemotional vs. the Emotional

Calm people have infrequent, moderate, and limited emotional states that they suppress rather than express. Emotional people have frequent, intense, and wide-ranging emotional states that they freely express.

Frequency of Emotional States

T	1.	I rather frequently find myself getting emotional about something.
T	2.*	I become emotional fairly easily.
T	3.	My feelings and emotions are very easily aroused.
T	4.	I experience rather frequent pleasant and unpleasant moods.
T	5.	I rather easily get stirred up.
T	6.	I am easily moved to laughter or tears.
T	7.	I am considered rather emotional by my friends.
F	8.	I am a rather objective and matter-of-fact person.
F	9.	My emotional life is marked by great moderation.
F	10.	I am moderate in my tastes and sentiments.
F	11.	I am almost never extremely excited or thrilled.
F	12.	It takes a great deal to make me emotional.
F	13.	I believe I am less emotional than most people.
F	14.	I find that my life moves along at an even tenor without many ups and downs.

Expression of Emotional States

T	15.	I like having someone with whom I can talk about my emotional problems.
T	16.	I am rather spontaneous in speech and action.
T	17.	I am a fairly impulsive person.
T	18.	I like to discuss my emotions with others.
T	19.	I sometimes speak on the spur of the moment without stopping to think.
T	20.	I have sometimes corrected others, not because they were wrong, but only because they irritated me.
F	21.*	I usually prefer to keep my feelings to myself.
F	22.	I suppress my emotions more often than I express them.
F	23.	I think much and speak little.
F	24.	I usually express myself objectively, with considerate caution and restraint.
F	25.	I never complain about my sufferings and hardships.
F	26.	I am practically always tolerant even in dealing with people I don't like.
F	27.	I consider most matters from every standpoint before I form an opinion.

Range of Emotional States

T	28.	Quite a few things make me emotional.
T	29.	I have occasional difficulty getting the temperature of my bath the way I like it.
T	30.	Sometimes I become so emotional that I find it a little hard to get to sleep.
F	31.	I am seldom disturbed by sexual matters.
F	32.	I almost always do about as well as I expected in competitions.
F	33.	I almost never notice minor physical injuries.
F	34.	I can stand pain better than the average person.
F	35.	I have never been seasick, plane sick, or car sick.

Intensity of Emotional States

| T | 36. | I have sometimes gotten so angry that I felt like throwing and breaking things. |

TABLE 5-1, continued

T	37.	I have occasionally had to make an effort not to cry.
T	38.	I have very strong likes and dislikes.
T	39.	I have sometimes screamed for joy.
F	40.	I usually do things in a leisurely sort of way, seldom getting excited.

Percentiles

	Unemotional									Emotional	
	0	10	20	30	40	50	60	70	80	90	99
Men	2	8	11	16	20	22	24	28	30	32	35
Women	5	13	20	21	23	25	28	30	32	34	40

The Present-minded vs. the Future-minded

"Now" people live in the moment, obeying their present feelings and ignoring the future. "When" people live for the future, setting hard goals for themselves and planning, working, and controlling their feelings to achieve them.

Present vs. Future Time

T	1.	I live more for the future than the present.
T	2.	I spend a great deal of time thinking about my plans for the future.
F	3.	I generally **seek** whatever makes me happy here and now.
F	4.	I like to be **with** people who are not preoccupied with the future.
F	5.	I am much more interested in activities that I can enjoy for their own sake than in activities that are of long-range benefit.

Impulsivity vs. Control

T	6.	I never lose my head.
T	7.	I always keep control of myself in an emergency situation.
T	8.	I can always do a good job even when I am very excited.
T	9.	I am considered extremely "steady" by my friends.
T	10.	I believe that what a person does about a thing is more important than what he feels about it.
F	11.	I frequently obey whatever impulse is strongest.
F	12.	I am greatly influenced in my minor decisions by how I happen to feel at the moment.
F	13.	I find that my minor likes and dislikes change rather frequently.
F	14.	I find it difficult to keep my mind on one detail for very long.
F	15.	I accept my feelings as the best guide for my actions.
F	16.	I have some difficulty in concentrating my thoughts on one thing for a long time.

Pleasure vs. Work

T	17.	I enjoy work more than play.
T	18.	I set very difficult goals for myself.
T	19.*	I am extremely ambitious.
T	20.	I am guided in all my conduct by firm principles.
T	21.	I really don't like to drink alcoholic beverages.
F	22.	Most of my spare money is used for pleasure.
F	23.	I believe that I have the disposition of a pleasure seeker.
F	24.	I like to be with people who don't take life too seriously.
F	25.	I feel that friendship is more important in life than anything else.

TABLE 5-1, continued

F   26.   I occasionally neglect serious things in order to have a good time.
F   27.   I believe in getting as much fun as I can out of life.
F   28.   I would rather see a musical comedy than a documentary film.

Less vs. More Planning

T   29.   I like to make a very careful plan before starting in to do anything.
T   30.   Whenever I have to undertake a job I make out a careful plan of procedure.
T   31.   I like to keep all my letters and other papers neatly arranged and filed.
T   32.   I am extremely systematic in caring for my personal property.
T   33.   I like to have my life so arranged that it runs smoothly and without much change in plans.
T   34.   I like to have my meals organized and a definite time set aside for eating.
T   35.   I keep my workplace very neat and orderly.
T   36.   I always finish one task before taking on others.
F   37.* I generally go from one thing to another in my daily life without a great deal of planning.
F   38.   I find it rather hard to keep to a rigid routine.
F   39.   I am not particularly methodical in my daily life.
F   40.   I am occasionally disorganized if I am called on suddenly to make a few remarks.

Percentiles

| | Present-minded | | | | | | | | Future-minded | | |
	0	10	20	30	40	50	60	70	80	90	99
Men	2	9	11	13	16	19	20	23	24	27	32
Women	5	8	11	13	15	16	19	21	23	25	32

The Artistic vs. the Practical

The artistic are introverted in their orientation, aesthetic in their attitudes, and artistic in their interests. The practical are extroverted in their orientation, practical in their attitudes, and economic in their interests.

Introverted vs. Extroverted Set

T   1.   I can deal much better with actual situations than with ideas.
T   2.   Sports generally interest me somewhat more than very intellectual affairs.
T   3.   I am mainly interested in ideas that are very practical.
T   4.   I only work for concrete and clearly defined results.
T   5.   I tend to judge people in terms of their concrete accomplishments.
F   6.   I like to discuss abstract questions with my friends.
F   7.   I sometimes think more about my ideas than about the routine demands of daily life.
F   8.   I spend a lot of time philosophizing with myself.
F   9.   My head is always full of imaginative ideas.
F   10.   I often think for a long time about an idea that has occurred to me.
F   11.   Daydreams are an important part of my life.

Aesthetic vs. Practical Attitude

T   12.   I am an extremely practical person.
T   13.*   I would rather be a salesman than an artist.
T   14.   I think there are few more important things in life than money.

TABLE 5-1, continued

T   15.   I would particularly enjoy meeting people who had made a success in business.
T   16.   I tend to accept the world as it is and not worry about how it might be.
T   17.   I am really only interested in what is useful.
T   18.   I believe that competitiveness is a necessary and desirable part of our economic life.
T   19.   I prefer the friends of my own sex to be very efficient and of a practical turn of mind.
T   20.   I always keep my feet solidly on the ground.
F   21.* Artistic experiences are of great importance in my life.
F   22.   I prefer friends who have well-developed artistic tastes.

Few vs. Many Artistic Interests

T   23.   I have never tried to collect pictures of paintings I like.
T   24.   Magazines such as *Arts and Decorations* bore me.
T   25.   I would rather read *Business Week* than *Atlantic Monthly*.
T   26.   In a discussion, I tend to lose interest if we talk about serious literature.
T   27.   I would rather see a movie than read a book.
T   28.   I have seldom enjoyed an art course.
F   29.   I enjoy going to art galleries very much.
F   30.   I would like to hear a popular lecture on contemporary painters.
F   31.   If I had unlimited leisure and money, I would enjoy making a collection of fine sculptures or paintings.
F   32.   I like to visit exhibits of famous paintings.
F   33.   I like abstract paintings.
F   34.   If I had the ability I would enjoy teaching poetry at a university.
F   35.   I like to read poetry.
F   36.   I would like to take a course in the modern novel.
F   37.   I like ballet performances.
F   38.   I think I would like to decorate a room with flowers.
F   39.   I get an intense pleasure from just looking at a beautiful building.
F   40.   I would rather read an article about a famous musician than a financier.

Percentiles

	Artistic									Practical	
	0	10	20	30	40	50	60	70	80	90	99
Men	2	8	10	12	14	16	20	22	26	29	33
Women	1	6	9	10	12	14	16	18	20	23	35

The Rationalistic vs. the Empirical

The rationalistic, putting their faith in principles developed through tradition, tend to be resistant to change, conforming, and religious. The empirical, putting their faith in facts developed by science, tend to be ready for change, individualistic, and skeptical.

Principles vs. Facts

T   1.   I am more interested in what I see and hear than in abstract principles.
T   2.   I am temperamentally more a skeptic than a believer.
T   3.   I believe that we should have less censorship of speech and press than we do now.

TABLE 5-1, continued

T   4.   Radical agitators should be allowed to make public speeches.
T   5.   In the long run, science provides the best hope for solving the world's problems.
T   6.   Science should have as much to say about moral values as religion does.
T   7.   I like to read scientific articles in popular magazines.
T   8.   I would enjoy the kind of work that a scientific research worker does.
F   9.   I am more interested in general ideas than in specific facts.
F   10.   I carry a very strict conscience about with me wherever I go.
F   11.   I think that I have a more rigorous standard of right and wrong than most people.
F   12.   I would rather be a salesman than a scientific research worker.
F   13.   Divine inspiration is an infallible source of truth.

Old vs. New Religions

T   14.   The world might benefit from a new kind of religion.
T   15.   It is possible that there is no such thing as divine inspiration.
T   16.   I have occasionally doubted the reality of God.
T   17.   I haven't yet reached any final opinion about the nature of God.
F   18.   It is necessary to retain the belief that God exists as a personal being.
F   19.   A person should develop his greatest loyalty toward his religious faith.
F   20.*   The idea of God must remain absolutely central to the whole plan of human purpose.
F   21.   My faith in God is complete for "though he slay me, yet will I trust him."
F   22.   It is absolutely vital to assume that there is a God behind the Universe.
F   23.   I have always been unalterably convinced of the reality of God.
F   24.   The thought of God gives me a complete sense of security.
F   25.   I trust in God to support the right and condemn the wrong.
F   26.   The idea of God means more to me than any other idea.
F   27.   It is as important for a person to be reverent as it is for him to be sympathetic.

Old vs. New Customs

T   28.   Compared to your own self-respect, the respect of others means little.
T   29.   I often act contrary to custom.
T   30.   Some of my friends think my ideas are a bit wild and impractical.
T   31.*   I believe that everybody would be happier if both men and women had more sexual freedom.
T   32.   The European attitude toward mistresses is more sensible than ours.
T   33.   I think that cremation is the best method of burial.
T   34.   Women should have as much right to propose dates to men as men to women.
F   35.   In matters of conduct I conform very closely to custom.
F   36.   I consider the close observance of social customs and manners as an essential aspect of life.
F   37.   I think that it is much more important to learn to control sexual impulses than to express them.
F   38.   I control my sexual impulses by instituting prohibitions and restrictions.
F   39.   No individual, no matter what the circumstances, is justified in committing suicide.
F   40.   I take pains not to incur the disapproval of others.

TABLE 5-1, continued

Percentiles

	Rationalistic 0	10	20	30	40	50	60	70	80	Empirical 90	99
Men	6	20	23	25	27	28	30	31	33	35	38
Women	7	13	17	20	22	24	27	29	30	33	37

MYTHIC VERSUS SCIENTIFIC CONCEPTS

The dictionary is a storehouse of personality concepts: abrupt, absent-minded, academic, accommodating, accurate, acquiescent, acquisitive, active, adventurous, etc. Some of these concepts bear the name of an actual person or literary figure: Beau Brummel, Cassandra, Don Juan, Lesbian, Narcissistic, Napoleonic, Rabelaisian, Sadistic, and Shylock. Of the approximately 20,000 possible trait names in the dictionary, about a fourth refer to temporary states: ablaze, alarmed, awed, etc. Another fourth tie nonhuman to human qualities: abysmal, autumnal, arctic, etc. A highly significant fourth describe feelings about a person rather than the person himself: asinine, addle-brained, atrocious, etc. Many are synonyms. Many are antonyms: sensitive and insensitive, active and inactive, pessimistic and optimistic, etc.

Every one of these words *simultaneously* describes a person, gives an emotional reaction to him, and implies a prediction about him. But each word has a different stress on these descriptive, emotional, and predictive qualities. "Sleepy" and "noisy" describe a person more than they indicate how we feel about him or expect him to behave. "Sincere" and "heartless" tell more about how we feel about him than they either describe or predict him. "Bold" and "emotional," in turn, are more predictive than either descriptive or evaluative.

The concepts we use to describe a person are not designed to refer to substantial things about him, independent entities which exist by themselves. They are determined rather by our perceptions, interests, and purposes. The world of myth is a dramatic world—a world of actions, of forces, of conflicting powers. When we perceive a person mythically, we perceive him emotionally. Our perceptions of him are impregnated with these emotions. They are surrounded by an emotional atmosphere—an atmosphere of joy or grief, of anguish, of excitement, of exultation or depression. The more mythic our perceptions, the more we use concepts with a high emotional loading.

Anderson (1968) determined the emotional loading of 555 traits from the ratings made by college students. He asked them to think of a person being described by a particular word and to rate the word according to how much they would like such a person. The average desirability of each word was calculated and the words ranked from 1 (most favorable) to 555 (least favorable). Table 5-2 is a representative sample from his list. Words like sincere, honest, and understanding have very high positive emotional loadings. Words like mean, phony, and liar have very high negative loadings. Words like bold, cautious, impulsive, and emotional are near the neutral middle of the scale. Few words were neutral; most were definitely desirable or undesirable.

What words do students find most meaningful? Anderson asked the students to rate the meaningfulness of words from 0 ("I have

TABLE 5-2
The Desirability of Trait Words
(Adapted from Anderson, 1968)

College students rated 555 personality-trait words on likableness as personality characteristics. The mean ratings of fifty of these are given below. The number in front indicates the rank among the fifty from the most desirable to the least desirable. The number in parentheses indicates the rank of that trait among the original 555.

1.	Sincere (1)	26.	Bold (237)
2.	Honest (2)	27.	Cautious (239)
3.	Understanding (3)	28.	Impulsive (252)
4.	Intelligent (7)	29.	Emotional (264)
5.	Open-minded (9)	30.	Opportunistic (274)
6.	Considerate (12)	31.	Conformist (306)
7.	Warm (16)	32.	Radical (307)
8.	Friendly (19)	33.	Unemotional (347)
9.	Responsible (28)	34.	Nervous (367)
10.	Ambitious (59)	35.	Pessimistic (140)
11.	Conscientious (65)	36.	Dominating (432)
12.	Cooperative (79)	37.	Neurotic (438)
13.	Capable (83)	38.	Cold (486)
14.	Punctual (93)	39.	Incompetent (492)
15.	Tolerant (100)	40.	Irresponsible (499)
16.	Calm (179)	41.	Unreliable (504)
17.	Artistic (183)	42.	Boring (514)
18.	Scientific (185)	43.	Hostile (523)
19.	Orderly (186)	44.	Selfish (532)
20.	Religious (195)	45.	Greedy (540)
21.	Nonconforming (212)	46.	Dishonest (551)
22.	Middleclass (221)	47.	Cruel (552)
23.	Talkative (226)	48.	Mean (553)
24.	Excited (227)	49.	Phony (554)
25.	Moderate (228)	50.	Liar (555)

almost no idea of the meaning of this word") to 4 ("I have a very clear and definite understanding of the meaning of this word"). The more emotional the word, the more likely a student was to report that it was meaningful. Nondescriptive but emotional meanings are clearer and more significant to students than unemotional but descriptive meanings.

The world of science is an *un*dramatic world. As a science, psychology aims to obliterate every trace of the personal, subjective, and emotional view characteristic of mythic thinking. Ideally, its concepts would be completely unemotional, completely predictive. The ideal, however, is only achieved with numbers or with letters. In approaching this ideal, psychology seeks concepts that have the minimum of emotional and the maximum of predictive meaning. Thus the names of the five traits in Table 5-1 are neutral in tone and the opposite poles are of equivalent desirability. Students, for example, rated "cautious" and "bold" in the middle of the desirable and undesirable scale and of almost identical desirability.

These trait names are neutral. More important, the traits are inherently neutral. The specific statements measuring each trait were written so that either the "true" or the "false" answer could be perceived as equally desirable. Their actual perceived desirability was checked by asking respondents in preliminary forms to answer, not as they would answer them, but as they thought it would be most desirable to answer them. Still, some people find it more desirable to say "true" than to say "false" to anything. To reduce the influence of acquiescence the statements measuring a trait are so designed that a person has to answer half of them "true" and half "false" to get the highest score.

Dynamic theorists have rarely bothered to remove the emotional element from their concepts. Quite the contrary. Freud, for example, wrote in a lively and exciting style. The id, the ego, and the superego have a dramatic quality about them. He never made an effort to measure empirically any of his concepts. Many resist measurement: How does one measure differences in the death wish or latent homosexuality? Clearly, concepts cannot be classified as mythic *or* scientific. Obviously, however, some are more mythic than scientific.

MYTHIC VERSUS SCIENTIFIC RELATIONSHIPS

A scientific theory is a set of concepts with *assumed* relationships between them. The more precisely these concepts are measured, the more explicitly these assumed relationships are defined, the better the theory. That is, the easier it is to find out whether these assumed relationships correspond to actual empirical relationships, the better.

The scales in Table 5-1, for example, indicate how boldness, emotionality, practicality, future-mindedness, and empiricism are to be measured. What relationships between these traits does the theory assume? It assumes that the traits are not related at all, that they are independent. It assumes that knowing where a person feels he stands on the cautious-bold trait tells us nothing about how he will feel about where he stands on any of the other traits. It thus assumes that knowing where a person places himself on one trait gives an entirely different kind of information than that given from knowing where he places himself on any of the others.

The assumed independence of the traits corresponds to their actual independence. The scores of 300 college men and women on the five traits were intercorrelated. Of ten possible interrelationships, only practicality and empiricism had any relationship at all. Even this relationship was due to the fact that men are more practical and empirical, women are more artistic and rationalistic (Grossman, 1967). Furthermore, the independence of the traits is not an artifact of poor measurement. All the scales have high internal consistencies and students have a strong tendency to get similar scores from one time to another.

The independence of the traits is not surprising, for Grossman developed the trait measures to *be* independent. He first gave measures of twenty-two well-established traits to a large group of students. He verified that the traits were stable and that they were relatively independent. Still, the traits clustered together. For example, students who scored high in dominance tended also to score high on the activity level, self-confidence, optimism, and gregariousness scales. The subheads in the trait scales in the table indicate the clusters for the other traits. Grossman finally devised the present scales as a measure of the cluster. Thus what were originally twenty-two relatively independent traits become five totally independent traits.

Actually, then, the traits are independent. However, people do not use the traits as if they were. The rankings of five sorority sisters provide a concrete example of the strength and variability of the relationships that can be assumed (Chelsea, 1965). Each sister ranked ten other members of the sorority on boldness, "1" being the boldest and "10" the most cautious. She then ranked them on each of the other traits. The rankings of each sister on each trait were then correlated with her rankings on the other traits. Table 5-3 gives the results. Boldness and practicality were assumed by all of the girls to be closely related (median *r* of .88). Generally, the group assumed no relationship between emotionality and future-mindedness. Evelyn, however, assumed that the more emotional a sister, the less empirical she was likely to be. The median correlations at the bottom of the table indicate that the general level of relationships between the traits

TABLE 5-3
Relation between Traits
Assumed by Five Sorority Sisters
                                          Correlations between Rankings for Traits

Traits	Anne	Babs	Clare	Donna	Evelyn	Median Corre- lation
Bold and practical	.86	.88	.89	.88	.79	.88
Future-minded and empirical	.78	.78	.79	.49	.65	.78
Bold and empirical	.23	.27	.50	.55	.68	.50
Bold and future-minded	.07	−.21	.43	.36	.45	.36
Practical and empirical	.14	.39	.18	.35	.71	.35
Emotional and empirical	.47	.01	.30	.30	−.60	.30
Future-minded and practical	.03	−.12	.23	.37	.57	.23
Bold and emotional	.30	−.30	.10	.09	−.59	.09
Practical and emotional	.05	.15	−.21	.20	−.79	.05
Emotional and future-minded	.20	.01	.43	−.13	−.60	.01
Median correlation	.05	.13	.22	.35	.62	

varied a great deal from girl to girl. Overall, for example, Anne assumed the least positive relationship between the traits (.05), whereas Evelyn saw the traits as closely related (.62). That is, Evelyn saw the boldest girl as also the most practical, empirical, future-minded and calm. As a consequence, each girl had a somewhat different set of correlations from every other girl, and some of the girls had conflicting sets. Anne, for example, saw emotionality and empiricism as being positively related, whereas Evelyn saw them as being negatively related.

The girls were victims of "illusory correlations," i.e., they assumed relationships that do not, in fact, exist. Illusory correlations are pervasive and universal, influencing psychologist and nonpsychologist alike. A university in Texas needed a new head for their psychology department and the president announced his choice without consulting the department. The psychologists in the department signed a petition protesting the appointment and saying that the proposed head was "unimpressive." The psychologists seem to assume a relationship between physical size and ability since discussion of his dwarflike physique played a large part in their deliberations. Nonetheless, the man was appointed and was so successful that he eventually became a dean. The country was combed for his replacement and there was general agreement on the best man for the job. It was incidentally remarked in the recommendations that "he tends to talk a great deal when he is nervous." He came, was interviewed, and was rejected because he was "arrogant, egotistical, and opinionated."

Psychologists are frequent victims of illusory correlations in their professional work. Clinicians, for example, classified mental patients into various categories of mental illness. The more confused the patient's thinking, the more frequently he was classified as schizophrenic. Almost all the patients that showed high confusion were put in this category. None of their classifications were correct (Hunt, Schwartz, and Walker, 1964). Clinicians commonly assume that patients who draw elaborate eyes in their drawings of a man are more likely to be paranoid. They are not (Machover, 1949). Furthermore clinicians report the same illusory correlations as do nonclinicians-(Chapman and Chapman, 1967). Laboratory studies show that concepts that are *emotionally* related are assumed to be empirically related (Chapman, 1967).

Time and again, illusory correlations have reduced many traits to one trait. Supervisors made ratings of their subordinates on a large number of traits. Factor analysis of these ratings showed that the same amount of information would have been obtained if the supervisors had given a single overall estimate of the performance of the employees on their present job (Ewart, Seashore, and Tiffin, 1941). Psychologists rated new graduate students on more than forty traits. Again, practically the same amount of information would have been obtained if they had just rated the students from least likely to most likely to succeed in graduate school (Kelly and Fiske, 1951). Psychiatrists rated interns on twenty traits. The results would have been the same if they had just rated the intern from bad to good (Holt and Luborsky, 1958). Stockbrokers follow a similar pattern in assessing the qualities of a stock (Slovic, 1968).

Why do we so readily assume mistaken relationships between traits? The general answer seems clear: Our conceptions reflect and intensify our perceptions. We perceive a person as an instant whole and then differentiate parts within the whole. The parts, however, are not independent of the whole but integrated with it. Our first verbal picture of a person, then, is a brief and simple whole. As we talk or write about him our picture becomes more elaborate and more differentiated. However, the words we use are intimately related to each other because they reflect the integrated whole we perceive.

The relationship between perceptions and conceptions is like the relationship between letters and numbers in the following cryptarithmetic puzzle:

$$
\begin{array}{r}
\text{SEND} \\
+\text{MORE} \\
\hline
\text{MONEY}
\end{array}
$$

Each letter stands for a particular number from 0 to 9. The problem is to infer the correct numbers. The theoretical system used in solving the problem concerns the arithmetic operations involved in addition. The solution is achieved when each letter has been replaced by a number and where collectively they satisfy the rules of addition. The puzzle solver begins by inspecting the pattern of letters, looking for some clue that will suggest a number for a letter. For example, in this puzzle, M can only be 1. The letters are gradually replaced by numbers until we finish with

$$\begin{array}{r} 9,567 \\ +1,085 \\ \hline 10,652 \end{array}$$

As in our reactions to a person, the letters represent the initial perception that attracts and holds attention. As in our personality theories, arithmetic allows us to find unity and meaning in the puzzle. As in our sketches of people, each possible number is tested for its fit to our theory and accepted or rejected on this basis. As in our efforts to understand people, the initial unity persists throughout the solving process. Each part of the puzzle is differentiated as one discovers the correct number for each letter until finally all the letters are replaced by numbers and the puzzle is solved. Finally, our perception becomes a conception.

Every part of our perception of a person is related to every other part. Consequently, every part of our conception tends to be related to every other part. For example, the concepts we use to describe appearance are related to the concepts we use to describe traits. McKeachie (1952) had six men rate six women on twenty-two different personality traits. They were told that the purpose of the study was to determine the reliability of personality ratings made on the basis of a ten-minute interview. Actually, the purpose was to determine the influence of lipstick on personal impressions. Each man interviewed three girls with and three without lipstick; each girl appeared in three interviews with the three without lipstick. Result: Without lipstick, a girl was more often judged as being conscientious, serious, talkative, and not interested in men. After the interviews the men were asked what things they thought had influenced their ratings. None mentioned lipstick. In a similar fashion, Thornton (1943) compared reactions to photographs of people with and without glasses. With glasses, they were seen as more intelligent, industrious, and honest.

The reverse is also true: Knowing the traits of a person generates a description of his physical appearance. Students were given these two descriptions (Secord, 1958):

A   This man is warmhearted and honest. He has a good sense of humor and is intelligent and unbiased in his opinion. He is responsible and self-confident with an air of refinement.

B This man is a ruthless and brutal person. He is extremely hostile, quick-tempered, and overbearing. He is well known for his boorish and vulgar manner and is a very domineering and unsympathetic person.

The students were then asked to rate thirty-two facial *features* of the two fictitious men on a seven-point scale. They not only did this quickly and without difficulty but also generally agreed on the differences between them. The warmhearted man had a more direct gaze, a smoother brow, more relaxed nostrils, and hair more neatly groomed. The ruthless man had a darker complexion, more tense face, a squarer jaw, and a rougher texture to his skin.

Relationships are structured: a few central concepts organize the peripheral ones within a unified framework. The warmth of a person is one of these central concepts. Asch (1946) read list A to one group and list B to another:

List A: Intelligent, skillful, industrious, *cold,* determined, practical, cautious

List B: Intelligent, skillful, industrious, *warm,* determined, practical, cautious

The two groups were asked to write an imaginative sketch of the kind of person who would have such a combination of traits. The substitution of "warm" for "cold" made a big difference in how the other traits were viewed. The following sketches are typical:

Cold Group:
A very ambitious and talented person who would not let anyone or anything stand in the way of achieving his goal. Wants his own way, he is determined not to give in, no matter what happens.

Warm Group:
A person who believes certain things to be right, wants others to see his point, would be sincere in an argument, and would like to see his point won.

The groups were also given a list of additional traits and asked to check those which fitted their impression of the person. The warm person was more often checked as generous, wise, happy, sociable, popular, and humorous. The cold person was more often checked as shrewd, irritable, ruthless, and self-centered. Asch concludes:

> *The moment we see that two or more characteristics belong to the same person they enter into dynamic interaction. We cannot see one quality and another in the same person without their affecting each other. . . . From its inception the impression has structure, even if rudimentary. The various characteristics do not possess the same weight. Some become central, providing the main direction; others become peripheral and dependent. Until we have found the center—that part of the person which wants to live and act in a certain way, which wants not to break or disappear—we feel we have not succeeded in reaching an understanding.*

What other traits besides "cold" and "warm" are central in our mythic theories? Koltur (1962) asked students to report the words that were most relevant to them in forming their impressions. The most relevant words were the emotionally meaningful words like "sincere" and "honest" or "cruel" and "mean." In other words, the concepts that dominate our theories are those that reflect the dominant feature of our perceptions, i.e., the expressive qualities that people have for us.

Theories do more than reflect impressions. They make them permanent. Perceptions of a person may be intense and vivid, but they are brief and ephemeral. We may recall how we perceived a person yesterday. In a week we may not remember at all. A spoken or written impression is an *expression* of a perception. This very fact implies a radical change. What hitherto was dimly and vaguely felt assumes a definite shape. What was a passive response becomes an active process. The novelist Proust (1922) has suggested the complex ways in which our conceptions may influence our perceptions:

> *Even the simple act which we describe as "seeing someone we know" is, to some extent, an intellectual process. We pack the physical outline of the creature we see with all the ideas we have already formed about him, and in the complete picture of him which we compose in our minds those ideas have certainly the principal place. In the end they come to fill out so completely the curve of his cheeks, to follow so exactly the line of his nose, they blend so harmoniously in the sound of his voice that these seem to be no more than a transparent envelope, so that each time we see the face or hear the voice it is our own ideas of him which we recognize and to which we listen.*

In mythic thinking, we are saying, everything tends to be related to and interchangeable with everything else *from the beginning.* In scientific thinking, on the other hand, concepts are initially unrelated. It is only through logical and empirical processes that they, in the end, can become related.

THE DISCRIMINATION OF MYTHIC FROM SCIENTIFIC THEORIES

How do we tell a mythic from a scientific theory? Marx (1951) has incisively stated the essential difference:

> Testability *is the absolutely essential characteristic of any scientifically useful hypotheses. . . . Without some degree of willingness to subject all concepts to a critical, operational analysis the essential self-correction processes in science can hardly function effectively. It is in just such a tight and exclusively speculative atmosphere that cultlike and anti-empirical tendencies thrive. . . . A major obstacle to more effective scientific progress seems to be a general disinclination to submit constructs and theories to a critical and rigorous operational analysis (whether or not that particular term is used) and corresponding failure explicitly to recognize the invidious infiltration of emotional beliefs and extra-scientific values throughout all phases of theory construction.*

Like scientific theories, mythic theories use concepts in describing people, assume relationships between these concepts, and from them make predictions about how a person will feel and behave. However, we are only dimly aware of our mythic theories. We use concepts without realizing it, assume relationships without stating them, and unconsciously make predictions about people based on these relationships. One good reason we do not test our mythic theories, therefore, is that we do not know we have them. Even if we knew, however, the mythic thinker " . . . possesses neither the impulsion nor the means to correct or criticize what is given here and now."

THE SELECTION OF A PERSONALITY THEORY

Mythic and scientific thinking, we have now said, are two different kinds of thinking. They generate different kinds of concepts and assume different kinds of relationships between concepts. We have also suggested that, while every theory is colored by mythic thinking, the paler these colors, the more useful for predictive purposes the theory is likely to be. In addition, we have implied that the five-trait theory embodies elements essential for the improvement of sensitivity. These elements are: (1) the theory forces the theorizer to adopt the perceptual point of view of the person he is seeking to understand; and (2) the concepts used in the theory are operationally defined and the assumed relationships are actual relationships, i.e., they have been empirically derived.

The only present empirical evidence for these last assertions come from the work of Fancher (1966). He studied the empirical consequences of the theories preferred by twenty-four male undergraduate Harvard students. All of them had had a course in personality theory. Each completed a test of sensitivity based on three individual case histories of students: Mr. X, Mr. Y, and Mr. Z. For each case, the experimenters prepared thirty-eight situations in which the man had been and asked the judges to choose between two alternatives what he had actually done in that situation. Each judge thus made more than 100 predictions for the three men together. His sensitivity score was the number of correct predictions.

In the test, each judge worked through each case, deciding between the two possible actions. After making each choice he would read what the correct response should have been. Thus he was provided in each case with an ever-increasing amount of information on which to base his subsequent choices. The group as a whole found the task very difficult. However, there were wide individual differences on each case, the most sensitive judge getting more than twice as many right choices as the least sensitive. Those who did well on one case tended to do well on the others.

After completing the cases, the judges filled out a questionnaire measuring their belief in eighteen different theoretical orientations, such as unconscious determinants, learning by contiguity, heredity, traits, structure, etc. Their answers were then related to their sensitivity scores. Most of the theoretical orientations had no relationship to sensitivity. A few seemed to have a negative one, i.e., proponents were less likely to be accurate in their predictions. The major finding of the study was that those who "used a trait approach and tried to take the points of view of the persons they were trying to understand" were more accurate predicters.

What are the virtues, if any, of the more dynamic and comprehensive approaches generally preferred by psychologists? The findings of Fancher (1967) in another phase of his study indicate that while the dynamic theorists cannot predict people better, they can talk about them better.

Fancher had each of his twenty-four judges write a personality sketch of Mr. X, Mr. Y, and Mr. Z using any technique that seemed appropriate to him. These seventy-two sketches were then given to seventy-two other students. These students were then asked to predict the responses of Mr. X, Mr. Y, and Mr. Z *from the sketches.* Three different students read each of the sketches. The average accuracy score of those who used the sketch determined the value of the sketch.

Some judges were consistently superior sketch writers. What was the relationship between the value of a judge's sketches and his sensitivity, i.e., the accuracy of his own predictions on the cases? The sensitivity scores of the judges were correlated with their sketch scores. Result: $r = -.41$. In other words, the less sensitive the judge, the *better* his sketches. In search of an explanation, Fancher compared the theoretical preferences of sensitive judges with theoretical preferences of effective sketchers. Compared to the sensitive, the best sketchers had different, and sometimes opposite, theoretical positions. In interpreting these results Fancher concludes that the good sketchers

> . . . may have tended to impose their own preexisting and subjective—but well-systematized—category systems upon the case material. Thus, they may have regarded the cases analytically, as objects to be evaluated and categorized. This kind of approach may have the advantage of facilitating systematic formulations of the cases and the disadvantage of inhibiting an intuitive "feel" for the cases.

The superiority of trait theories oriented toward the perceptions of the person to be understood is supported by the few lonely research findings. In addition, trait theories have great practical advantages in sensitivity training. Their narrowness permits the setting of limited but realistic training goals. These goals can be more quickly communicated than the more abstract goals of comprehensive theoretical "systems." The stress upon the other person's impressions of himself provides convenient measures of predictive accuracy. These, in turn, facilitate the giving of feedback to trainees.

The trait approach requires the use of specific traits that fit the particular kinds of people the trainees want to understand. Thus a trait theory that is suitable for mothers would not be suitable for graduate students trying to understand hospitalized patients. A trait theory that is suitable for policemen trying to understand juvenile delinquents would not be suitable for undergraduates trying to understand each other. Whatever the traits are, they must be developed from empirical study of particular groups. They cannot be effortlessly inferred from a master theory.

CHAPTER 6

THEORETICAL TRAINING

THEORETICAL sensitivity is the ability to select and use theories to make more accurate predictions about others. A scientific theory is like a nutcracker that opens the shell of a person and reveals the kernel. Psychology abounds with theoretical nutcrackers. In fact, the time of students is so taken up with acquainting themselves with the range of these theoretical riches that they seldom have time to practice applying them to actual people. When their skill is put to the test, as it turns out, they do no better with their elaborate crackers than the ordinary man with a hammer.

The central difficulty in theoretical training is the ease with which a scientific theory can be absorbed into a mythic way of thinking. This difficulty is intensified by the fact that the most popular scientific theories are those that encourage their users to continue their mythic orientation, their preoccupation with expressive qualities, their illusionary correlations, and their avoidance of empirical checks. Part of the solution lies in the use of theories that encourage the trainee to take the point of view of the other person, to reduce the grip of expressive qualities, and to verify his predictions. Empirically derived trait theories seem most suited to the achievement of these ends. We introduced a five-trait theory that follows this model in the last chapter.

The trait road seems to be the right road; it is not a short or an easy road, as the evidence in Table 6-1 testifies. At the beginning of a course, the author had more than a hundred students in a lecture class rate him on five traits. They had had these traits defined and had completed the inventory (Table 5-1) measuring these traits. They were instructed:

> *Your instructor completed the same personality inventory as you did. How do you think his scores compare with those of the men in this class? Rate him on each of the traits as either LOW (25th percentile or less), AVERAGE (26th to the 75th percentile) or HIGH (76th percentile or higher).*

During the course, the students received a profile of scores showing their own position on each of the traits; they read a chapter in the text describing details of each trait; and they spent several sessions interviewing and rating individual members of the class and receiv-

TABLE 6-1
**Theoretical Sensitivy of Students
to an Instructor**

		Percent			
Traits		Low	Average	High	Total
Cautious vs. Bold	Before training	29	41	30	100
	After training	26	31	43	100
	Improvement			+13	
Unemotional vs. Emotional	Before training	67	19	14	100
	After training	54	26	20	100
	Improvement	−13			
Present-minded vs. Future-minded	Before training	17	40	43	100
	After training	15	23	62	100
	Improvement			+19	
Artistic vs. Practical	Before training	23	28	49	100
	After training	44	24	32	100
	Improvement	+21			
Rationalistic vs. Empirical	Before training	13	25	62	100
	After training	10	23	67	100
	Improvement			+5	

ing feedback on their accuracy. At the end of the course, they again
rated the instructor. The before and after results are shown in the
table. The students showed only a modest gain on four traits, a loss
on the fifth. These results suggest that it is hard to adopt the
orientation of another person even when the theory that the trainees
are using encourages them to do so. The vividness of expressive
qualities and the pervasiveness of illusionary correlations persist.
Empathic influences also persist, students seeing the instructor as
very like or very different from themselves at the beginning continue
to see him in much the same way at the end. In this chapter, we
consider ways of shifting trainees from a self to an other orientation,
of getting them to discriminate emotional from descriptive qualities,
and of improving their empathic accuracy.

THE MEASUREMENT OF THEORETICAL SENSITIVITY

The first requirement of theoretical training is that trainees learn the
theory. In most training, it is the only real requirement. Students
spend the course or the seminar mastering the theoretical concepts
and their assumed relationships. If they master one theory, they are
likely to go on to another. If any time is spent in efforts to apply the

theory to the understanding of actual persons, these efforts are casual and anecdotal.

Trait theories are generally simple and therefore easy to learn. Learning success is also relatively easy to measure. Thus success in learning the definitions of the five traits described in the last chapter, the cluster of subordinate traits related to each, the independence of the traits, and their known antecedents and consequences may be satisfactorily measured by the use of the usual types of achievement tests. It is a realistic goal of trait training, therefore, to expect trainees to achieve quick mastery of the concepts and relationships they are to apply.

Intellectual mastery of a theory, however, is purely a means to the end of improved trainee sensitivity. In dynamic and comprehensive theories, the measurement of a trainee's ability to apply them ranges from hard to impossible. By contrast, the measurement of a trainee's ability to apply the trait theory is simple. Correct application of the theory requires that the trainee correctly predict how another person has described himself. The ultimate criterion is not what the person is "really like"; it is what he says he is.

Table 6-2 presents items for the measuring of trait sensitivity based on a matching model. Charlotte, Joan, and Susan took the five-trait test. One of the profiles below each thumbnail sketch matches the actual profile of the woman. The three items are arranged in order of the fineness of the discriminations required, the first being the easiest and the last the hardest. Items of this type may be used as a test of theoretical sensitivity or as part of a programmed learning approach to its development.

TABLE 6-2
Items Measuring Trait Sensitivity

DIRECTIONS: This is a test of your ability to apply a theory to actual persons. The task is to identify the profile of the person in the sketch. First read the sketch of the person. One of the profiles below the sketch is that of the person. Mark the one that you think is correct.

The Case of Charlotte Adams

Charlotte is a forty-seven-year-old junior majoring in social work. She was often ill as a child, and this was resented by her foster parents who raised her. Her mother punished her often and sometimes unjustly, and avoided handling her if she could help it. She ran away from home a number of times and only survived her childhood because her foster father liked her, showed her some consideration, and tried to help her. Charlotte has difficulty getting along with women, especially her superiors at work. She likes to be in a helping relationship with any person, male or female.

She believes in God but not in a formal religion, and her moral views are narrow: "Intent to wrong is almost like doing." Her first goal is to someday teach creative writing; now she writes poetry and prose for pleasure and profit. Improvising is

TABLE 6-2, continued

something she does well because of her versatility, and she has a great deal of perseverance. However, she is somewhat egocentric, and feels she often talks more than she should, especially in class. She feels she may be losing something by not participating in college activities, and is anxious to complete her education and get to work.

Check below the percentile score that you think Charlotte obtained when compared with other college women.

Trait	Profile A	Profile B
Cautious vs. Bold	30	70
Calm vs. Emotional	10	90
Present-minded vs. Future-minded	90	10
Artistic vs. Practical	20	80
Rationalistic vs. Empirical	90	10
Your Prediction	*	_____

*Indicates correct answer.

The Case of Joan Dollard

Joan is a sophomore majoring in psychology, and is twenty years old. She has three older brothers, and all the children were raised by her grandmother because her mother was working. Her mother always compared her to her brothers, and she never measured up to their achievements. Her father, the vice-president of a small company, was respected and obeyed by all the children, and gave no physical disciplining. Her brothers considered her as the "kid" or a tagalong. Joan had negative feelings toward her grandmother because she sided with her mother and often berated Joan's father. She had few friends as a child, and got along better with boys than with girls.

Joan says her ideas on religion are in the process of changing, but she is anti-organized religion. She is a curious person, doesn't get bored easily, is interested in practically everything, and likes to read and learn. But she is inconsistent, often needs reassurance from her close friends and relatives, and is sometimes frightened by external conditions like the possibility of World War III.

Check the profile that you think is Joan's.

Trait	Profile A	Profile B	Profile C
Cautious vs. Bold	10	90	50
Calm vs. Emotional	90	50	10
Present-minded vs. Future-minded	30	60	90
Artistic vs. Practical	10	60	80
Rationalistic vs. Empirical	85	20	40
Your Prediction	*	_____	_____

*Indicates correct answer.

The Case of Susan Edgar

Susan is a nineteen-year-old social work major, and is in her sophomore year. Her family was not very close because the members were individualistic and shared few

TABLE 6-2, continued

common interests. At an early age she developed a liking for animals and had as many as varied an assortment of pets as her parents would allow. Her parents didn't understand where this interest came from (they were both teachers) and disliked her spending so much time with her animals. Susan says, "I told my animals my secrets and how I felt, and can't see why I should tell people who might take it the wrong way or not understand."

Susan didn't date much till she came to college, and gets along better with older people than with people of her own age group, who seem immature to her. She believes in two religions—God and Mother Nature—and understands the latter better; "I just don't know what side God is on." She likes cooking, skating, swimming, and horseback riding. Her interests are broad, and she feels she often expects too much of herself. She respects other people's beliefs, is persistent, and is depressed a lot of the time. She says she can be a tomboy or a lady when called for.

Check the profile that you think is Susan's.

Trait	Profile A	Profile B	Profile C	Profile D
Cautious vs. Bold	30	90	60	10
Calm vs. Emotional	80	40	5	60
Present-minded vs. Future-minded	10	30	75	50
Artistic vs. Practical	90	10	45	80
Rationalistic vs. Empirical	50	70	40	90
Your Prediction	___	___	*	___

*Indicates correct answer.

THE DIAGNOSIS OF INTERPERSONAL ORIENTATION

Those people are most sensitive who use a theory that takes the point of the view of the other person (Fancher, 1967). The five-trait theory assumes this view. It requires that the user of the theory find out how a person sees himself and the world. The basic question is not: What do I think of him? It is not: What do others think of him? It is not: How does he behave? It is: What does he think of himself?

Not only the novice in psychology but also the man in the street recognizes the desirability of taking the point of view of another person. Both also tend to assume that they have this desirable ability. If the experienced professional has any advantage over them, it lies in his greater appreciation of the obstacles involved in even partially and temporarily seeing the world as another person sees it.

How can the trainee's point of view be changed? The question is largely unasked and certainly unanswered. The development of skill in using a trait theory oriented toward others may, in the long run, be the best answer. A more direct approach, however, would be to diagnose the orientations of trainees, to feed back this knowledge to them, and to provide individual training based on the diagnosis.

The Orientation Test in Table 6-3 is a step in these directions. In his original form of this test, Linden (1965) assumed that people would take one of three orientations toward other people:

First Person Orientation: What does he think of me?

Second Person Orientation: What does he think of himself?

Third Person Orientation: What do other people think of him?

He developed a series of ambiguous social situations and asked respondents to report what they thought would be the feelings of individuals in those situations. The respondents chose from three alternatives representing the three orientations.

Analysis of scores on the test showed that people were not consistent in their choices of a second-person versus a third-person orientation. They were, however, highly consistent in their choice of the first-person versus either a second- or a third-person orientation. Each situation in the final form of the test, therefore, contrasts a first-person choice with either a second- or a third-person choice. In this form, the mean score among 150 college students was 15 and the range was practically from bottom to top (2 to 27). The internal consistency was satisfactory ($r = .80$).

How valid is the test? Small but consistent correlations indicate that those scoring high in their other orientation are more observant and more sensitive. They are less impulsive, less likely to assume similarity between themselves and others, and more considerate and responsible in their attitudes toward others. Perhaps most significant, those with another orientation are observant in their perceptual style rather than evaluative (Table 4-2).

The test seems to have some value as a diagnostic device. It has immediate value as a device for making trainees more aware that there are different orientations. Of course, all the methods for developing observational sensitivity (Chapter 4) are directly relevant to changing points of view.

TABLE 6-3
The Orientation Test
(Linden, 1965)

This is a scale measuring opinions about how people react in different situations. In many cases it may be difficult to choose an answer, but please mark a choice for each one.

The Case of Hans: The Place: Munich, Germany. The time: 1922. Hans Meyerhoff, a poor shopkeeper, has been invited to a secret meeting of a small organization headed by Adolf Hitler. Hans is bewildered throughout the meeting.

(1) Hans becomes enthralled with Hitler and tries to convince one of his customers, Rudolph, to join the Party. Why is Rudolph hesitant?

TABLE 6-3, continued

    1.   Hans himself doesn't know what he is joining.*
    2.   I wonder why Hans wants me to join the Party.

(2) In time, however, Hans's friend, Rudolph Hess, joins the Party and becomes one of Hitler's most trusted aides. For some reason, in the middle of World War II, Rudolph Hess flew alone right over London only to be shot down. What were Hitler's thoughts about this?
    1.   He did it to embarrass me before the world.
    2.   He did it to show the others he wasn't a coward like they said.*

The Case of the Babe: Besides being one of baseball's great heroes, Babe Ruth had a sincere interest in children. He once had an interview with Tommy Smith, reporter for his high school paper.

(3) What was Tommy thinking during the interview?
    1.   I hope he thinks I'm doing a good job.
    2.   I wonder if he knows how admired he is.*

The Case of Martha: Martha is an orphan. She is fifteen years old and is being considered for adoption through a social-work agency. The interested couple is talking with a social worker.

(4) The social worker decides to recommend the adoption. What might she be thinking during her conference with her supervisor?
    1.   He seems to respect my views.
    2.   His experience makes him a keen judge of adoption cases.*

(5) Her supervisor's thoughts?
    1.   She's done a good job of analysis.*
    2.   She knows she has to convince me.

(6) Martha is adopted by the couple. What is the social worker thinking after her twelfth and final monthly visit?
    1.   They all seemed terribly grateful to me.
    2.   Her parents and friends have grown to love her.*

(7) Two years later Martha falls in love with a college senior named Bill. What do her parents think about this?
    1.   Bill seems to love her too; he treats her like a queen.*
    2.   She doesn't need us like she used to.

(8) Martha talks to her social worker for advice about leaving her parents so soon. Martha's thoughts?
    1.   I hope she doesn't think I let her down.
    2.   A social worker would be a good person to talk to now.*

(9) The social worker talks with Martha's parents. Their thoughts?
    1.   She will be good to talk to now.*
    2.   She probably thinks we let her down as parents.

(10) Martha and Bill decide to get married. Her parent's thoughts now?
    1.   They make a great couple and have happy days ahead.*
    2.   Hope she still loves us.

*Indicates other-oriented (second- and third-person) responses; those not starred are self-oriented (first-person) responses.

TABLE 6-3, continued

(11)   What is Bill thinking now?
    1.   Her parents still love her and understand her.*
    2.   I hope she loves me as much as I love her.

The Case of Lou: Lou is the father of three college-age children. He has been acting rather cold toward his wife as of late. His wife is worried. They had always gotten along well in their twenty-six years of marriage, and were able to discuss their problems with each other.

(12)   What might Sally be thinking? She is his favorite child.
    1.   He must be depressed because I left for college.
    2.   I guess adults have periods of depression just like us kids.*

The Case of Albert: Little Albert is a schoolboy in Germany. He is doing below-average work in math and sees his teacher for help.

(13)   What is Albert thinking during the conference?
    1.   He is one of my best teachers.*
    2.   I wonder if he's interested in helping me.

(14)   Poor Albert failed his math course. How did his teacher feel?
    1.   I hope he doesn't feel resentful toward me for failing him.
    2.   I hope this doesn't hurt his self-confidence too much.*

(15)   How did his teacher feel a few years later when his former student formulated an equation $E = mc^2$, changing world history?
    1.   Einstein will go down as one of the great thinkers.*
    2.   I wonder if he thinks I was a poor teacher.

The case of Samuel Reshevsky: Mr. Reshevsky is a world champion chess player. He recently played fifty players simultaneously.

(16)   What were his opponents thinking as they sat down to play him?
    1.   He is truly one of the world's great players.*
    2.   Does he really think that I'm a challenge?

(17)   One of the players, a fifteen-year-old boy, beats the master. His name is Bobby Fischer, current U.S. chess champion. As they played the second time, what was Reshevsky thinking?
    1.   I don't think success has gone to Bobby's head.*
    2.   He seems to look at me differently than he did the last time.

(18)   What did Bobby think after he defeated the Master again?
    1.   His one mistake at the end cost him the game.*
    2.   He must think I'm his equal now.

The Case of Cathy: Cathy and her roommate are sophomores at a large university. They just had a fight about keeping the room neat, Cathy claiming her roommate is not neat enough.

(19)   What did Cathy think after talking to her housemother about it?
    1.   I can see why girls think she is so understanding.*
    2.   I wonder what she thought of me and my side of the argument.

*Indicates other-oriented (second- and third-person) responses; those not starred are self-oriented (first-person) responses.

TABLE 6-3, continued

The Case of Bob: Bob is a college senior majoring in math and plans to go to graduate school next year. His math teacher, Mr. Lewis, is retiring.

(20) His wife's thoughts about the news of her husband's retirement?
    1.   He has a feeling of real satisfaction after these thirty years.*
    2.   Maybe he will need me more now that he is not working.

(21) Mr. Lewis is replaced by a young Ph.D. She is bright, good-looking and single. What is Bob thinking as she walks into class?
    1.   I hope she likes my work.
    2.   This should be an interesting course.*

(22) Bob goes to talk to her about his work. Her thoughts?
    1.   He seems upset at me for marking so hard.
    2.   He seems genuinely interested in improving his work.*

(23) Bob gets straightened out and ends up with an A in the course. What are his thoughts now?
    1.   She thinks I really know the material now.
    2.   This was a very beneficial course.*

The Case of Leon: Leon Winters is captain of his bowling team. His team loses its first three matches and he resigns as captain. Under his successor, Al, the team wins its next four games.

(24) What are Al's thoughts now?
    1.   His bowling has improved lately, as has the team's.*
    2.   He resents me for taking over his job.

The Case of Jan: Jan is a high school dropout. He gets a job on a construction project.

(25) His foreman's thoughts at first:
    1.   This boy needs to gain some self-confidence.*
    2.   He'll be depending on me to help get him started.

(26) Jan gets in a fight with another worker. The foreman then thought:
    1.   Jan will probably worry what I'll do to him about the fight.
    2.   These things happen on any job.*

The Case of Mr. Moore: Alan Moore is in the market for a new car. He is deciding between a Lincoln and a Cadillac.

(27) What might he be thinking as he is talking to one of the salesmen?
    1.   I wonder if he thinks I'm an easy customer to sell.
    2.   I've heard he's a well-respected salesman.*

The Case of Ellen: Ellen has been dating a boy steadily for three months. They are both freshmen and have decided to stop seeing each other for a while.

(28) How does Ellen feel?
    1.   I hope he still likes me even though we're not dating.
    2.   It's best for both of us because we're too young to get serious.*

*Indicates correct answer.

THE CONTROL OF GOODNESS

The expressive quality that we perceive in a person which is dominated by a perception of his badness or goodness is not just a subjective appendage. It is not just accidentally added to the objective content of sensation. On the contrary, it is part of the essential fact of perception. Consequently, it can never be entirely eliminated. It is only with difficulty that we can learn to discriminate what we see about a person and hear him say from this expressive quality. Under emotional strain, we lose the ability to discriminate that we have learned.

It is more difficult still to discriminate the descriptive from the expressive elements in our trait words. Words are symbolic tools that we use to intensify, illuminate, and harmonize our perceptions. The dominant element in our perceptions is their expressive quality; the dominant element in our words is their expressive quality. Consequently, we find expressive words like "sincere," "honest," and "understanding" more meaningful than descriptive words like "bold," "emotional," or "practical."

All the efforts of scientific thought are directed to the aim of reducing and controlling these expressive elements. Thus the five-trait theory uses words that are neutral in their emotional quality and stress how people describe themselves rather than how they evaluate themselves. Such an approach contributes to sensitivity. It also confuses potential users, for they do not find words like "bold" and "practical" very meaningful.

TABLE 6-4
The Goodness in Words

College men and women were given 555 trait words and asked to think of a person being described by the word and to rate the word according to how much they would like the person (Anderson, 1968). The average goodness of each word was calculated and the words ranked from 1 (most favorable) to 555 (least favorable). "Sincere" ranked number 1 and "liar" ranked last.

First: In the pretest *circle* the adjective that you think the *typical student* ranked as the most desirable (or the least undesirable) trait.

Second: Complete the five questions labeled "very easy." When you have finished, the instructor will read and discuss the correct answers. Put an "X" through the answers read. *After* the discussion, complete the five labeled "easy." Again, after scoring your answers and hearing the discussion, complete the five labeled "hard." When the last group, labeled "very hard," is completed and scored, return to the endtest and answer these questions again. Finally, the instructor will read the answers to these so that you can determine your improvement during the exercise.

TABLE 6-4, continued

Pretest	Endtest								
1 2 3	1 2 3	1.	(1)	insincere	(2)	untrustworthy	(3)	hostile*
1 2 3	1 2 3	2.	(1)	restless*	(2)	rebellious	(3)	dependent
1 2 3	1 2 3	3.	(1)	sarcastic	(2)	indifferent	(3)	timid*
1 2 3	1 2 3	4.	(1)	greedy*	(2)	untrustworthy	(3)	obnoxious
1 2 3	1 2 3	5.	(1)	loyal	(2)	honest*	(3)	friendly
1 2 3	1 2 3	6.	(1)	ambitious*	(2)	artistic	(3)	tolerant
1 2 3	1 2 3	7.	(1)	unreliable	(2)	snobbish	(3)	incompetent*
1 2 3	1 2 3	8.	(1)	kindhearted	(2)	considerate*	(3)	helpful
1 2 3	1 2 3	9.	(1)	careful	(2)	frank*	(3)	practical
1 2 3	1 2 3	10.	(1)	observant	(2)	capable*	(3)	self-reliant

_____   _____   Gain _____

Very Easy

1 2 3	11.	(1)	self-conceited	(2)	conceited	(3)	overconfident*
1 2 3	12.	(1)	amusing	(2)	pleasant*	(3)	witty
1 2 3	13.	(1)	silent*	(2)	indecisive	(3)	clumsy
1 2 3	14.	(1)	timid*	(2)	withdrawn	(3)	insecure
1 2 3	15.	(1)	lazy*	(2)	nosy	(3)	cold

_____   Number Correct

Easy

1 2 3	16.	(1)	possessive	(2)	impractical*	(3)	oversensitive
1 2 3	17.	(1)	pessimistic*	(2)	boastful	(3)	egotistical
1 2 3	18.	(1)	opportunistic	(2)	impulsive	(3)	bold*
1 2 3	19.	(1)	depressed	(2)	moody*	(3)	wasteful
1 2 3	20.	(1)	shrewd	(2)	talkative	(3)	persuasive*

_____   Number Correct

Hard

1 2 3	21.	(1)	impulsive	(2)	daring*	(3)	persistent
1 2 3	22.	(1)	nervous	(2)	unemotional*	(3)	superstitious
1 2 3	23.	(1)	orderly	(2)	punctual*	(3)	scientific

*Indicates correct answer.

TABLE 6-4, continued

1 2 3	24.	(1)	ill-mannered	(2)	discourteous*	(3)	disrespectful
1 2 3	25.	(1)	ill-mannered*	(2)	insincere	(3)	loudmouthed

_____ Number Correct

Very Hard

1 2 3	26.	(1)	irritating*	(2)	self-centered	(3)	cold
1 2 3	27.	(1)	excitable	(2)	aggressive	(3)	self-critical*
1 2 3	28.	(1)	clever*	(2)	witty	(3)	ingenious
1 2 3	29.	(1)	unemotional*	(2)	noisy	(3)	conformist
1 2 3	30.	(1)	talented	(2)	competent	(3)	creative*

_____ Number Correct

*Indicates correct answer.

Table 6-4 demonstrates an effort to improve the ability of trainees to recognize and to discriminate the emotional loadings of words. The discriminating value was determined by item analyses of the response of college students, the pretest and endtest items being the most discriminating. The correct answers are asterisked. In a single session, the average student improves his score significantly. However, some students seem to find the task disturbing, and others report difficulty in differentiating their evaluation of the words from the evaluations of the typical student. Consequently, the exercise is more effective when it is preceded by one in which students rate words on a scale from "very bad" to "very good" and discuss their ratings.

The five traits are a distillation and a systemization of the different kinds of things that people say about how they perceive themselves. But expressive qualities dominate our perceptions of others; they also dominate our perceptions of ourselves. We only incidentally describe ourselves; primarily, we evaluate ourselves, reporting how bad or how good a person we think we are. Consequently, a word we use to describe ourselves is more likely to be loaded with evaluation than with description. The trainee seeking to describe a person as that person describes himself must first learn to identify the expressive quality that the person perceives in himself.

The task of determining a person's self-evaluation is simplified by the fact that the degree of a person's boldness *is* just such an evaluation. The dominating, self-confident, energetic, and optimistic person perceives himself as a very desirable, worthy, and good person. So the trainee who knows a person's boldness knows how he evaluates himself. The task is complicated by the fact that how bad or how good a person sees himself to be has little or no relationship to objective evidence of goodness—intelligence, beauty, achievement, morality, etc. The task is most complicated, however, by the conflict of expressive qualities. The person who perceives another person to be "bad" has great difficulty feeling, perceiving, thinking, or imagining that the other person can and does see himself as "good."

The last complication might be reduced by making trainees aware of the goodness they tend to think other people see in themselves. But who are those who think that most other people have good opinions of themselves? The author had a large group of students make predictions about what a variety of people would say about themselves. The twenty-five students who made the most consistently favorable predictions were matched with twenty-five students of the same sex and intelligence who made the most consistently *un*favorable predictions. The answers of these two groups to each of the 200 statements in the five trait scales (Table 5-1) were compared. The forty-eight statements on which they differed the most were answered by a second "favorable" and a second "unfavorable" group. An inspection of the twenty-four of the forty-eight statements that again sharply distinguished those who felt that others would have a good opinion of themselves suggests the following composite picture:

> *He is a quiet and orderly person who is very aware of his own limitations and worried about his personal future. He is amiable toward other people and tolerant of their weaknesses. He is inclined to accept them as they are and not to worry about what they "ought" to be. He is firm in his religious beliefs and inclined to accept rather than to rebel against society.*

Skill in applying the trait theory also requires that the trainee learn to translate the emotional words of everyday usage into the language of the (trait) theory. Table 6-5 is an example of a training exercise designed to develop the trainee's skill in translation. Since George is one of the film cases developed by Cline (1955), the film is commonly shown before students complete the exercise. Again, the adjectives have been selected by item analysis. Again, the typical student improves from the pretest to the endtest, but only modestly.

TABLE 6-5
The Self-image of George

How well can you predict what George, a middle-aged married man, will say about himself? Below is a transcript of a brief interview with him. After studying it, circle "T" in the pretest column if you think George checked the adjective in describing himself; circle "F" if you think he did *not* check that adjective. Before returning to the endtest, we will complete the exercises on the other side which are designed to improve your understanding of him.

TABLE 6-5, continued

Psychologist:	"What sort of person are you?"
Mr. George:	"Just an average person. I like the normal things most people do. I like sports, I like to dance and play around that way. Of course, I don't run around, I'd say I was getting into a stable class. I'm over the younger fling."
Psychologist:	"What would you consider your greatest personality handicap?"
Mr. George:	"Well, maybe too reserved."
Psychologist:	"In what way?"
Mr. George:	"Well, especially in business. I think I take too much of what the boss says, and do it. And, though maybe I can do it better, I do it the way he says to avoid trouble. In other words, I try to get along with people, which is good. But maybe sometimes I should say more about it to maybe help me and the others."
Psychologist:	"Assert yourself a little more?"
Mr. George:	"Yes."
Psychologist:	"Do you ever lose your temper?"
Mr. George:	"Well, very seldom with the person. I may become upset. I try my best not to let them know it."
Psychologist:	"What would you do if someone told a lie about you?"
Mr. George:	"Well, what kind of a lie—that I did something I didn't?"
Psychologist:	"Yes, a lie that perhaps would be damaging to your character."
Mr. George:	"Well, I don't know, but I imagine I'd try and find out why the person said it. Maybe, as far as he knew, he was telling the truth."

After the interview, he was given a long adjective check list with these instructions:

> Put a check-mark in front of each adjective you would consider to be self-descriptive. Do not worry about duplications, contradictions, and so forth. Work quickly and do not spend much time on any one adjective. Try to be frank, and check those adjectives which describe you as you really are, not as you would like to be.

He was asked on two later occasions to perform the same task. All the adjectives below are those that he never checked or that he checked every time.

Pretest	Endtest		
T F	T F	1.	Self-confident (T)
T F	T F	2.	Emotional (T)
T F	T F	3.	Methodical (T)
T F	T F	4.	Cheerful (T)
T F	T F	5.	Dignified (F)
T F	T F	6.	Aggressive (T)
T F	T F	7.	Quick (F)
T F	T F	8.	Unassuming (F)
T F	T F	9.	Clever (F)
T F	T F	10.	Artistic (F)

Number
Right ____   ____   Gain ____

TABLE 6-5, continued

Exercise A.   How Good Does George Think He Is?

The adjectives to the right are favorable. Circle the answer George did. George's actual answers will then be read and discussed.	T F	11. Sincere (T)
	T F	12. Understanding (F)
	T F	13. Mature (T)
	T F	14. Considerate (T)
	T F	15. Responsible (T)
	T F	16. Healthy (T)
	T F	17. Capable (T)
	T F	18. Insightful (F)
	T F	19. Handsome (F)
	T F	20. Sophisticated (F)

Exercise B.   How Bold Does George Think He Is?

Bold:

The adjectives to the right are arranged according to whether they suggest boldness *and* according to their favorableness. Answer as you think George did.	T F	21. Courageous (T)
	T F	22. Enthusiastic (T)
	T F	23. Active (T)
	T F	24. Conceited (T)
	T F	25. Arrogant (F)

Cautious:

T F	26. Shy (T)
T F	27. Meek (F)
T F	28. Worrying (F)
T F	29. Pessimistic (F)
T F	30. Submissive (F)

Exercise C.   How Emotional Does George Think He Is?

Unemotional:

The adjectives to the right are arranged according to whether they suggest emotionality *and* according to their favorableness. Answer as you think George did.	T F	31. Contented (T)
	T F	32. Peaceable (T)
	T F	33. Aloof (F)
	T F	34. Apathetic (F)
	T F	35. Hardhearted (F)

Emotional:

T F	36. Sympathetic (T)

TABLE 6-5, continued

T	F	37.	Nervous (T)
T	F	38.	Defensive (T)
T	F	39.	Anxious (T)
T	F	40.	Fearful (F)

Exercise D.   How Future-minded Does George Think He Is?

Present-minded:

The adjectives to the right are arranged according to whether they suggest future-mindedness *and* according to their favorableness. Answer as you think George did.

T	F	41.	Spontaneous (T
T	F	42.	Uninhibited (F)
T	F	43.	Distractible (F)
T	F	44.	Careless (F)
T	F	45.	Lazy (F)

Future-minded:

T	F	46.	Ambitious (T)
T	F	47.	Dependable (T)
T	F	48.	Organized (T)
T	F	49.	Deliberate (T)
T	F	50.	Painstaking (F)

THE CONTROL OF EMPATHY

My empathy with a person is the degree to which I assume that he is like me. It forms the foundation of my understanding of him; also, of my *mis*understanding of him. I may assume that a person in my social group has the same traits I do when he does not. I may assume that a person I like has the same traits I do when he does not. I may assume that a person who is like me on one trait will be like me on others when he is not. I may assume that most people are like me when they are not. Or I may assume that most people are not like me when they are. In general, it is not my empirical similarities to a person but my rationalistic understanding of him—the degree to which I feel close to, sympathetic with, or identified with him—that determines my empathy with him. If I feel close to a person, I assume he is actually like me.

Discriminating rationalistic from empirical empathy, assumed from actual similarity, is mechanically, intellectually, and emotionally a strenuous task. The model in Table 6-6 analyzes the task and the training problems involved in developing empathic accuracy.

TABLE 6-6
A Model for Training in Trait Empathy

Traits	Percentiles for college women (B & C)						Assumed similarity Difference RANK₁		Actual similarity Difference RANK₂		Empathic accuracy R_1–R_2
(A)	0	20	40	60	80	99	(D)	(E)	(F)	(G)	(H)
Bold	4	10	15	20	25	38	___	___	___	___	___
Emotional	5	20	23	28	32	40	___	___	___	___	___
Future-minded	5	11	15	19	23	32	___	___	___	___	___
Practical	1	9	12	16	20	35	___	___	___	___	___
Empirical	7	17	22	27	30	37	___	___	___	___	___

Total Empathic Accuracy Score (I) ___

A. Traits

When we speak of empathy, we generally mean an emotional identification with another person, not a high degree of empirical similarity. Bakan (1956) makes this difference clear:

> It should be apparent from this that when we say that we are all pretty much alike it does not mean that we must all be psychotic, nor that we must all have children, nor that we must all have had the experience of our parents dying. Not in point of fact need we have had these experiences. But rather in the way in which all yearning is the same, and all pain is the same, and all fantasy is the same, etc.—only in this way need we have had these experiences. And the method whereby we may become aware of the relationship between experience and behavior is through the use of systematic self-observation.

It is possible to measure emotional empathy. Stotland and Dunn (1963), for example, had students watch another student undergoing a humiliating experience. A psychogalvanometer measured their emotional empathy with the student. The authors compared the emotional responses of first-born students with students who had older siblings. Students with older siblings were more responsive: "The first and only born . . . react as if they only use the other person's performance level as a guide to self-evaluation and do not really 'feel with' him." They also compared cautious with bold students. The bold students identified more with the humiliated student: "These results are reminiscent of the clinician's belief that only those who really love themselves can love others."

Emotional empathy, however, is *not* empirical empathy. The emotion we feel for a person may not be the emotion he is experiencing. In fact, he may not be experiencing any emotion at all. Thus the apparently humiliated student was really a trained assistant. Even if the emotional states of two people are actually similar, the similarity may vanish in moments. In any case, the problem of measuring the actual degree of similarity of emotional states in training situations is nearly impossible. A focus upon trait empathy offers a feasible alternative.

B & C. The Measurement of Traits

To develop their empathic accuracy, trainees must be given detailed feedback on their empathic errors. The trait scales (Table 5-1) provide a practical way of doing this. Suppose that the trainee and the person he is judging have both completed the scales. Then the trainee has a concrete idea of what he is assuming similarity about. He also sees where he himself stands on the trait scale as well as a way of seeing the similarity he is assuming to the person. Specifically, he may insert his own score on each scale with a circle, and the score he assumes for the person with an X.

D. Assumed Similarity

Once the trainee and the person's scores are inserted, a measure of empathy can be obtained by subtracting the scores. The process is cumbersome. Experience has shown us, however, that alternatives quickly sink into a maze of arithmetic complexities. These intensify a strong resistance to making any discrimination at all between assumed and actual similarity.

E. Ranking

Now it is easy for the trainee to rank from "1" (the trait on which he assumes the greatest similarity with the person) to "5" (the trait on which he assumes the least). The small shift from a rating system ("he is very like me" to "he is very different from me") to a ranking makes a large difference in the task of the trainee. More important, it can make a tremendous difference in the trainee's perception of the other person. For this reason, the rating-versus-ranking issue requires detailed consideration.

We differ a great deal in the goodness we perceive in the same people. One instructor sees a student as mediocre while another sees him as outstanding. Furthermore, the first instructor may find few students that are commendable while the second finds many. In the same manner, one clinician finds few signs of abnormality in people while another finds many; one sales manager searches intensely for qualified salesmen but finds few; another manager, equally conscientious, finds many. Ratings reflect these differences in perceived goodness: Some people are hard raters; some people are easy raters.

We differ in the variations in goodness we see among people. Some see people as "pretty much alike" while others divide the world into saints and devils. The narrow or wide spread of goodness we see is quite distinct from the general level of goodness we see. Thus the low leveler may see everyone as "bad" or he may see some as "extremely bad" and an occasional person as "not so bad." The higher leveler may see everyone as "good" or he may see some as "extremely good" and an occasional person as "not so good." These level and spread differences have nothing to do with differences between the rated; they have all to do with differences between the raters.

Ranking *eliminates* level and spread differences. In rating, a judge rates a *man* from low to high on a trait; in ranking, he ranks *men* from low to high on the trait: Tom Jones, first; Dick Thomas, second; Harry Smith, third, etc. Every ranker must use every rank. Consequently, it is impossible to have low and high rankers as we have low or high raters; it is impossible to have narrow or wide rankers as we have narrow or wide raters.

Psychologists know about the superiority of ranking. They have, in fact, proved it. Albrecht, Glasser, and Marks (1964), for example, had two staff members of a firm of consultants use an intensive interview, personal history data, and scores on a variety of ability and personality tests to predict the success of thirty-one recently promoted managers. On the basis of this information, each consultant rated the probable success of each manager. He also *ranked* the managers from the one most likely to be most successful to the one least likely. The ratings and the rankings of the two consultants were combined and correlated with a composite criterion of actual success on the job. The ratings were not related to success ($r = .09$); the rankings were ($r = .46$). The authors concluded: "The rating-form procedure, in contrast to ranking, adds the uncertainty of interpretation of a scale with the possibility for central tendency or leniency biases to enter the picture."

Still, psychologists prefer to rate. In a hundred studies of sensitivity, for example, the present author found one out of two researchers had used ratings. It seems that the psychologist, like everyone else, perceives people as having a basic quality of goodness or badness. He finds that ranking forces him away from his perception of the world. The generous rater is forced by ranking to put someone at the bottom, to see him as "bad"; the tough rater is forced to put someone at the top, to see him as "good." Ranking forces the narrow spreader to discriminate between people whom he "sees" as alike; the wide spreader is not allowed by ranking to push people as far apart as he sees them. Judges only reluctantly yield the freedom they have in rating.

Ranking among individuals results in more valid predictions. Ranking within individuals, as proposed in Table 6-6, directs the trainee away from the rating question: How much is he like or different from me? It directs him toward the ranking question: In what way is he most like me and in what is he most different? The development of a ranking orientation thus tends to internalize the control of empathy. Instead of encouraging him to form a global impression of his similarity, ranking encourages the trainee to discriminate between the ways in which he is like and the ways in which he is unlike another person.

F & G. Actual Similarity

The trainee has now recorded and ranked his assumptions of similarity. He is next given the actual scores of the person he is judging so that they may be inserted in the table. The subtraction of his own scores from the actual scores of the person tells him how much he is actually like him. These actual differences can now be ranked. When he has done this ranking, the trainee knows the trait in which he is most like the person he has judged as well as the trait on which he is least like him.

H & I. Empathic Accuracy

The subtraction of R_1 from R_2 gives an index of the empathic accuracy of the trainee, i.e., the degree to which his original assumptions of similarity fit his actual similarities to that person. The total of these differences for all traits, in turn, gives a general index of empathic accuracy.

The details of the model make clear the major elements involved in making empathic judgments as well as the training necessities. It is simple enough to be used in training. After a few trials, the mechanical details become routine. It is not essential that the detailed steps be strictly followed. The important things are that the trainee focus on the empirical ways which he is like and unlike the other person and that he get feedback on the accuracy of his assumptions of similarity.

CUE TRAINING

How does a trainee learn to identify correctly the traits of a person? In general, he learns to identify the cues that the person gives him that are related to his position on the traits. The most valid cues are verbal, i.e., the person tells the trainee where he stands on the traits. The importance of such cues are especially obvious in the five-trait theory, for it focuses upon the question: How does the person perceive himself? *The closer the trainee sticks to what the person says about himself, the more accurate he is likely to be.*

It is hard to practice this simple principle. Giedt (1955) studied the cues that psychologists, social workers, and psychiatrists used in making predictions about the traits of patients. On the whole, they wandered much too far from what the patient said about himself. Thus they incorrectly judged a person to be high in emotionality because he moved around in his chair and smoked a lot. They incorrectly judged a patient to be submissive because he lapsed into silence, made lengthy responses to questions, or was "acting like a little boy before a parent figure." They sometimes totally ignored what the patient said about himself. They rated a patient low in emotionality even though he said he was so anxious that he could not work. A related kind of error grew out of the tendency of interviewers to believe "in the almost magical power of confession and catharsis." That is, the interviewers tended to underestimate a patient on undesirable traits that he confessed. An incorrect rating of high friendliness was rationalized on the basis that a patient "expressed dislike of father with embarrassment." A too-high rating on future-mindedness of a patient was rationalized on the basis that the patient reported feeling guilty about his impulsiveness and had resolved to do better in the future. A too-high rating on warmth for a patient was rationalized because the patient was "able to express hostility in the interview." The raters were more accurate when they based their judgments "directly on what the patient said as to his feelings, preferences, or past behavior. When the observers tried to use more devious interpretations or to infer from direct behavior, they tended to err."

The increase in errors of the trainee when he fails to stick to what the person says about himself is not merely due to factual or logical errors. It arises from the radical change that occurs when the trainee shifts from the other person's point of view to his own. At that point the empathy he has for the person and the expressive qualities that he perceives become more dominant. This dominance determines the illusory correlations he finds, for the correlator seeks to squeeze and distort the cues to fit his perceptions of the person.

People, of course, tell us about themselves by their actions as well as by their words. Bold people talk louder, write with greater pressure, volunteer to speak before groups more often, and look at people more directly than do the cautious. Emotional people blink their eyes more rapidly than do the calm. Artistic people reveal their interests by their dress and appearance. The future-minded are neater than the present-minded, and the empirical behave in nonconforming ways. We will know more about the relationship between the nonverbal cues to traits in the future. At present, however, most of the considerable research work on nonverbal behavior deals with problems of "communication." At best, such work tells us primarily how one person is relating to another person at a given moment and in a particular situation. It tells us little about the stable and enduring traits of the person. In general, the communication perspective is a self-oriented perspective. It does not try to answer the question "What does he think of himself?" It focuses on the question "What is he feeling and thinking about *me*?"

In Chapter 2 we proposed general guidelines for the development of more effective sensitivity training: (1) formulate more realistic goals, (2) sequence the goals, (3) reduce defensiveness, (4) fit the method to the goal, and (5) evaluate the success of training. In this chapter we have shown how they might be applied in the development of procedures for improving theoretical sensitivity—the ability to select and use a theory that will result in greater predictive accuracy.

In applying these guidelines, we have advanced the general hypothesis that the mastery of an empirically derived trait theory should be the basic goal (Table 6-2). As subgoals we have assumed that the trainee must first become aware of his general orientation to other people and learn to adopt an other-orientation (Table 6-3). Next, he must learn to discriminate the emotional loading of trait words that are commonly used to describe oneself and others (Table 6-4). He must learn to translate these words into the traits of the theory (Table 6-5). Finally, he must learn to recognize the actual similarities and differences between the traits he ascribes to himself and the traits that others ascribe to themselves (Table 6-6). These subgoals, we have assumed, can best be achieved by following the sequence indicated. We have implied that breaking the task into subgoals reduces defensiveness. We have suggested quite different methods for achieving the different subgoals. And we have indicated how the overall success of the training might be evaluated (Table 6-1).

We still have doubts about the effectiveness of such training. We doubt it because it has had only limited objective evaluation. We doubt it even more because of the great difficulty of the learning task. It demands that a trainee shift from his powerful and immediately satisfying mythic way of thinking about others to the relatively weak, unsatisfying, and emotionally meaningless scientific way of thinking about others. In making this shift, he must give up many personal idiosyncrasies and comfortable fallacies. He already feels that he understands others. However, he can only actually understand them by applying the laws that govern his own person perceptions.

We doubt, then, that the training procedures that we have outlined are adequate for accomplishing this personal upheaval. We do not doubt, however, that the road we have suggested is more likely to lead to success than present theoretical training practices, which encourage trainees to continue to think mythically while giving them the illusion that they are thinking scientifically.

NOMOTHETIC SENSITIVITY

CHAPTER 7

GROUP PERCEPTION

NOMOTHETIC sensitivity is the ability to learn about a group and to use this knowledge in making more accurate predictions about its individual members. Reade (1938) argues that we can only think scientifically about a person *by* placing him in a group:

> It is obvious, surely that when "individual" signifies uniqueness neither from it nor to it can there be any inference whatever. . . . If we propose to make an inference from one man, one triangle, or one anything else to others it can only be by virtue of what is common to two or more. The moment we touch the unique all inference (and indeed all science) comes to an end.
>
> What, then, is the "particular" for the purposes of inference? Paradoxical as it may sound, it seems that it cannot be anything but the universal. Dissect or analyze the individual, dissolve Plato into "man," "Athenian," "philosopher," and he can become apparently the goal or source of many inferences. But leave as Plato, the unique and unapproachable, and he will mock at deduction, induction, and all similar pretenses. Before the individual can be brought within range of inference it has to be transformed into a specimen, an example, an instance. . . .

In mythic thinking, at the other extreme, the individual *is* his group and cannot be separated from it.

Predicting an individual from his group membership puts psychologists in a dilemma. On the one hand, they decry the use of "stereotypes," standardized mental pictures of what the typical member of a group is like, and call the users of such pictures racists, sexists, and dogmatists. On the other hand, their efforts to train people to suppress their stereotypes and to become sensitive to individuality has never improved predictive accuracy. It often has resulted in a significant decrease in sensitivity.

Gough (1968), for example, had several hundred Americans complete a sixty-four-item questionnaire as they thought a typical Italian male and a typical Italian female would fill it out. They then saw filmed interviews with two Italian men and two Italian women. Before showing the films it was explained that the interviews were in Italian and that the observers must therefore depend principally on inflection of voice, facial expressions, tone, and incidental cues. After the films had been shown, discussions revealed that observers found the films rich with informative clues. They then answered the same questionnaire as they thought each of the four Italians had. The accuracy of their predictions after seeing the individual Italians was compared with the accuracy they would have achieved if they had simply used their stereotypes of the typical Italian man and woman. Their mean individual accuracy was 33; their mean stereotype accuracy was 37, significantly *higher.*

Crow (1957) showed medical students pictures of physicians interviewing patients. He then had them predict the feelings and attitudes of the patients. Afterward, the students took an extensive training program designed to sensitize them to individual differences among patients. They took the film test again. Result: "Contrary to expectations, a training program in interpersonal relations for medical students decreased the trainees' accuracy in judging others."

Idiographic training has not improved idiographic sensitivity. Such training may not even improve nomothetic sensitivity. Twenty students were told that a survey of attitudes of 400 faculty members toward their university magazine had been conducted (Olmsted, 1962). They were shown the questionnaire form and asked to estimate what percentage of the surveyed group had answered the question in various ways. A second group of students made the same estimates. Each of the students in the second group had the experience of actually interviewing fifteen of the faculty members who completed the survey. In spite of this experience, they were no better at predicting the replies of the faculty than the first group.

The task of training, then, is not to eliminate stereotypes but to improve their accuracy. In general, we perceive groups as we perceive persons. Consequently, we shall again consider the structure of group impressions as we did individual impressions, the dominance of goodness in that structure, and the large influence of empathy on both goodness and the accuracy of observation.

THE FORMATION OF GROUP IMPRESSIONS

The perception of a group forms as a simple whole and then simultaneously differentiates and integrates details within that whole. The irreducible unit of this perception is its expressive quality, the perception of the group as familiar or strange, as friendly or hostile, as helpful or threatening. The verbalization of the impression reflects, intensifies, and stabilizes the original perception.

The Instant Whole

We can form an instant whole impression of a group from a shadowy clue. Haire (1950) gave fifty people shopping list I that had seven items: "Pound and a half of hamburger, bunch of carrots, 5 pounds of potatoes, Nescafe instant coffee," etc. He gave another fifty people shopping list II that was identical except that "1 lb Maxwell House

Coffee" was substituted for the Nescafe. Both groups read these instructions:

> Read the shopping list below. Try to project yourself into the situation as far as possible until you can more or less characterize the woman who bought the groceries. Then write a brief description of her personality and character.

The Nescafe women were much more often described as lazy, disorganized, spendthrifts who were not good wives. Here is a typical description of the Nescafe woman:

> This woman appears to be either single or living alone. I would guess that she had an office job. Apparently, she likes to sleep late in the morning, basing my assumption on what she bought, such as instant coffee which can be made in a hurry. She probably also has peaches for breakfast, cans being easy to open. Assuming that she is just average, as opposed to those dazzling natural beauties who do not need much time to make up, she must appear rather sloppy, taking little time to make up in the morning. She is also used to eating supper out, too. Perhaps alone rather than with an escort. An old maid probably.

In a follow-up study, "Blueberry Fill Pie Mix" was substituted for the instant coffee with similar results: "There seems to be little doubt that the prepared-food-character, and the stigma of avoiding housewifely duties is responsible for the projected personality characteristics. . . ."

We can form elaborate impressions of a group with *no* perceptual clues. Katz and Braly (1933) showed that college students had stereotypes of a wide variety of minority and nationality groups. Furthermore, there was no relation between the elaborateness and uniformity of these stereotypes and the amount of contact with the group in question. The students, for example, had as rich stereotypes of Turks and Japanese, who were quite unknown to them, as they had of American Negroes, who were far more familiar. Research done in the 1930s showed that whites with no personal acquaintance with Negroes held, if anything, more elaborate stereotypes of them than did whites who had Negro acquaintances (Campbell, 1967).

Differentiation and Integration

We tend to see members of other groups as homogeneous parts of a whole. We meet one Australian and talk about Australians; we meet one Indian and talk about Indians. However, we see members of our own group in a highly differentiated way. Orwell (1954, p. 266) has described the differences between in-group and out-group perspectives:

> It is quite true that the so-called races of Britain feel themselves to be very different from one another. A Scotsman, for instance, does not thank you if you call him an Englishman. You can see the hesitation we feel on this point by the fact that we call our islands by no less than six different names, England, Britain, Great Britain,

the British Isles, the United Kingdom, and, in very exalted moments, Albion. Even the differences between north and south England loom large in our own eyes. But somehow these differences fade away the moment that any two Britons are confronted by an European. It is very rare to meet a foreigner, other than an American, who can distinguish between English and Scots or even English and Irish. To a Frenchman, the Breton and the Auvergnat seem very different beings, and the accent of Marseilles is a stock joke in Paris. Yet we speak of "France" and "the French". . . . So also with ourselves. Looked at from the outside, even the cockney and the Yorkshireman have a strong family resemblance.

Knowing that a person is an Englishman or a member of the instant-coffee group, we can quickly generate a detailed picture of him. That is, we have "stereotypes."

In 1798, a London paper announced that "the celebrated Didot, the French printer, with a German, named Herman, have announced a new discovery in printing which they term stereotype." The process involved printing from a plate of type metal cast from a set of type instead of from the type itself. Gradually, the term came to be used in a more figurative sense to mean "something continued or constantly repeated without change." Before 1900, for example, psychiatrists were referring to the highly repetitive motions of the arm or body by patients as "stereotyped movements." Now, the term means "something conforming to a fixed or general pattern, especially a standardized mental picture" representing a judgment of a group that is applied to every member of the group.

We have stereotypes that can give us a detailed picture of a person. We also have implicit theories—traits with assumed relationships between them—that, given one trait about a person, can generate a detailed picture of him. Which is the chicken and which the egg? Does the stereotype dominate the theory or the theory dominate the stereotype? Secord and Berscheid (1963) attacked this question by presenting seventy-nine students with traits sometimes assumed to be characteristics of the typical Negro (lazy, dishonest, happy-go-lucky, superstitious, and deeply religious) and also with traits not commonly associated with the Negro specifically (sportsmanlike, sincere, generous, conceited, moody, and quarrelsome). The assumed relationships between each pair of traits was measured by having the students fill out ratings like the following:

A person is *lazy.* How likely is it that he is *also:*

Sportsmanlike
0   1   2   3   4   5   6   7   8   9   10
Impossible   Certain

Each trait was rotated into the "lazy" and "sportsmanlike" slots. The mean rating for a pair was the measure of the assumed relationship. The ratings were repeated, but this time the students were asked to assume that the person was a Negro. That is: "A Negro is *lazy.* How likely is it that he is. . ." If the assumed relationships of the theory changed with the shift, it would mean that the racial stereotype was stronger than the theory. Result: No change. Conclusion: "If implicit personality theory biases remain unaffected in the type of quantitative judgment employed here, as they seem to, they will be even more likely to operate in the everyday situation where there is usually little pressure for precision in judgment and more freedom for biases to operate." It seems that the mythic theory is the chicken.

For an implicit theory to generate a differentiated and integrated picture of a group it must have at least a few real characteristics of the group. In his study of stereotypes and the perception of group differences, Campbell (1967) concludes: "The greater the real differences between groups on any particular custom, detail of physical appearance, or item of material culture, the more likely it is that the feature will appear in the stereotyped imagery each group has of the other. . . . The more opportunities for observation and the longer the exposure to the outgroup, the larger the role of real differences in the stereotypes."

Campbell assumes that when an in-group and out-group agree on a trait of the in-group, that trait is very likely to be real. Thus since both the Masai group in East Africa and neighboring groups agree that the Masai are usually hot-tempered and sexually promiscuous, it is safe to assume that the Masai really exhibit these qualities. Through fortuitous circumstances, there are real differences between some groups in literacy, technical skills, and familiarity with the subtleties of the monetary economy. As a consequence, the more modernized groups may be perceived as progressive, intelligent, wealthy, and clean. The less acculturated groups may be perceived as backward, stupid, poor, and dirty. Another type of social reality lying behind the mutual stereotypes in East Africa is ethnic specialization in the economic life. Thus farmers in mountainous areas where there is heavy rainfall so that they can plant continuously, see the coastal farmers who have much less rain as physically weak and lazy.

Given a few real differences to work with, mythic thinking generates through illusory correlations a host of unreal differences. The most obvious of these is in the degree of difference perceived. Thus an average IQ of 95 for Negroes and 103 for Jews generates the conclusion that all Negroes are dumb and all Jews are smart. The emotional language of mythic thinking is so fluid that a difference in any direction can be anathematized, i.e., the Negroes can be hated because they are too dumb and the Jews can be hated because they are too smart.

It is in the generation of erroneous causal relationships, however, that mythic theories carry their users furthest from reality. Why are

Negroes uneducated? It is because of their hereditary inferiority, not because of their inferior environment. Why are outgroup members hated? It is their traits that cause the ingroup to hate them; it is not because the ingroup hates them to begin with and opportunistically interprets all differences as despicable and gives most attention to the most plausibly despicable traits.

Expressive Quality

The expressive quality that a person has for us, though sometimes vivid, fluctuates. The expressive quality of a group is more stable. The perceptual quality of a person is like a text that is written in such small letters that it is illegible. The perceptual quality of his group, however, is in large capital letters.

What expressive quality, for example, do women perceive in men? The answer is obscure when one examines the way one woman perceives one man. It becomes clearer when one examines the impressions of the typical woman of the typical man. Steinman and Fox (1966) asked more than 800 women, among them artists, lawyers, Negro professionals, physicians, business women, nurses, members of philanthropic organizations, as well as undergraduates in private and public educational institutions, the role they perceived themselves as actually playing. They completed a thirty-four-item attitude scale that measured the relative stress they placed on family activities versus career activities. The items asked for their attitude toward work ("I would rather be famous than have affection," etc.), toward marriage ("I would like to marry a man I could look up to," etc.), toward child rearing ("I would rear children to believe in the equality of the sexes," etc.), and toward themselves ("I argue against people in authority," etc.). Results: The women saw themselves as playing a role that was almost exactly balanced between intrafamily and extrafamily activities. The artists saw themselves as somewhat more career-oriented and undergraduate women at expensive colleges saw themselves as more family-oriented. However, the average differences among the various groups were small.

The women also filled out the scale not as they thought they actually were, but as they would like to be. The differences between their perceptions of their actual role and their ideal role were calculated. The undergraduates of public colleges saw themselves as more family-oriented than they would like to be; the Negro professionals saw themselves as being more career-oriented than they would like to be. Again, the differences were small. The large majority of these women saw themselves as actually leading very close to the kind of life they would ideally like to lead.

More than 400 men from the same professional groups also filled out the attitude scale as they would like their ideal woman to fill it out. The ideal woman of male lawyers was more family-oriented than female lawyers actually wanted to be. The ideal woman of male undergraduates of public colleges was more career-oriented than female undergraduates at those colleges wanted to be. In general, however, the ideal woman of men was extremely close to the ideal woman of women.

Finally, the women were asked to fill out the scale for the ideal woman *as they perceived the typical man to want her to be.* The results shatter the apparent harmony of male with female ideals. All groups of women perceived all groups of men as wanting women to be much more family-oriented than they wanted to be. They perceived men as wanting them to be more interested in affection, more interested in having women look up to men, more interested in child rearing, and more interested in giving in to authority than they wanted to be. Women quite uniformly seem to perceive men as having a strange, competitive, and threatening quality.

GOODNESS IN GROUP IMPRESSIONS

The core of the expressive quality perceived in groups, as in individuals, lies along the bad-versus-good dimension. We see our own group as "good" and an opposing group as "bad." Consequently, the pictures that members of opposing groups have of each other often seem to have little similarity. Haire (1955), for example, studied the perceptions that labor and management leaders had of each other. He concluded:

> It seems clear that labor and management are not talking to the same people when they confer with one another. Labor sees itself and management so differently and management sees itself and labor so differently that, although they are only two people in the room, four people seem to be involved in the conversation. Consider, for example, the meaning of a statement like "we are anxious to work with you." Let us suppose it is made by Mr. B, a labor representative. He is seen by labor to be honest, dependable, and efficient. However, by management he is seen as persistent, opinionated, argumentative, and outspoken. He is seen by labor to have high thinking ability, to be dependable, and to see the other's side of the problem. He is seen by management to be a less clear thinker than management is, to be relatively undependable, and to fail to see management's side of the problem. Under these circumstances, it seems hardly possible that the statement can mean the same thing to both parties. Though only one man speaks, the masks through which the statement comes are so different that it is hardly the same thing any longer. . . .

There could not be a greater contrast than that between these perceptions that are dominated by qualities of good and evil and the understanding of groups sought by science. In its quest for an empirical picture these emotional perceptions fade away. Furthermore, in the development of such a picture, as in the development of an empirically derived trait theory, the perceptions of the group of itself play the central role. What is sought in these self-perceptions of groups is the different ways that they describe themselves.

Guilford (1967) exemplifies the course and the results of the search for empirically derived group portraits. She was interested in the common perceptions which life insurance salesmen, engineers, clergymen, journalists, or physicists shared with each other and did *not* share with the other groups. Successful members of each of these groups completed a 653-item questionnaire that covered their personal history, their interests, and their temperament. By the use of inverse factor analysis she isolated the unique ways in which each group described itself. Here are those descriptions.

Life Insurance Salesman
The typical salesman did not so much choose his career as drift into it. He is ambitious and desires success, money, and luxuries. He likes activities which involve either selling or business and dislikes aesthetic and scientific activities. He tends to be aggressively hostile and is sociable on a large scale and dependent on others for advice and companionship. He is conservative and authoritarian in his attitudes. He tends to think poorly of others and often suspects their motives. He is not sensitive to criticism and is stable emotionally. He is sometimes impulsive. He is a doer rather than a thinker. When profitable, he may take advantage of others. He sees other members of his occupation as having these same characteristics.

Engineer
The typical engineer is distinguished primarily by his fondness for all activities which are mechanical or manipulative and for studies in the area of mathematics and science. He is antagonistic towards aesthetic and verbal activities and occupations as well as toward those which deal with people on a personal basis. He is socially independent, neither avoiding nor seeking out social contacts. He is unusually free from concern for his health or welfare and enjoys taking risks. He likes to assume responsibility and is thorough in his work. He has very high ethical standards. He does not like to be the center of attention. He likes a regulated life and has little need for freedom. He is a realistic thinker with a practical approach to life. His occupational stereotype agrees with his self-perception.

Clergyman
The typical clergyman seems to have led a rather righteous and well-supervised life as a child. He has high athletic interests and prefers occupations closely allied to his own, such as administrative or teaching occupations. He seeks personal relationships and likes to help others. He rejects occupations related to selling or business as well as those which involve mechanical work. He likes to "play it safe" and avoid danger. He evidences attitudes of humility appropriate to his calling in not being irritated by or speaking out in reaction to personal affronts. He has a high regard for the ethical behavior of others, to the point of naivete. He is unusually sociable and likes to have a wide circle of acquaintances. He is quite conventional in his attitudes. He likes to live a well-regulated life and does not object to restrictions on his freedom. Religion is very important to him and his religious beliefs are orthodox. He is self-confident, emotionally healthy, and objective. He has some need for recognition from others, but is not ambitious for success in the conventional sense. He sees his fellow clergyman as being like himself.

Journalist
The journalist comes from an unhealthy emotional climate. There is a history of unsatisfactory family relationships and poor adjustment to the demands of society. His interests are solely in aesthetic areas, while his antipathies for almost all other activities (mechanical, scientific, business, and particularly mathematical) are numerous. He is particularly irresponsible when it comes to money and material goods. Unconventionality is a major characteristic of the journalist, who seems to rebel against the institutions of society (e.g., church, penal systems) and rejects public opinion as an influence over his behavior. He is emotionally unstable, pessimistic, and excitable. He broods about himself and makes impulsive decisions. He is sociable with close friends and sexually aggressive toward women. His habits are irregular and he needs to feel free to come and go as he pleases. He views his fellow journalist as fitting this pattern.

Physicist
The physicist's background and personality reveal social isolation; his feelings of being "different" as a child and his tendency to avoid personal relationships are evidence of withdrawal. His major interests are in scientific and mechanical areas with all forms of mathematics as favorite subjects of study. Any occupation which might involve leadership, selling, or dealing with people in any way would be very distasteful to him. He lacks self-confidence and does not take the initiative in social situations even when it is appropriate. He does not like to be conspicuous. His decisions are cautiously made. He tends to be nervous and to eat poorly. He would avoid any situation which might require him to be responsible for anyone else. He is a persistent, careful worker. He feels uncomfortable with women and is disinterested in religion. Emotions are not his concern. He is a realistic and logical thinker. He tends to see other physicists as being much like himself.

The more specific these empirically derived group pictures become, the better they predict the feelings of persons in that group. Such pictures of even the broadest groups, however, can lead to surprisingly accurate predictions. Stelmachers and McHugh (1964), for example, had forty-two psychologists, psychiatrists, and psychiatric social workers predict the responses two men and two women made to 171 items on the Minnesota Multiphasic Personality Inventory (MMPI). One of the women was a normal college sophomore; the other was an elderly woman with a long medical and psychiatric history and the diagnosis of "conversion reaction." One of the men was a teen-age homosexual with a lengthy criminal record; the other, a psychiatric patient with a diagnosis of "depressive reaction." To aid them in making their predictions, the experts were given information from a biographical questionnaire, an interest and activities questionnaire, and a sentence completions test, as well as hospital records and psychiatric interviews. The responses of these four individuals were also predicted from an accurate knowledge of how the typical man and the typical woman would answer these questions. The norms of the MMPI handbook give the percentage of each of these groups answering "true" and "false" to the 171 items in the prediction test. A special key was then made for each group where an item was called "true" if 50 percent or more of the group answered it true and "false" if 49 percent or less answered it true. The keys were applied to each of the four subjects. For example, if the college girl answered a statement "true" and the typical college girl had also answered it "true," the item was counted as correct, etc.

Table 7-1 compares the accuracy of expert predictions with that based on special keys. In three out of the four cases, the keys win. The authors conclude: "It is truly surprising how powerful these keys turn out to be! . . . Apparently even a very approximate matching on a very few variables between subject and population can lead to a significant improvement in predictive accuracy. . . ."

It is clear that the trainee who masters an empirically derived self-portrait of a group can significantly improve his sensitivity to individual members of that group. Thus if he masters the Guilford portrait of a life insurance salesman, he can make better predictions about individuals in that occupational group. His mastery, among other things, will eliminate the constant errors he makes in judging all members because of his too unfavorable or too favorable view of the group. Cronbach (1955) has stressed the value of eliminating such errors:

> An argument can be presented for concentrating attention on constant processes, taking up interactions between J and O only after the constant processes characteristic of J are dependably measured. Constant processes in the perceiver have potentially great importance because they affect all his acts of perception. Individual differences in constant processes need to be measured dependably so that their influence can be discounted in studies of variable processes. Moreover, identifying constant errors should permit training to eliminate such biases; this may be the most effective way to improve the social perception of leaders, teachers, and diagnosticians.

But the obstacles to such mastery are great. The trainee does not have to change merely his opinion of the group; he has to change his

TABLE 7-1
Expert Predictions Compared with Empirical Predictions
(Adapted from Stelmachers and McHugh, 1964)

Subjects Whose MMPI Responses Were Predicted	Accuracy of Experts	Accuracy of Special Keys
1. Normal female sophomore (college female norms)	127	144
2. Elderly female patient (adult female norms)	106	129
3. Adult male depressive (adult male norms)	98	67
4. Criminal teen-age homosexual (adult male norms)	102	116

perception of it, for it is this perception that his opinions reflect. In this process, he has to learn to perceive the group as it perceives itself.

EMPATHY WITH GROUPS

In Chapter 3 empathy was defined as "the degree of similarity that one person assumes between himself and another person." But we did not stop to consider the baffling question of *how* we make these assumptions. Lipps (Cassirer, 1957, p. 83), the father of empathy theory, implied that what we know about another person can never be an original but only a borrowed reality: "The other psychological individual is . . . made by myself out of myself. His inner being is taken from mine. The other individual or ego is the product of a projection, a reflection, a radiation of myself (or of what I experience in myself, through the sense perception of an outside physical phenomenon) into this very sensory phenomenon, a peculiar kind of reduplication of myself."

Lipps' explanation has a fundamental weakness. It presupposes as fact what is theory: It accepts the splitting of reality into an outside and an inside as a fact, without inquiring into the conditions under which this splitting is possible. It is quite clear that such a division is *not* possible for the infant. He is conscious, but not self-conscious. He treats his own body as if it were foreign to him. His toes are his toys, and he may claw his own face until it bleeds. He has no bodily self, no social self, and no material self. The boundary between him and not-him, between his and not-his is unestablished.

Many theorists have stressed the slowness and difficulty with which the individual develops a consciousness of his self. Rank (1941), for example, viewed the development of the self as determined by the resolution of the conflict between the fears of life and death. The "fear of life" is the fear of separation from the whole, a fear first experienced as the infant separates from his mother at birth. In later life the same fear is evidenced by the individual's fear of having to stand alone or be alone, of becoming himself or being himself, of standing out sharply from the mass of other people. The fear drives the individual back toward groups more powerful than he, back toward dependence on others, back toward his mother. The "fear of death" is the fear of the loss of personal identity. The closer one's attachment to the mother, the more dependent one is on others, and the more one is lost in the crowd, the more the fear is stimulated. To reduce the fear, the individual strives to separate himself from others and to establish his own uniqueness.

Cassirer (1946) stresses the slowness and difficulty with which mankind as a whole has developed an awareness of a self that is separate from the group. In primitive societies, the pressures do not push the child to differentiate himself from the group but to identify himself with the group (p. 38):

> It is a deep and ardent desire of the individuals to identify themselves with the life of the community and with the life of nature. This desire is satisfied by the religious rites. Here the individuals are melted into one shape—into an undistinguishable whole. If in a savage tribe the men are engaged in warfare or in any other dangerous enterprise and the women who have stayed at home try to help them by their ritual dances—this seems to be absurd and unintelligible when judged according to the standards of empirical thought and "causal laws." But it becomes perfectly clear and comprehensible as soon as we read and interpret this act in terms of our social rather than of our physical experience. In their war dances the women identify themselves with their husbands. They share their hopes and fears, their risks and dangers. This bond—a bond of "sympathy," not of "causality"—is not enfeebled by the distance that lies between them; on the contrary it is strengthened. The two sexes form one indivisible organism; what is going on in one part of this organism necessarily affects the other part. A great many positive and negative demands, of prescriptions and taboos, are nothing but the expression and application of this general rule. The rule holds not only for the two sexes, but for all the members of the tribes. When a Dayak village has turned out to hunt in the jungle, those who stay at home may not touch either oil or water with their hands; for if they did so the hunters would all be "butter-fingered" and the prey would slip through their hands. This is not a causal but an emotional bond. What matters here are not the empirical relations between causes and effects, but the intensity and depth with which human relations are felt.

The members of a tribe assume that they are like the other members of their tribe; they assume that other members are like them. When a member knows what he is like, he assumes that other members are like him. When he knows what another member is like, he assumes that he is like that member. For him, empathy is more realistically defined as the degree of similarity he assumes between himself and a group member. The more closely he identifies himself with the group, the more similarity he assumes with its members, and vice versa: the less he identifies with the group, the less similarity he assumes. At the extreme, he assumes no similarity between himself and a member of any enemy group.

In the same way, members of our society assume that a member of their group is like them and that they are like the typical member of their group. Burnstein, Stotland, and Zander (1962) brought more than a hundred junior high school boys together in the school gymnasium and asked them to complete a "describe yourself questionnaire." One part of the questionnaire required them to rate their excellence in swimming, ability to hold breath under water, etc. Two weeks later, the boys were addressed in groups of a dozen by a "deep-sea diver" (one of the authors) who described his career and stressed his excellence in swimming, ability to hold his breath under water, etc. In some groups, he stressed that he was similar to the boys: He was born and raised in their rural neighborhood, went to the same school, had a father who worked in the same factory that employed most of the fathers of the boys, etc. In other groups, the diver stressed that he was dissimilar: He was born and raised in a big city, went to a large school, had a father who was a fisherman, etc. At the end of each group meeting, the diver asked the boys to rate themselves again on their excellence in swimming, etc. Result: The boys who had heard the "low-similarity" diver rated themselves about as they had two weeks before; the boys who heard the "high-similarity" diver changed their ratings of themselves so that they were more like those that the diver described himself as possessing.

The bad-versus-good dimension dominates group impressions. Like the goodness of individual impressions, the goodness of group impressions is heavily influenced by the degree to which an individual assumes similarity to the group. In general, the in-group is good; the out-group, bad. Table 7-2 offers an example of these tendencies. In all twenty statements, the "true" answer reflects more favorably on the group than a "false" answer. The average college student answers "true" for the ten statements about the typical college student. He is correct, for the typical college student does answer "true" to all the statements. The average college student answers "false" for the ten statements about the typical worker. He is entirely mistaken, for the typical worker answers "true" to all the statements about workers.

TABLE 7-2
A Demonstration of Goodness in Group Perceptions

The Typical Student

A group at this university was asked to give their impression of the typical undergraduate student here by answering the following statements. Some of the group answered "true" and some answered "false" to each of them. Answer each of these statements, not as you would, but *as you think the majority of the group answered them.*

T F 1. The average student really enjoys learning.

T F 2. He takes pride in his work.

T F 3. He rarely worries about being suspended.

T F 4. He thinks he should learn as much as he can while in college.

T F 5. He believes his education is supported because society will benefit from it.

T F 6. He believes that everyone would benefit if each student did the best he could.

TABLE 7-2, continued

T F   7. He is more interested in relevant than in "snap" courses.

T F   8. He would rather be graded on his performance than on some automatic grading system.

T F   9. He thinks the future of society will be influenced by how much students get out of college.

T F   10. He is seriously interested in learning rather than in just "getting by."

The Typical Worker

Several thousand workers in 150 small and large companies, some of which were unionized and some of which were not, answered the statements below. Some of the group answered "true" and some answered "false" to each of them. Answer each of these statements, not as you would, but *as you think the majority of the workers described the typical worker.*

T F   11. The average worker really enjoys his work.

T F   12. The average worker takes pride in what he does on his job.

T F   13. The average worker thinks that wages are increased primarily because he is able to produce more and needs more to live.

T F   14. The average worker only occasionally worries about being laid off.

T F   15. The average worker feels that the company's investment in new labor-saving equipment generally makes it possible for him to earn more money.

T F   16. The average worker thinks he should be advanced by ability rather than by seniority.

T F   17. The average worker in a plant should turn out as much work as he can.

T F   18. The average worker feels that his company's growth and prosperity depends upon whether he does his work well or not.

T F   19. The average worker feels that his work is important to the company's customers.

T F   20. The average worker believes that everyone on the job would benefit if each worker did the best he could.

Table 7-3 (Campbell, 1967) shows the simple scheme that forms the frame of typical intergroup judgments. With the aid of the emotional loading of words, judgments simultaneously describe real differences yet give a good evaluation of an in-group and bad evaluation of an out-group. Thus the English describe themselves as "reserved, respect the privacy of others." Yankees describe the English as "snobbish, cold, unfriendly." Yankees describe themselves as "friendly, outgoing, open-hearted." The English describe Yankees as "intrusive, forward, pushing."

Subgroups among the English continue the process. Warr and

TABLE 7-3
The Goodness Component in Reciprocal Descriptions of Two Groups
(Adapted from Campbell, 1967)

Descriptions by	Descriptions of Group A	Group B
Group A	Good	Bad
Group B	Bad	Good

Knapper (1968) gave Catholic, Anglican, and nonaffiliated English undergraduates a 350-word description of a church official within a small community that contained details of his opinions and attitudes as well as his standing with local residents. When the official was identified as a Roman Catholic priest, Catholics rated him higher on such traits as humane, warm, generous, and kind and Anglicans rated him higher on such traits as irritable, ruthless, blunt, and unjust. The reverse occurred when he was identified as an Anglican parson.

In general, whether we are "in" or "out" of a group determines the goodness we see in the group. The more we feel we belong to a group, the more favorably we view the group. Byrne, Clore, and Worchel (1966) introduced eighty-four students of low or high socioeconomic status to each other in small groups for a short time. Each student was later asked to indicate his liking for other group members. Those of low status preferred those of low status; those of high status preferred those of high status. The authors conclude from this study and an extensive series of similar studies: "It seems quite possible that in any type of social comparison with other human beings (e.g., traits, tastes, income, overt behavior, etc.) similarity is preferred to dissimilarity."

Campbell suggests that "pot-calling-the-kettle-black" reciprocal perceptions generate a set of universal stereotypes that can be used to describe real differences between any groups with opposite evaluations:

THE GOOD IN-GROUP Description	THE BAD OUT-GROUP Description
1 We have pride, self-respect, and reverence for the traditions of our ancestors.	They are egotistical and self-centered. They love themselves more than they love us.
2 We are loyal.	They are clannish, exclude others.
3 We are honest and trustworthy among ourselves,	They will cheat us if they can. They have no honesty

but we're not suckers when foreigners try their tricks.	or moral restraint when dealing with us.
4 We are brave and progressive. We stand up for our own rights, defend what is ours, and can't be pushed around or bullied.	They are aggressive and expansionistic. They want to get ahead at our expense.
5 We are peaceful, loving people, hating only our vile enemies.	They are a hostile people who hate us.
6 We are moral and clean.	They are immoral and unclean.

One significant exception: oppressed groups tend to idealize the oppressing group and to take an unfavorable view of their own group. Thus 240 Negro students at Howard University answered the Guilford-Zimmerman Temperament Survey in terms of "the average Negro male," "the average white male," "the average Negro female,"and "the average white female" (Bayton, Austin, and Burke, 1965). In every instance where differentiation of racial groups occurred, the differences were in favor of whites. Thus whites were judged as having a higher level of general activity, of restraint, of ascendance, of emotional stability, and of objectivity.

THE OBSERVATION OF GROUPS

Hit on the back of the head, we *sense* blinding flashes of light and color. Hit in a slightly different place, we *perceive* stars and butterflies. Sensation is the registration of stimuli in the brain; perception is an awareness of objects, persons, or groups by way of these sensations. We sense heat but perceive fire, we sense loudness but perceive a drum, and we sense sourness but perceive vinegar. Perception, then, is the interpretation of sensations, prediction from sensory cues. A group can never be so completely unstructured as to make perception of it depend solely upon the perceiver; but it can never be so sharply and clearly organized as to obliterate individual differences among perceivers. To some degree, we always observe what we want to observe, what we expect to observe, and what we have learned to observe.

We observe what we want to observe. When we are hungry, we observe food-related things. McClelland and Atkinson (1948) had 108 candidates for submarine training look at ambiguous stimuli projected on a dimly lit screen. They were told what to look for: "Three objects on a table" or "All the people in the picture are enjoying themselves. What are they doing?" Forty-four of the sailors took the test one hour after eating; twenty-four took it four hours after eating; and forty took it sixteen hours after eating. The hungrier the subject, the more food-related objects he reported.

We observe what we expect to observe. Siipola (1935) flashed on a screen for a tenth of a second such nonsense syllables as "chack," "sael," and "dack." Each of 180 subjects wrote down what he thought the words were. Half of them were told in advance that the words to appear would have to do with animals or birds; the other half was told that the words would have to do with travel or transportation. The first group gave animal or bird responses 63 percent of the time: "chick," "seal," "duck," etc. The second group gave travel or transportation responses 74 percent of the time: "check," "sail," "deck," etc. Police expect to see violence; they see it. Toch and Schulte (1961) showed police trainees and college students the same nine pairs of slides in a modified stereoscope. They saw a violent scene with one eye and a peaceful scene with the other. The subjects saw each pair for only a fraction of a second and invariably reported seeing only one of the two scenes. The police saw twice as many scenes of violence as the students.

We observe what we have learned to observe. Bruner and Postman (1949) quickly flashed playing cards before subjects and asked them to name the cards. Some of the cards were especially manufactured to reverse the usual relation between color and suit: a black six of hearts, a red four of spades. Most persons saw what they had previously learned to see: a six of spades and a four of hearts. In another experiment, Bruner, Postman, and Rodrigues (1951) cut a lemon, a carrot, and a tomato from the same sheet of paper. Subjects looked at each piece and then turned around and set a color wheel to match the color of the paper. When the paper was identified as a lemon, the matching color was yellower; when the paper was identified as a tomato, the matching color was redder.

Members of a group learn to observe members of their group. Jews are more accurate in identifying Jews than are non-Jews (Toch, Rabin, and Wilkins, 1962). Mexicans observe Mexicans more accurately than Americans; Americans observe Americans more accurately than Mexicans (Bagby, 1947). Women are more observant of women than men; men are more observant of men than women (Forsythe, 1970).

Finally, it is possible for the person we are observing to change without our observing it. Two photographs, each of a different face, were mounted in a stereoscope so that subjects saw one with the left eye and the other with the right eye at the same time (Engel, 1961). At first, the observer saw just one of the faces with normal illumination. Next, he was given the first face normally lit, with the second face under very low illumination. The procedure was repeated with slight increases in light on the second face until the observer was seeing both faces with normal lighting. At each step he was asked whether any change had taken place in what he saw. Most reported that they saw no change. The light on the first face was then reduced by small steps to zero. At this point, the observer was looking at the quite different second face. Observers still continued to report that they were looking at the same face.

CHAPTER 8

NOMOTHETIC TRAINING

SUCCESSFUL nomothetic training requires: (1) knowledge of what the typical member of a particular group is like; (2) mastery of this knowledge by the trainees; and (3) skill in using the knowledge in making predictions about individuals in the group. Psychologists devote a large part of their research efforts to discovering the distinctive characteristics of the typical man and the typical woman, the typical Negro and the typical white, the typical lower-class and the typical upper-class citizen, the typical neurotic and the typical normal person, the typical two-year-old and the typical four-year-old, the typical moronic and the typical bright person, the typical Japanese and the typical American, etc. The experimental- and control-group design is an incisive way of establishing accurate stereotypes.

Psychologists devote a large part of their teaching efforts to imparting knowledge of groups to students. The ability of our students to understand what they learn is much less than we would like to think. The author, for example, gave seventy-two students a test measuring accuracy of knowledge of the differences between the interests of psychologists and of men in general. For the next six meetings he lectured on psychologists: their education, their places of work, the kinds of problems they worked on, and their methods of solving the problems. The test was administered again. Result: No improvement.

A more intensive effort was slightly more successful. A hundred male and female students first completed the Men and Women Test (Table 8-1). They were then given feedback on their total accuracy score compared to other members of the class. Then they heard lectures, read text material, and discussed the general interests, traits, and interpersonal behavior of men and women. On the pretest the average scores of men and women were the same. On the posttest, the men showed no change in their scores, but the women improved significantly.

Why should there be such difficulty in improving sensitivity to groups? Much of the answer lies in the fact that we are naive realists. We say "I believe what I see with my own eyes" about another group even though most of what we "see" has been taught us by our own group. Campbell (1967) has not only eloquently answered the question but also stated the basic problem of nomothetic training:

> Awareness that one's own preoccupations have projectively contributed to the content, that fallible communication and knowledge processes are involved, that the image could be totally wrong, or even where correct, can be selectively distorted and emphasized—all such awareness is lacking. For many a social psychologist, his own overcoming such an ethnocentric enculturation is a deeply experienced revelation, and one he wants to communicate. In so doing, the message that stereotypes contain a large portion of error and projection becomes overcompensated into an implicit denial of group differences. The message that stereotypes of groups or images of specific others contain a projective contribution from one's own (or one's ingroup's) personality, either in fabricated content or in selective attention to perjorative content, is an unsuspected lesson which every normal undergraduate needs to learn. But it must be taught without denying group differences.

How are trainees to be taught the lesson? We again assume that the first requirement is the development of satisfactory measures of nomothetic sensitivity. We further assume that a trainee's progress will be enhanced by learning about and correcting the constant errors he makes in judging all groups. However, learning about a particular group is only a means to the end of learning about individuals in that group. Consequently, he must learn to apply his knowledge of a group to persons in that group. This chapter reports the state of our efforts to develop instruments and procedures for fulfilling each of these requirements.

THE MEASUREMENT OF NOMOTHETIC SENSITIVITY

Stereotypes are countless. They range from broad to narrow—from men in general to men in the United States, to male psychologists in the United States, to older male experimental psychologists in New York, etc. The groupings may, and do, cover age, sex, race, occupation, and religion, as well as physical and mental health groups. The problems of internal consistency, repeat reliability, independence, validity, and practicality arise in the effort to measure sensitivity to these groups as they arise in all measurement efforts.

Nomothetic sensitivity is specific, not general; a person knows a group, not groups. Johnson (1963), for example, correlated scores on a test measuring sensitivity to the interests of psychologists with scores on similarly constructed tests of men versus women, young men versus old men, and unskilled versus professional men. All of these tests had reliabilities around .70, indicating that perceivers varied widely and consistently in their knowledge of each of these groups. Still, the median intercorrelation was only .21 and the highest only .30. Both Zavala (1960) and Silkiner (1962) obtained similar results. The fact that a perceiver knows a great deal about one group tells us little about his knowledge of other groups, even when the groups are as broad and as well known as men versus women, young versus old men. The more specialized the groups, the more obvious the conclusion becomes. Why should people who understand Australians understand Mexicans? Why should people who understand engineers understand morticians? Why should people who understand clerks in an insurance company understand coal miners in Kentucky? Some individuals understand many groups well and are adept at learning about new groups. On the whole, however, stereotype accuracy is highly specific.

The test in Table 8-1 is the best measure of nomothetic sensitivity that we have developed. It is a measure of sensitivity to two broad social groups, i.e., men and women. Scores on the men test have internal consistencies ranging from .60 to .68; the women test, from .59 to .66. Since scores on the two parts of the test are relatively independent, the overall reliability is only slightly higher (.67 to .77). The reliabilities for foreign students are higher, for they have a wider range of scores and score significantly lower than American students (Silkiner, 1962). The test is not a concealed measure of either reading ability or intelligence, for measures of these have no relationship to the scores (Shook, 1971). Unlike tests based upon understanding of one person, this test reflects knowledge accumulated from many similar experiences with many men and women. In general, considering the ease with which tests of this sort may be administered and scored, they offer the most convenient single measure of overall sensitivity.

TABLE 8-1
Test of Nomothetic Sensitivity to Men and Women

This is a test of your knowledge of the likes, dislikes, and self-ratings of the typical man (Part I) and the typical woman (Part II). The correct answers are based on the analysis of replies to the *Strong Vocational Interest Blank*. In taking this test the respondent is asked to "disregard considerations of salary, social standing, future advancement, etc. . . . consider only whether or not you would enjoy the interest regardless of any necessary skills, abilities, or training which you may or may not possess."

Part I Understanding Men

The correct answers are the actual replies of thousands of American men, primarily those in business and professional occupations. They checked whether they would "like" or "dislike" many different occupations, amusements, activities, and kinds of people. They also answered statements about what kind of persons they thought they were.

TABLE 8-1, continued

Likes

Three interests are listed opposite each question below. Only one of the three was liked by *more than half* of the men. Mark on the separate answer sheet the one that you think more than 50 percent of the men *said* they would "like."

Example

(1) *travel movies* (2) cashier in a bank (3) people who borrow things

80% of the men said they liked "travel movies," 20% "cashier," and 2% "people who borrow things." Therefore, "travel movies" is the correct answer.

1. (1) pet monkeys (2) geography* (3) military drill
2. (1) civil service employee (2) carpenter (3) psychology*
3. (1) literature* (2) botany (3) shop work
4. (1) agriculture (2) typewriting (3) chemistry*
5. (1) performing sleight-of-hand tricks (2) educational movies* (3) full-dress affairs
6. (1) bargaining (swapping) (2) taking responsibility* (3) drilling soldiers
7. (1) being pitted against another as in a political or athletic race (2) meeting and directing people* (3) teaching children
8. (1) spendthrifts (2) cripples (3) conservative people*
9. (1) J. J. Pershing, soldier (2) opportunity to make use of all one's knowledge and experience* (3) secretary of a social club
10. (1) headwaiter (2) lighthouse tender (3) emphasis on quality of work*

Dislikes

Only *one* interest in each group below was actively *disliked* by *more than half* of the men. Mark the one that you think that most men said they disliked.

11. (1) factory manager (2) undertaker* (3) geometry
12. (1) physician (2) life insurance salesman* (3) economics
13. (1) thrifty people (2) history (3) music teacher*
14. (1) magazine writer (2) chemist (3) auctioneer*
15. (1) school teacher (2) watchmaker* (3) governor of a state
16. (1) floorwalker* (2) stock broker (3) reporter
17. (1) editor (2) railway conductor* (3) surgeon
18. (1) author (2) store manager (3) pharmacist*
19. (1) auto salesman* (2) interior decorator (3) scientific research worker
20. (1) printer* (2) wholesaler (3) astronomer
21. (1) making a radio set (2) pet monkeys* (3) *Atlantic Monthly*
22. (1) repairing a clock (2) acting as a yell leader* (3) giving first aid
23. (1) interviewing men for a job (2) opening conversation with a stranger (3) looking at a collection of rare laces*
24. (1) doing research work (2) climbing along edge of a precipice* (3) looking at shop windows.
25. (1) sick people (2) irreligious people (3) side-show freaks*
26. (1) very old people (2) people who don't believe in evolution (3) men who use perfume*
27. (1) people easily led* (2) people who assume leadership (3) deaf mutes
28. (1) people who get rattled easily* (2) people with protruding jaws (3) people with hooked noses

*Indicates correct answer.

TABLE 8-1, continued

29. (1) fashionably dressed people (2) nervous people* (3) emotional people
30. (1) interest the public in a machine through public addresses* (2) steadiness and permanence of work (3) chairman, program committee

Self-ratings

The men also answered statements about what kind of persons they thought they were. Mark the one statement in each group below that you think was answered *"yes"* by *more than half* of the men.

31. (1) practically never make excuses (2) get "rattled" easily (3) follow up subordinates effectively*
32. (1) am approachable* (2) lose my temper at times (3) usually ignore the feelings of others
33. (1) worry very little (2) win confidence and loyalty* (3) when caught in a mistake usually make excuses
34. (1) tell jokes well (2) discuss my ideals with others* (3) best-liked friends are superior to me in ability
35. (1) get "rattled" easily (2) worry considerably about mistakes (3) can correct others without giving offense*
36. (1) am always on time with my work* (2) lend money to acquaintances (3) have mechanical ingenuity (inventiveness)
37. (1) stimulate the ambition of my associates* (2) have mechanical ingenuity (inventiveness) (3) best-liked friends are superior to me in ability
38. (1) lend money to acquaintances (2) lend only to certain people (3) rarely lend money*
39. (1) usually ignore the feelings of others (2) consider them sometimes (3) carefully consider them*
40. (1) when caught in a mistake usually make excuses (2) seldom make excuses* (3) practically never make excuses

Part II   Understanding Women

Over four thousand women, many in professional positions, checked whether they would "like" or "dislike" different occupations, amusements, activities, and kinds of people.

Likes

Three interests are listed opposite each question below. Only one of the three was liked by *more than half* of the women. *Mark* the one that you think more than 50 percent of the women said they would "like."

Example

   (1) interior decorator (2) mechanical engineer (3) cheer leader

   Since 65 percent of the women said they would like being an "interior decorator," this is the correct answer.

41. (1) wife* (2) office manager (3) music composer
42. (1) probation officer (2) dancing teacher (3) vocational counselor*
43. (1) confectioner (2) buyer of merchandise* (3) postmistress
44. (1) solving mechanical puzzles (2) plays* (3) cashier

*Indicates correct answer.

TABLE 8-1, continued

45. (1) *Reader's Digest* (2) conventions (3) poker
46. (1) interviewing clients (2) decorating a room with flowers* (3) open conversation with a stranger
47. (1) organizing a play (2) arguments (3) looking at shop windows*
48. (1) discussing politics (2) entertaining others* (3) buying at an auction sale
49. (1) attending church* (2) doing research work (3) making a speech
50. (1) costume designer (2) emotional people (3) people who are natural leaders*
51. (1) self-conscious people (2) irreligious people (3) optimists*
52. (1) methodical people (2) thrifty people* (3) very old people
53. (1) opportunity to understand just how one's superior expects work to be done (2) opportunity to make use of all one's knowledge and experience* (3) opportunity for promotion
54. (1) activities of a conservative nature (2) travel with someone who will make the necessary preparations for you (3) be married*
55. (1) be married with small income (2) going to a play* (3) order others
56. (1) psychology* (2) chemistry (3) Bible study
57. (1) geography* (2) bookkeeping (3) calculus

Dislikes

Only one interest in each group below was *disliked* by *more than half* of the women. Mark the *one* that you think more than 50 percent of the women said they would "dislike."

58. (1) factory worker* (2) athletic director (3) physician
59. (1) milliner (2) life insurance salesman* (3) judge
60. (1) manufacturer (2) traveling saleswoman* (3) illustrator
61. (1) manager, women's style shop (2) naturalist (3) dentist*
62. (1) laboratory technician (2) telephone operator* (3) social worker
63. (1) public health nurse (2) criminal lawyer* (3) opera singer
64. (1) YWCA secretary (2) tea-room proprietor (3) bookkeeper*
65. (1) author of a novel (2) accountant* (3) graduate general nurse
66. (1) illustrator (2) typist* (3) interpreter
67. (1) statistician* (2) secret service women (3) social worker
68. (1) stage actress (2) mechanical engineer* (3) editor
69. (1) dean of women (2) proofreader* (3) kindergarten teacher
70. (1) *Good Housekeeping* magazine (2) afternoon teas (3) *True Story* magazine*
71. (1) mannish women* (2) surgeon (3) methodical people
72. (1) absent-minded people* (2) fashionably dressed people (3) people who assume leadership
73. (1) writing personal letters (2) looking at a collection of rare laces (3) interest the public in building their own homes through public addresses*

Self-ratings

The women also answered statements about what kind of persons they thought they were. Mark the *one* statement in each group below that you think *more than half* of the women answered "yes."

74. (1) can discriminate between more or less important matters* (2) remember faces and incidents better than the average person (3) can correct others without giving offense

*Indicates correct answer.

TABLE 8-1, continued

75.   (1) usually liven up the group on a dull day (2) lend money to acquaintances (3) win confidence and loyalty*
76.   (1) borrow frequently (2) borrow occasionally (3) practically never borrow*
77.   (1) worry considerably about mistakes (2) worry very little* (3) do not worry
78.   (1) feelings easily hurt (2) feelings hurt sometimes* (3) feelings rarely hurt
79.   (1) have mechanical ingenuity (2) can write a well-organized report (3) able to meet emergencies quickly and effectively*
80.   (1) tell jokes well (2) smooth out tangles and disagreements between people* (3) feelings easily hurt

*Indicates correct answer.

THE FORM OF GROUP IMPRESSIONS

The bad-good dimension dominates group as it does individual impressions. Individuals vary widely in the level and spread of the expressive qualities they perceive in groups. Some see Negroes, Jews, and Mexicans as generally bad; some, as neither bad nor good; and some as generally good. Those at the same level of goodness vary in their spread around this level. That is, some who are average in their level may see Negroes, Jews, and Mexicans as neutral or may see one group as bad, one as neutral, and one as good. Trainees need to be aware of the influence of goodness on group impressions, of their own level and spread tendencies, and of the influence that these tendencies have upon the accuracy of their predictions.

The Group Impressions Test (Table 8-2) was designed with these needs in mind. It has been used as a measure of nomothetic sensitivity, as a diagnostic device, and as a training method. Each of the three parts of the test has three subparts: low ratings, average ratings, and high ratings. These subheadings are shown to aid the reader in understanding the construction of the test. The low rating score is obtained by counting the total number of correct answers for the three parts of the test (1–12 + 61–72 + 89–96). Average and high rating scores are obtained in a similar manner. The internal consistencies of low and high scores are approximately .70, of average scores, much lower. The norms at the end of the table are based upon scores obtained from several hundred college students.

Inspection of an individual's pattern of scores provides a basis for diagnosing a respondent's level and spread tendencies. The clearest and most significant of these patterns is the bimodal one, i.e., the student is very accurate on the low and high ratings, very inaccurate on the average ratings. The pattern indicates the respondent is a wide spreader—he makes many very low (1) and many very high (5) ratings but few average ones. The reverse pattern indicates the narrow spreader—many average responses, few extreme. The "step-up" pattern where the respondent is very inaccurate on the low ratings, moderately accurate on the average ones, and highly accurate on the high ones indicates a high leveler. The "step-down" pattern indicates the low leveler, i.e., the person who assumes that most men and women have few interests and that college men have a low opinion of themselves.

Using the test as a remedial device, trainees first complete the Interests of Men part, score their replies, and discuss weaknesses in their general rating patterns. The following two parts are then used as practice in remedying these weaknesses and giving feedback on the successes.

TABLE 8-2
The Group Impressions Test

Our impression of an individual is influenced by our impression of the groups to which he belongs. Consequently, the more accurate our picture of the group, the more accurate our picture of the individual: the better we understand men, the better we understand a man; the better we understand women, the better we understand a woman; and the better we understand students, the better we understand a student.

The accuracy of our stereotypes, the standardized mental pictures we have of groups, is quite specific. That is, the person who understands men very well may not understand women or students at all well. However, the accuracy of all of these group pictures is influenced by the general way we go about taking a "picture" of a group. It is the purpose of this session to give you a diagnosis of the way you go about taking your group pictures and the consequences for your predictive accuracy.

Part I   The Interests of Men

Thousands of men checked whether they liked or did not like the occupations, activities, subjects, and types of people below. For each item the question is: About what percentage of men said they would "like" the interest? Circle the number in front of each interest that corresponds to your estimate of the actual percentage of men who said they would like it. CIRCLE as follows: (1) 10 percent or less, (2) 30 percent, (3) 50 percent, (4) 70 percent, (5) 90 percent or more.

Low Ratings

1 2 3 4 5   1. Office clerk (1)

1 2 3 4 5   2. Advertiser (2)

1 2 3 4 5   3. Auctioneer (1)

1 2 3 4 5   4. Sculptor (1)

1 2 3 4 5   5. College professor (2)

1 2 3 4 5   6. Secretary, chamber of commerce (1)

1 2 3 4 5   7. Railway conductor (1)

1 2 3 4 5   8. Auto salesman (2)

1 2 3 4 5   9. Buyer of merchandise (2)

TABLE 8-2, continued

1	2	3	4	5	10.	Bookkeeper (1)
1	2	3	4	5	11.	Bank teller (1)
1	2	3	4	5	12.	Printer (1)

High Ratings

1	2	3	4	5	13.	President of a society or club (4)
1	2	3	4	5	14.	Arithmetic (4)
1	2	3	4	5	15.	Educational movies (4)
1	2	3	4	5	16.	Thrifty people (4)
1	2	3	4	5	17.	Can discriminate between more or less important matters (said "yes") (5)
1	2	3	4	5	18.	Can carry out plans assigned by other people (said "yes") (4)
1	2	3	4	5	19.	Usually get other people to do what I want done (said "yes") (4)
1	2	3	4	5	20.	Energetic people (5)
1	2	3	4	5	21.	Progressive people (5)
1	2	3	4	5	22.	History (4)
1	2	3	4	5	23.	Mathematics (4)
1	2	3	4	5	24.	Musical comedy (5)

Average Ratings

1	2	3	4	5	25.	People who make fortunes in business (3)
1	2	3	4	5	26.	Scientific research worker (3)
1	2	3	4	5	27.	Golf (3)
1	2	3	4	5	28.	Looking at shop windows (3)
1	2	3	4	5	29.	Contributing to charities (3)
1	2	3	4	5	30.	Raising flowers and vegetables (3)
1	2	3	4	5	31.	Bridge (3)
1	2	3	4	5	32.	People who assume leadership (3)
1	2	3	4	5	33.	Observing birds (nature study) (3)
1	2	3	4	5	34.	Picnics (3)
1	2	3	4	5	35.	Inventor (3)
1	2	3	4	5	36.	Author of technical book (2)

Part II   The Interests of Women

Thousands of women checked whether they liked or disliked the interests below. Circle the number in front of each interest that corresponds to your estimate of the actual

TABLE 8-2, continued

percentage of women who said they would like it. CIRCLE as follows: (1) 10 percent or less, (2) 30 percent, (3) 50 percent, (4) 70 percent, (5) 90 percent or more.

Low Ratings

1 2 3 4 5   37. Minister (1)

1 2 3 4 5   38. Men who drink (1)

1 2 3 4 5   39. Bank teller (1)

1 2 3 4 5   40. Stockbroker (1)

1 2 3 4 5   41. Whoesaler (1)

1 2 3 4 5   42. Dentist (1)

1 2 3 4 5   43. Artist's model (1)

1 2 3 4 5   44. Politician (1)

1 2 3 4 5   45. Real estate saleswoman (1)

1 2 3 4 5   46. Telephone operator (1)

1 2 3 4 5   47. Afternoon teas (2)

1 2 3 4 5   48. Waitress (1)

High Ratings

1 2 3 4 5   49. Philosophy (4)

1 2 3 4 5   50. Museums (4)

1 2 3 4 5   51. Can discriminate between more or less important matters (said "yes") (5)

1 2 3 4 5   52. Poetry (4)

1 2 3 4 5   53. People who are natural leaders (5)

1 2 3 4 5   54. Music (4)

1 2 3 4 5   55. Psychology (4)

1 2 3 4 5   56. Energetic people (5)

1 2 3 4 5   57. Cooking (4)

1 2 3 4 5   58. *Reader's Digest* magazine (5)

1 2 3 4 5   59. Dancing (5)

1 2 3 4 5   60. Decorating a room with flowers (5)

Average Ratings

1 2 3 4 5   61. Educational Director (3)

1 2 3 4 5   62. Tennis (3)

1 2 3 4 5   63. Zoology (3)

1 2 3 4 5   64. Hostess (3)

TABLE 8-2, continued

1 2 3 4 5   65. Psychiatrist (3)

1 2 3 4 5   66. Florist (3)

1 2 3 4 5   67. Physician (3)

1 2 3 4 5   68. Foreign correspondent (3)

1 2 3 4 5   69. Writing personal letters (3)

1 2 3 4 5   70. Dramatics (3)

1 2 3 4 5   71. Office manager (2)

1 2 3 4 5   72. Radio program director (2)

Part III   The Self-Images of College Students

Each of several hundred Midwestern college men rated himself as he thought he compared with other men on a series of traits. The average rating of all the men on each trait was determined. *Rate the average college man* as you think he rated himself. CIRCLE as follows: (1) the lowest 25 percent, (2) the middle 50 percent, (3) the highest 25 percent.

Low Ratings

1 2 3   73. Rebellious (1)

1 2 3   74. Impractical (1)

1 2 3   75. Unrealistic (1)

1 2 3   76. Unpredictable (1)

1 2 3   77. Socially poised (1)

1 2 3   78. Easily upset (1)

1 2 3   79. Timid (1)

1 2 3   **80.** Irresponsible (1)

High Ratings

1 2 3   81. Cooperative (3)

1 2 3   82. Friendly (3)

1 2 3   83. Ambitious (3)

1 2 3   84. Adaptable (3)

1 2 3   85. Wide range of interests (3)

1 2 3   86. Liberal (3)

1 2 3   87. Adventurous (3)

1 2 3   88. Trustful (3)

Average Ratings

1 2 3   89. Stubborn (2)

1 2 3   90. Egotistical (2)

TABLE 8-2, *continued*

1 2 3   91. Shy (2)

1 2 3   92. Affectionate (2)

1 2 3   93. Serious (2)

1 2 3   94. Talkative (2)

1 2 3   95. Imaginative (2)

1 2 3   96. Aggressive (2)

| | | | | | Percentiles | | | | | | |
Accuracy Scores	0	10	20	30	40	50	60	70	80	90	99
Low Ratings	0	3	4	5	6	7	8	9	10	12	19
Average Ratings	2	5	6	7	8	9	10	11	12	14	18
High Ratings	0	2	3	3	4	4	5	6	7	7	9
Total Accuracy	8	16	17	19	20	21	23	24	25	27	31

In this special test, the wide spreader is not at a disadvantage. In general, however, the wider a person spreads his ratings, the more inaccurate his predictions are likely to be. Unfortunately, training usually encourages a trainee to increase the spread of his ratings. Medical students, for example, saw films of physicians interviewing patients and made predictions about how the patients would rate themselves (Crow, 1957). They then completed an intensive training course designed to increase their sensitivity to patients as individuals. They saw the films and made predictions about their ratings again. Result: "Contrary to expectations, a training program in interpersonal relations for medical students decreased the trainees' accuracy in judging others." Why? Most of the students increased their spread during training, and the increase seemed responsible for the decline in accuracy.

A follow-up study established the relationship more precisely (Crow and Farson, 1961). Air Force officers and civilian supervisors attended a week-long course designed to increase their sensitivity. The core of the program involved the use of the T-group method. The predictive accuracy of the members was measured before and after training.

Accuracy was measured in the following way. Prior to training, the trainees were assigned at random to eight testing groups of eight members each. The groups were composed so that only two members of the same training group were included in a testing group. At the end of the week the trainees were again assembled into entirely different eight-man testing groups. Trainees in each testing group became as well acquainted with each other as they could in thirty

TABLE 8-3
The Relationship between Changes in Spread and Changes in Sensitivity
(Adapted from Crow and Farson, 1961)

	Smaller Spread after Training, percent	Larger Spread after Training, percent
More sensitive after training (N = 38)	73	54
Less sensitive after training (N = 22)	27	46
Total	100	100

minutes. Each trainee then rated himself on a variety of rating scales. Finally, each trainee rated the other seven members of the group as he thought they had rated themselves. The agreement between a trainee's rating for the other members and the ratings the other members gave themselves was the measure of sensitivity. This time, as Table 8-3 shows, more trainees decreased than increased their spread. Among those who had a larger spread after training, about as many decreased as increased their accuracy. Among those who had a smaller spread after training, almost three times as many increased their accuracy.

Among the medical students, spread increased: among the Air Force officers, it declined. Neither change was anticipated. It is clear, however, that sensitivity will become more effective as those involved become more aware of the potent influence of spread. With only minor reservations, the trainee should be guided by this principle: The person who decreases his spread will increase his accuracy.

STEREOTYPIC TRAINING

The universal use of stereotypes is not a problem in the development of sensitivity. The problem is that stereotypes are so often incomplete, erroneous, and distorted. The solution requires the development of more accurate stereotypes. The first obstacle to achieving this solution is that the trainers generally do not, themselves, have an accurate stereotype to teach (Stelmachers and McHugh, 1964):

> Psychologists would do well studying the base rates of various types of behavior in as many separate populations as is practicable. Apparently even a very approximate matching on a very few variables between subject and population can lead to a significant improvement in predictive accuracy if the population norms are known to the judge. For most pieces of behavior assumed to be relevant in personality assessment, such norms are not available. Therefore, it seems that the establishment of them for a select number of broadly defined populations could be beneficial to the clinicians' performance in the area of behavior prediction.

The second obstacle to the development of an accurate stereotype is that it is hard to teach trainees about a group in such a way that they will retain what they have learned and use their learning in making additional inferences about a group.

Lectures, reading, and discussions seem to do only a little to overcome these obstacles. By contrast, the methods used by Spier (1969) resulted in the rapid learning of the typical differences between the happily married, the unhappily married, and the divorced woman. His program involved diagnosis of error tendencies, practice in making predictions, and discussion of trait differences between the groups. It was stressed in the discussion, for example, that the typical divorced woman was bolder and more artistic than women in the other groups, that the unhappily married were more emotional and impulsive, and that the happily married were more religious, conservative, and conforming.

Table 8-4 shows the materials passed out at the beginning of the single session program for several hundred students. In addition to training exercises, these included an evaluation of the session's effectiveness in improving the accuracy of the female stereotypes and in generalizing this improvement to male groups. The gains on the women test were highly significant and the gains on the men test were just as high. Furthermore, retests seven weeks later showed no decline in scores. The work of Johnson and Terman (1935) provided the essential facts about the marital groups. The specific training materials, particularly the short but reliable tests, were developed after considerable pretesting of items. Similar results were obtained for a similar session devoted to developing an accurate stereotype of the typical psychologist.

TABLE 8-4
**Training in Nomothetic Sensitivity
to Marital Groups**
(Spier, 1969)

This exercise is designed to improve your understanding of the typical happy, unhappy, and divorced husband and wife. The correct answers throughout are based on an analysis of the replies of members of each of these groups to lengthy and confidential questionnaires. For example, 100 happily married, 100 unhappily married, and 100 divorced women answered the question: "Do you prefer a play to a dance?" Results:

    81 percent of the happily married women answered "yes"
    58 percent of the unhappily married women answered "yes"
    44 percent of the divorced women answered "yes".

Therefore, the correct answer to the statement "Most apt to prefer a play to a dance," is "happily married women." The exercise follows this sequence:

A.   *Men pretest* Answer statements *1 through 16* for men.

TABLE 8-4, continued

- B. *Women pretest* Answer the statements *33 through 44* for women.
- C. *Training Period* STOP when you have completed the pretests. The instructor will now provide information giving you a more accurate understanding of the typical happily married, unhappily married, and divorced woman. The statements in the training materials are indicated on the other side by "A," "B," etc.
- D. *Woman Posttest* After the training, answer the statements in the woman test again, following the numbers in parentheses, i.e., "33" is (45), "34" is (46), etc.
- E. *Man Posttest* Can you apply what you have learned about women to men? To find out, answer the statements in the men test again, this time following the numbers in parentheses, i.e., "1" is (17), "2" is (18), etc.

A. Men Pretest and Posttest

Mark: "1" if you think the correct answer is "happily married men"
"2" if you think the correct answer is "unhappily married men"
"3" if you think the correct answer is "divorced men".

Correct

2	1.	(17) Least interested in artistic activities.
2	2.	(18) Most dislikes foreigners.
3	3.	(19) Most apt to like the occupation of novelist.
1	4.	(20) Most apt to like religious people.
2	5.	(21) Slowest in making decisions.
2	6.	(22) Most dislikes modern languages.
3	7.	(23) Most often experiences feelings of loneliness.
2	8.	(24) Least often takes the lead to enliven a dull party.
2	9.	(25) Least interested in the occupation of teacher.
1	10.	(26) Most likely to organize a club or team.
3	11.	(27) Most likely to enjoy competition.
1	12.	(28) Most meticulous and methodical in work.
1	13.	(29) Most likely to stress quality in his work.
3	14.	(30) Most likely to enjoy taking risks.
3	15.	(31) Most prefers fashionably dressed people.
1	16.	(32) Most prefers to make plans with others.

B. Women Pretest and Posttest

Mark: "1" if you think the correct answer is "happily married *women*"
"2" if you think the correct answer is "unhappily married *women*"
"3" if you think the correct answer is "divorced *women*"

Correct

3	33.	(45) Most willing to be unconventional.
3	34.	(46) Most interested in being an inventor.
2	35.	(47) Most often troubled by feelings of inferiority.
2	36.	(48) Most apt to arrive late for work.
3	37.	(49) Most prefers work that makes heavy demands.
2	38.	(50) Most interested in avoiding technical responsibilities.
1	39.	(51) Most apt to like religious people.
2	40.	(52) Least effective in emergencies.
3	41.	(53) Most ambitious.

TABLE 8-4, continued

1   42. (54) Most apt to like old people.
1   43. (55) Most conservative in social and political opinions.
1   44. (56) Most apt to like people who never drink.

C. *Training Materials*

The materials are designed to give you practice and feedback in applying the principles outlined in the training discussion. Do *not* answer any of these statements until told to do so. "H" stands for happy, "U" for unhappy, "D" for divorced women.

					Pretest Difficulty
H	*U**	D	A.	Most often has spells of dizziness.	6
H	U	D	B.	Most likes picnics and excursions.	11
H	*U*	D	C.	Most likely to consider herself as nervous.	13
H	U	*D*	D.	Most interested in change and travel.	26
H	U	D	E.	Most apt to like music.	28
H	*U*	D	F.	Least willing to work things out for herself.	29
H	U	*D*	G.	Most prefers taking chances to playing it safe.	30
H	U	*D*	H.	Most self-assertive and self-reliant.	33
H	*U*	D	I.	Least methodical.	49
H	U	D	J.	Most apt to dislike working in isolation.	50
H	U	D	K.	Most dislikes quick-tempered people.	55
H	U	*D*	L.	Most apt to like playing chess.	67

D. *Women Posttest*

After you have answered the training statements and corrected them, answer the Women Test again to determine whether your stereotype accuracy has improved. Use the numbers in parentheses, i.e., (45) instead of "33", etc., in recording your answers.

E. *Men Posttest*

Try, finally, to apply what you have learned about women to men. Answer again the statements in the Men Test. This time, however, use the numbers of the statements in parentheses, i.e., (16), (17), etc., in recording your answers.

F. *Final Feedback*

The correct answers for both the Men and Women Tests will be read to you at the end of the exercise.

*Answers in italics are correct.

The marital group training materials are a big step along the road toward a programmed learning approach to stereotypic training. Ideally, such a program would systematically apply learning principles to the process of learning about a particular group so that the trainee could quickly and completely master it. A list of the things the programmer wants the trainee to know at the end of the program is called a *specification of the terminal behavior for the program*. A specification of both the initial behavior and the terminal behavior tells the programmer what skills the program must teach. His task is to change the trainee's initial behavior until it matches the terminal behavior. In stereotype training the task would be to increase the trainee's knowledge of a particular group.

DEVIATION TRAINING

Nomothetic sensitivity requires that the trainee know what a particular group is like. The knowledge is not enough, however, for he must also learn to apply it to particular members of that group. The application is difficult. It is made much more difficult by the tendency of both trainers and trainees to put the cart before the horse: They assume that they are most likely to err by sticking too closely to the stereotype; in fact, they are most likely to err by deviating too far from the stereotype. As a consequence, they generally make no more errors, and often fewer, when they only know an individual's group identification than when they have a great deal of information about him. Stelmachers and McHugh (1964), for example, gave different judges widely different amounts of information upon which to base their predictions. Result: "The comparatively elaborate and individualized personality sketches failed to produce accurate predictions, were in fact no better than the knowledge of subjects' age and sex."

When should a trainee deviate from an accurate stereotype? The theoretical answer can be stated with precision. Assume that five judges are rating the intelligence of ten people. Assume, further, that the average IQ of the ten is 100, that all the judges know this, and that the actual ratings of each of the judges turns out to average 100. Assume, finally, that all the judges know the actual spread of IQs in the group to range from a low of 70 to a high of 130 and to have a standard deviation of 16. Will a judge's errors be smallest if he rates ten people at an IQ of 100, spreads his ratings from 70 to 130, or compromises somewhere between the minimum and maximum spread?

The correct answer varies with how well the judge knows the ten people. If he knows nothing about them, errors will be smallest if he rates them all at an IQ of 100. If he knows them perfectly, the errors will be smallest if he spreads the ratings over the entire range. While the answer is definite, it is neither complete nor very helpful, for we seldom rate people whom we know nothing about and we never rate people whom we know everything about. The critical question thus becomes: What is the relationship between amount of spread, degree of accuracy, and amount of knowledge about the people being rated?

Cronbach (1955) has given an exact and general answer to the last question. The spread accuracy is greatest when

$$SDj = SDa \times rja$$

Applied to the ten people, j is the judge's estimate of their intelligence, a is their actual intelligence, SD is the standard deviation (the most widely used statistical measure of spread) and r is the correlation between the judge's estimate of intelligence for the ten people and their actual intelligence. Thus if a judge knows nothing about the intelligence of the ten people, his ratings will be guesses, his guesses will have no relationship to the actual intelligence of the people, and rja will be zero. Zero times the SDa, which in this case is 16, will also be zero; consequently, SDj will also be zero. We reach the conclusion that we stated in the last paragraph: If a judge knows nothing about the people he is rating, he will make the fewest and smallest errors by assuming that *everybody* is average. The formula also applies to the opposite extreme, i.e., if the correlation between the judge's estimate of intelligence and actual intelligence is perfect (rja is 1.00), then he will make the fewest errors by having his spread (SDj) equal the actual spread (SDa, which is 16).

The formula fits our commonsense conclusions about the extreme cases. Much more important, it leads to some unexpected conclusions about the in-between cases that make up practically all life situations. As an example, let us continue our assumptions about the case of the ten people. Assume that our five judges have brief interviews with each of the ten people and then rate their intelligence. Assume further that the correlation between the *best* judge's estimates of intelligence and actual intelligence is .50. What does the formula indicate as his optimum spread? The answer would be 16 × .50 or 8 ($SDa \times rja$). If he followed this recommendation, he would rate seven of the ten people between 92 and 108 and none of them as low as 76 or as high as 124.

When and how can a perceiver "beat the formula"? Meehl (1954) used only a global measure of predictive accuracy. Cline and Richards (1962) in a careful analytical experiment compared the accuracy of mechanical predictions with the clinical predictions of fifty-six judges. As they expected, the mechanical predictions were more accurate in differentiating between groups and were, overall, more accurate. The judges, however, were more accurate in differentiating between individuals. Conclusion:

Contrary to common opinion among clinicians, the activity at which clinicians are most likely to exceed the actuary is not making predictions about an "unique individual." . . . appropriate activity for clinicians is predicting differences among persons who are grouped into the same class by statistical predictions, and it is easy to suggest many ordinary activities of clinicians that are of this type. An example of this might be a mental hospital in which ten patients had roughly the same statistically derived "predicted benefit from psychotherapy" score, but which had such a limited staff that only three of these patients could actually be given psychotherapy. The results of this study suggest that the clinician might be quite successful in picking the three "best bets" although all ten had been given an "equal" rating by the statistical prediction procedure.

In general, then, trainees should be taught to stick to their stereotypes unless there is a good reason for deviating from them. That is, they should at least start with the assumption that a man is like men, a woman like women, a psychologist like psychologists, or a patient like patients. The most obvious reason for not sticking to a stereotype is that it is irrelevant. Thus if the judge must predict differences between members of exactly the same group, he is entirely free from restraints imposed by stereotypic knowledge. Even if they are members of approximately the same group, he has considerable freedom. He should be taught to restrain himself most severely when he has only his subjective impressions as a basis for deviating from the stereotype.

The cases of Morgan Johnson and Professor Brown (Table 8-5) can be used to acquaint trainees with the difficulty of deviating successfully from stereotypic information. The average student does not do as well on the first exercises in these cases as he would if he gave all stereotypic responses. By the third ones, he does a little better.

TABLE 8-5
Deviations from Stereotypes

Learning the typical behavior of a group and applying this knowledge in predicting the behavior of individuals in the group improves the accuracy of our judgments of these individuals. Of course, no individual is entirely typical. The improvement of sensitivity, therefore, requires the ability to predict when a person will and when he will not behave in a typical fashion. The aim of this session is to improve this ability.

The Case of Morgan Johnson

The Strong Vocational Interest Blank consists of hundreds of vocations, school subjects, hobbies, and kinds of people to which the respondent answers "like" or "dislike." For the items in the exercises below the answer given by the majority of thousands of American men is printed in CAPITALS.

Morgan Johnson, a 23-year-old unmarried American man who is a college senior majoring in psychology, completed the Strong test. Morgan's parents died when he was four, and he and his younger brother were raised by permissive grandparents in Brooklyn. Of his childhood, Morgan said, "As I grew up, I always had the feeling that I was inferior to everybody else because I had no parents. In grade school, I was very loud and boisterous and made persistent attempts to dominate my peers and to excel in everything I did." Today he places stress on being a "well-rounded scholar." About his values, he now says:

TABLE 8-5, continued

> *I do not believe there are any determining forces in the universe that make us what we are; everybody rules his own destiny. I can think of nothing more important than being a good friend or having good friends, but I don't think it is possible to have more than a few really close ones. I place little value on material things: cars, clothes, etc.*

In *six out of ten* of the items in each of the exercises below Morgan answered in the same way as the majority of men. Thus if you predict that Morgan answered *all* of the items as men in general did, you would have 60 percent correct. Your task is to do better than 60 percent.

Exercise A

Circle the answer that you think Morgan made. Afterward, his actual answers will be given and discussed. Remember that Morgan gave the answer in capital letters six out of ten times.

LIKE*	Dislike	1.	Philosophy
LIKE*	Dislike	2.	Literature
LIKE*	Dislike	3.	Meeting new situations
LIKE	Dislike*	4.	Regular hours of work
LIKE	Dislike*	5.	Progressive people
Like	DISLIKE*	6.	Quick-tempered people
Like	DISLIKE*	7.	Pet monkeys
Like	DISLIKE*	8.	Auctioneer
Like*	DISLIKE	9.	Spendthrifts
Like*	DISLIKE	10.	Politician

Exercise B

LIKE	Dislike*	11.	Arithmetic
LIKE*	Dislike	12.	Driving an automobile
LIKE*	Dislike	13.	Contributing to charities
LIKE*	Dislike	14.	Adjusting difficulties of others
LIKE	Dislike*	15.	Saving money
Like	DISLIKE*	16.	Drilling in a company
Like*	DISLIKE	17.	Auto racer
Like*	DISLIKE	18.	Poet
Like	DISLIKE*	19.	Snakes
Like	DISLIKE*	20.	Auto repairman

Exercise C

LIKE*	Dislike	21.	Sporting pages

*Indicates Morgan's answer.

TABLE 8-5, continued

LIKE	Dislike*	22.	Operating machinery
LIKE	Dislike*	23.	Economics
Like	DISLIKE*	24.	Acting as yell leader
Like	DISLIKE*	25.	Printer
Like	DISLIKE*	26.	Clergyman
Like	DISLIKE*	27.	Auto salesmen
Like*	DISLIKE	28.	People who always agree with you
Like*	DISLIKE	29.	Sick people
Like	DISLIKE*	30.	Consul

The Case of Professor Brown

Several hundred college men answered 200 statements in a personality inventory. In the statements below, more than two-thirds of these men gave the answer printed in CAPITAL letters.

Professor Brown, a middle-aged social science professor, also completed the inventory. His score on the empiricist scale, which measures readiness for change, interest in science, independence, and nonconformity of ideas, was higher than that of any of the men who took the test. His scores also indicated that he had a higher interest in the arts than 90 percent of the men. He also saw himself as less emotional, better organized, and more energetic than most college men.

In *six out of ten* of the statements in each exercise below, Professor Brown answered in the same way as the large majority of college men. If you predict that he answered *all* of the statements in the way that the typical man answered them, you would have 60 percent correct. Your task is to do better than 60 percent.

Exercise A

Circle the "true" or "false" as you think *Professor Brown* did. The answer in capitals is that given by the typical college man. Brown gave this answer on six of the ten statements.

TRUE†	False	1.	I am generally active in my everyday life.
TRUE†	False	2.	I always keep control of myself in an emergency situation.
TRUE†	False	3.	I occasionally neglect serious things in order to have a good time.
TRUE	False†	4.	I am always taking on added social responsibilities.
TRUE	False†	5.	I believe that competitiveness is a necessary and desirable part of our economic life.
True	FALSE†	6.	I prefer quiet games to extremely active ones.
True	FALSE†	7.	I am considered rather emotional by my friends.
True	FALSE†	8.	Divine truth is an infallible source of truth.
True†	FALSE	9.	I enjoy work more than play.

*Indicates Morgan's answer.
†Indicates Professor Brown's answer.

TABLE 8-5, continued

True†   FALSE   10. I think cremation is the best method of burial.

Exercise B

TRUE†   False   11. I sometimes think more about my ideas than about the routine demands of daily life.

TRUE†   False   12. I am practically always tolerant even in dealing with people that I don't like.

TRUE†   False   13. I like to discuss abstract questions with my friends.

TRUE†   False   14. Radical agitators should be allowed to make public speeches.

TRUE†   False   15. I believe that what a person does about a thing is more important than what he feels about it.

True   FALSE†   16. I always finish one task before taking on others.

True†   FALSE   17. Compared to your own self-respect, the respect of others means little.

True†   FALSE   18. I think I would like to decorate a room with flowers.

True†   FALSE   19. I never complain about my sufferings and hardships.

True†   FALSE   20. I prefer friends who have well-developed artistic tastes.

Exercise C

TRUE   False†   21. I am a very adventurous person.

TRUE   False†   22. I have never been seasick, plane sick, or car sick.

TRUE   False†   23. I believe in getting as much fun as I can out of life.

TRUE   False†   24. I would rather see a movie than read a book.

TRUE†   False   25. I occasionally neglect serious things in order to have a good time.

True   FALSE†   26. I have occasional difficulty getting the temperature of my bath the way I like it.

True   FALSE†   27. Artistic experiences are of great importance in my life.

True   FALSE†   28. Quite a few things make me emotional.

True   FALSE†   29. I would rather be a salesman than a scientific research worker.

True   FALSE†   30. The thought of God gives me a complete sense of security.

†Indicates Professor Brown's answer.

STRESS TRAINING

The development of nomothetic sensitivity generally requires not just that the trainee learn an accurate stereotype but that he change a stereotype he already has. The change process can be extremely stressful. A common professional response to erroneous stereotypes is to deny that differences exist between the groups. Campbell (1967) suggests that such denials may do more harm than good:

> In southern legislatures in the last 100 years, the alleged intellectual inferiority of Negroes has played an important role. Removing the belief that Negroes are inferior would not, however, remove the hostility, although it would change the content of the stereotype. Had the World War I test results showing northern Negroes to be more intelligent than southern whites been effectively publicized in the South, opportunistic hostility could certainly have created an image of the northern Negro carpetbagger whose opprobrious traits included shrewdness, trickiness, and eggheaded intellectuality. . . . The most ubiquitous fallacious aspect of stereotypes is not so much the falsity of the descriptive content as it is in the several causal misperceptions that accompany them. Remedial efforts focused on denying group differences are apt to be unwittingly endorsing the most mischievous of these causal misperceptions—wrongly agreeing that the particular group differences cause the hostility, unwittingly agreeing that were the actual group differences to exist, discrimination would be justified.

Those who deny differences, in other words, are implicitly agreeing with the mistaken causes and consequences of such differences that the prejudiced person perceives.

The serious but not unsolvable problems involved in changing a person's stereotypes are exemplified by the efforts of a staff psychologist to hire older women in a garment factory (Marrow and French, 1945). The supervisors of older women perceived them as inferior to younger ones. They and the management therefore resisted the proposal. The psychologist then proposed a research project to answer the question: How much money is being lost through the employment of older women? The project was accepted. The results: women over thirty were higher producers, faster learners, less often absent, and less likely to quit than women under thirty. The management was excited by the results and notified the employment agencies that women over thirty were to be given the same opportunity as younger women.

The supervisors still resisted. They did not challenge the results but countered with the fact that older women were not strong enough to stand the pace. They expressed satisfaction with individual older workers but would not change their belief that older women were generally inadequate workers. Conferences of supervisors were arranged to discuss the research results. The discussion centered around the origin of their attitudes toward older women and the possible motivations for maintaining them. The groups finally decided to recommend that an effort be made to train older workers. Eventually, the idea of hiring older women workers gained support. The authors concluded that if supervisory stereotypes are sufficiently strong they can withstand prestige suggestions by psychologists, personnel managers, or presidents. They can withstand facts, be they specific examples, general arguments, or the results of scientific

TABLE 8-6
Variations in Stress with Methods of Training

	Low Stress	Average Stress	High Stress
Presentation of the group member	Written case	Filmed interview	Social interaction
Type of prediction	Nonpersonal	Second person	First person
Recording of predictions	Rating	Matching	Ranking

research. Only group involvement and group decision can succeed in altering them.

It is widely assumed that high stress is inevitable if perceptions of a group are to be changed. It seems to be a dubious assumption, for stress increases resistance. An alternative approach is to gradually increase the stress as trainees develop the ability to manage it. Table 8-6 indicates some of the dimensions along which stress may be varied. Finding out about a group member from a written case, the table assumes, is less stressful than seeing him in a film which, in turn, is less stressful than making judgments based on interaction with him. Thus training would deal with low-stress case studies until trainees could deal with feedback on their errors at this stress level. It is also assumed that making predictions about the age, education, and background of the group member would be less stressful and, therefore, would come earlier in training than the questions: What does he think of himself? What does he think of you? Ranking may force the trainees to decide which good quality a group member has the most of and which he has the least of. Rating, which does not force such a choice, is less stressful than ranking and should be used at the beginning of training.

All the methods for developing observational sensitivity discussed in Chapter 4 are applicable to stress training: the diagnosis of perceptual style, the discrimination of sensory from expressive qualities, and the development of ability to play the observer role. Stress might begin at the lowest level with the observation of a person who is not a member of the group about whom the trainees have misperceptions.

5

IDIOGRAPHIC SENSITIVITY

CHAPTER 9

THE DEVELOPMENT
OF UNDERSTANDING

ASSUME that we meet Mr. A for an hour. Assume, also, that we observe him and remember what we have observed, that we are able to integrate our observations into a sound theoretical system, and that we have a comprehensive knowledge of the age, educational, and occupational groups to which he belongs. As a result of our keen observational, theoretical, and nomothetic sensitivities, let us say, we can now make accurate predictions about his feelings, thoughts, and behavior. Is any other component involved in determining our sensitivity to him? We suggest that there is and that it is the ability to *continue* to observe, theorize, and apply our nomothetic knowledge about him hour after hour and year after year so that our predictive accuracy continues to improve. We have called this component "idiographic sensitivity": the ability to use increasing exposure to and information about a person in making increasingly accurate predictions about him.

The mountain that blocks us from the valley of idiographic sensitivity is our conviction that we are already in it. As we become more and more familiar with a person, we feel more and more confident that we understand him better and better. This misplaced confidence arises from our persistent confusion of rationalistic with empirical understanding. Thus the first task in this chapter is to distinguish these quite different kinds of understanding and their quite different antecedents and consequences.

Some people learn little after much exposure to a person. Some learn a great deal. What accounts for the difference? We suggest that idiographic sensitivity depends upon two independent but complementary traits: consideration and responsibility. A person's degree of *consideration* is the degree to which he knows and respects the rights and feelings of others. His degree of *responsibility* is the degree to which he feels and acts as if he were holding himself accountable for what happens in a situation or to a person. These terms are defined much as a dictionary would define them. The most significant deviation is that "responsibility" ordinarily refers to the person's accountability to some outside agency. As defined here, it stresses what the person holds *himself* accountable for. The person of lowest idiographic sensitivity is he who neither knows nor respects the rights and feelings of another person and has no concern for what happens to him. The person of highest idiographic sensitivity is he who has the fullest respect for the separateness of the other person and also holds himself accountable for what happens to him.

Later in this chapter, we examine how differences in consideration and responsibility might be measured, their relationship to sensitivity, and their implications for training in idiographic sensitivity.

RATIONALISTIC UNDERSTANDING

We, as perceivers, have a degree of rationalistic understanding of others, i.e., we *feel* some degree of closeness to, sympathy with, and emotional understanding of other people. The desire to have such feelings seems to be among the strongest of human impulses, and the satisfaction of the desire seems to create the highest states of human happiness. In its most general and extreme form, rationalistic understanding is akin to a mystical experience. The following is one among many such experiences cited by James (1902, pp. 390–91). The brief but joyous experience that has enduring consequences is typical:

> I had spent the evening in a great city, with two friends, reading and discussing poetry and philosophy. We parted at midnight. I had a long drive in a hansom to my lodging. My mind, deeply under the influence of the ideas, images, and emotions called up by the reading and talk, was calm and peaceful. I was in a state of quiet, almost passive enjoyment, not actually thinking, but letting ideas, images, and emotions flow of themselves, as it were, through my mind. All at once, without warning of any kind, I found myself wrapped in a flame-colored cloud. For an instant I thought of fire, an immense conflagration somewhere close by in that great city; the next, I knew that the fire was within myself. Directly afterward there came upon me a sense of exultation, of immense joyousness accompanied or immediately followed by an intellectual illumination impossible to describe. Among other things, I did not merely come to believe, but I saw that the universe is not composed of dead matter, but is, on the contrary, a living Presence; I became conscious in myself of external life. It was not a conviction that I would have eternal life, but a consciousness that I possessed eternal life then; I saw that all men are immortal; that the cosmic order is such that without any peradventure all things work together for the good of each and all; that the foundation principle of the world, of all the worlds, is what we call love, and that the happiness of each and all is in the long run absolutely certain. The vision lasted a few seconds and was gone; but the memory of it and the sense of the reality of what it taught has remained during the quarter of a century which has since elapsed. I knew that what the vision showed was true. . . .

A hundred years ago James was well aware that this yearning for identification with others and the happiness in achieving it were influenced by drugs: "The sway of alcohol over mankind is unquestionably due to its power to stimulate the mystical faculties of human nature, usually crushed to earth by the cold facts and dry criticisms of the sober hour. Sobriety diminishes, discriminates, and says no; drunkenness expands, unites, and says yes."

Feeling close to, sympathetic with, and understanding of another person is an extremely satisfying experience for physicians and psychotherapists as well as for men in general. The poet and physician, William Carlos Williams (1951) describes his response to his patients (p. 357):

> . . . it is the rest, the peace of mind that comes from adopting the patient's condition as one's own to be struggled with toward a solution during those few minutes or that hour or those trying days when we are searching for causes, trying to relate this to that to build a reasonable basis for action which really gives us our peace . . . . often after I have gone into my office harassed by personal perplexities of whatever sort, fatigued physically and mentally, after two hours of intense application to the work, I come out at the finish completely rested (and I mean rested) ready to smile and to laugh as if the day were just starting.

Rogers (1961) has described similar feelings resulting from his experiences with his disturbed clients:

> I find that when I am working with clients in distress, that to understand the bizarre world of a psychotic individual, or to understand and sense the attitudes of a person who feels that life is too tragic to bear, or to understand a man who feels that he is a worthless and inferior individual—each of these understandings somehow enriches me. I learn from these experiences in ways that change me, that make me a different and, I think, a more responsive person.

It is also extremely satisfying to feel that others are close to, sympathetic with, and understanding of us.

The longer we know someone, the higher our rationalistic understanding of him is likely to be. What is new and strange is likely to be perceived as threatening and hostile; what is old and familiar is perceived as benign and friendly (Harrison, 1969). The law of propinquity states: "As the frequency of interaction between two persons increases, the degree of their liking for one another increases." The law is pervasive. Beier and Stumpf (1959) started out to determine the influence of various kinds of cues on judgments of intelligence, sociability, and other personality characteristics. To do so, over 200 students were presented with four subjects one at a time under different conditions: (1) They heard only the voices of the subjects from behind the screen; (2) they then heard the subjects and saw them making gestures but did not see their faces; (3) they heard their voices and saw them in person making the gestures; and (4) they had all of these cues and also heard the subject discuss a topic for three minutes. They rated the subjects four times: (1) with only the voice as a cue; (2) with voice and gestures; (3) with voice and gestures and face; and (4) with voice and gestures and face and discussion. Major result: The more familiar students became with a subject the more favorable their ratings became.

The longer we know a person, the more we assume he is like us. Students were brought into a room two at a time and seated at desks in such a way that they could not see each other (Bieri, 1953). Each of them took a test which pictured twenty-four situations with three possible responses. Each chose the response that he would make in each situation. They were then briefly introduced to each other and asked, even though they did not know each other very well, to fill out the test as they thought their partner had filled it out. Assumed similarity was measured by determining the number of the twenty-four situations in which a student picked the same response for his partner as he had picked for himself. The pairs were then given two topics to discuss for twenty minutes. Afterward, each member of the pair was asked to answer the test as he thought his partner had. Result: Higher assumed similarity after interaction.

The more we assume someone is like us, the more we like him. Newcomb (1956) had students in a cooperative house fill out a variety of inventories and rate themselves on various traits. They also filled out the inventories and ratings as they thought each of the other sixteen members would fill it out. The author measured the degree of similarity each student assumed to each of the other members. He also had the students indicate how much they liked each of the other members. Result: The more similarity they assumed, the more they liked him. In fact, though, there was no relationship between their assumed and actual similarity.

The more we like a person to begin with, the more we like him at the end. Mettee (1971) gave one group of individuals strong positive reinforcement on their task performance followed by minor criticisms $(++/-)$. Another group was given minor criticism to begin with followed by strong positive reinforcement $(-/++)$. Individuals in both groups, before and after, were asked: "How much, in general, did you like the experimenter?" To begin with, of course, those who were given strong positive reinforcement liked him much more than those who were given minor criticism. Those who were initially given minor criticism liked him somewhat more after he gave them positive reinforcement. But those who were initially given positive reinforcement liked him *more* even after he gave them minor criticism.

The more familiar a person becomes, the more we assume he is like us, and the more we like him, the higher our rationalistic understanding of him, i.e., the closer to, the more sympathetic with, and the more understanding of him we feel. Familiarity, empathy, and attraction may operate independently. Normally, however, they are intimately interwoven.

IDIOGRAPHIC SENSITIVITY

The relationship between familiarity and rationalistic understanding is linear: the longer we know a person, the better we feel we understand him. The relationship between familiarity and idiographic sensitivity is *not* linear: we quickly hit the peak of our ability to predict what a person will feel, think, and do. In fact, the relationship is sometimes curvilinear: the accuracy of our predictions declines with increasing exposure to him.

Our degree of confidence is a dubious measure of our degree of empirical understanding. Psychologists were given increasing amounts of information about a person (Oskamp, 1965). They first studied just a few general facts about a man and then predicted how he would behave in twenty-five different situations. Afterward, they were asked: How many of your predictions do you think were correct? The average psychologist expected 33 percent to be correct; 26 percent were actually correct. The psychologists were given increasing amounts of information. They repeated their predictions after each additional bit of information. They also reported the number of predictions they thought they had made correctly. At the final stage, they read more than a thousand words about the person. The more they read, the more confident they became about the accuracy of their predictions. In fact, however, their accuracy did not increase at all. Thus, at the final stage, the typical psychologist expected to get 53 percent of his predictions correct; he actually got 28 percent. Conclusion: "The judges' confidence ratings show that they became convinced of their own increasing understanding of the case. . . . Their certainty about their own decisions became entirely out of proportion to the actual correctness of those decisions."

Meehl (1959) showed that clinicians also reach an early saturation point in the amount of exposure and information they can use. He measured the accuracy with which therapists could predict the *Q*-sort responses of clients after the first, second, fourth, eighth, sixteenth, and twenty-fourth sessions. Peak accuracy was obtained between the second and fourth interview. Hunt and Walker (1966) asked experienced clinicians to diagnose thirty patients as schizophrenic, psychoneurotic, mental retardates, brain damaged, or normal. They were sometimes given vocabulary test scores, sometimes comprehension test scores, and sometimes both. Their predictions were just as accurate using one of the tests as using two. A similar result was obtained from clinicians using scores on the Rorschach and Thematic Apperception Tests alone and in combination (Golden, 1964).

Oakes and Corsini (1961) compared the accuracy with which students after one hour and thirty-six hours in an instructor's class could describe the instructor as he had described himself. The students did rather well after one class (a median correlation of .54 between the way they thought the instructor had sorted adjectives to describe himself and the way he actually had). They did only slightly better after thirty-six hours ($r = .63$). The authors compared this result with the results obtained by husbands and wives attempting to describe each other in the same way on the same test. Result: "Exposure to an instructor in a classroom for 36 hours seems to result in an average accuracy of perception of his self comparable to the average perceptiveness of a mate's self attained through six years of exposure in marriage." Taft (1966) found that students were better in judging acquaintances than strangers—but not much better.

In an unpublished study, George Baker compared the accuracy with which twenty-four engaged couples could predict each other's ranking of Rokeach's eighteen terminal values ("a comfortable life," "an exciting life," "mature love," etc.). The couples had been engaged from one month to five years. There was no correlation between duration of engagement and accuracy. The correlation between length of engagement and accuracy for those engaged for less than eighteen months was .60; for those engaged for more than eighteen months, .60. Dymond (1954) also found no relationship between duration of marriage and predictive accuracy.

THE TRAINING PROBLEM

The problem with rationalistic understanding and sensitivity is not that they are entirely different kinds of understanding that follow different principles in their development. The problem is that they are so universally assumed to be the same. This problem and its consequences are concretely demonstrated by the results of Kurtz and Grummon (1971). These investigators studied thirty-one college counselors and their thirty-one clients. After the third of an average of twelve interviews each client rated his therapist's understanding of him. He repeated the rating at the end of therapy. The rating instructions and the rating items were similar to the following:

Below are listed a variety of ways that your counselor might have felt or behaved in relation to you. Circle the number under the column that corresponds to how *you felt about him.*

F   PF   ?   PT   T

1   2   3   4   5   1. He tried to see things through my eyes.

1   2   3   4   5   2. He was interested in knowing what my experiences meant
                              to *me*.

1 2 3 4 5   3. He tried to understand me from my own point of view.

1 2 3 4 5   4. When I did not say what I meant at all clearly, he still understood me.

1 2 3 4 5   5. He could be deeply and fully aware of my most painful feelings without being distressed or burdened by them himself.

1 2 3 4 5   6. Sometimes he thought I felt a certain way because *he* felt that way.

1 2 3 4 5   7. His own attitudes toward some of the things I said or did stopped him from really understanding me.

1 2 3 4 5   8. He did not understand how strongly I felt about some of the things we discussed.

1 2 3 4 5   9. He understood what I said from a detached and objective point of view.

1 2 3 4 5   10. At times he jumped to the conclusion that I felt more strongly or more concerned about something than I actually did.

_____ Total Score (Add all the numbers that you have circled above.)

After the third interview, each counselor also rated his understanding of his client on the same scale, but with the substitution of "I" for "he" ("*I* tried to see things through *his* eyes," "*I* was interested in knowing what his experiences meant to *him*," etc.).

What was the relationship between the counselor's rating of his understanding of his client and the client's rating of the counselor's understanding of him? Essentially, zero. The counselor's rating of himself had no significant correlation with the client's rating of him after the third interview ($r = .20$). The correlation did not increase with the client's final rating ($r = .21$).

How were the counselor's and the client's ratings correlated with those of independent judges? Two judges listened to segments of the tape-recorded counseling sessions of each counselor and client. They then rated the understanding of the client on a five-point scale from level 1 ("the therapist's responses either do not tend to or detract significantly from the expressions of the client") to level 5 ("the therapist's responses add significantly to the feelings and meanings of the client in such a way as to express accurately feelings and meanings which the client himself is unable to express clearly.") The ratings of the two judges were almost perfectly related to each other ($r = .96$). However, their combined ratings were completely unrelated to those of the counselor and the client. In fact, the ratings of the judges and the ratings of the counselor were negatively related ($r = -.24$). The ratings of the judges were positively related to client ratings made after the third interview ($r = .31$), but these sank to zero with ratings made at the end of therapy.

How were the ratings made by the client, the counselor, and the independent judges related to the sensitivity of the counselor, i.e., the degree of his accuracy in predicting his client's responses? Each of the thirty-one counselors filled out an interpersonal check list containing 134 descriptive phrases as he thought his client had filled it out. Each also filled out the Kelly Role Concept Repertory Test as he thought his client had. The therapist's empirical understanding of his client was related to his client's rating of his understanding of him. The results were quite simple: no significant relationships of any kind. In fact, five of the eight possible correlations were negative, emphatically stressing the complete lack of relationship.

The results are quite consistent with those found by Lewis and Wigel (1964). They asked high school students who had worked together in groups of eight for months to rank from 1 ("the person who you feel understands you the best") to 7 ("the person who you feel understands you least"). Each student also filled out a scale for himself and as he thought each of the other members would fill it out. The empirical understanding of each student for every other student was measured by comparing the way he thought each of the other students would fill it out with the way each of the others actually had. These empirical scores were then related to the original subjective rankings. There was no relationship: "A person who is seen by a subject as being most understanding is no better able to make accurate predictions about how the subject will complete a Semantic Differential than is one who is seen as not being understanding."

In general, the low and unpredictable relationships between subjective measures and objective measures are a repetitive finding. The subjective estimates of students of how much they had learned in a course had no relationship to their gains on an objective test given at the beginning and end of the course (Armour, 1954). The subjective estimates of workers of their job performance had no consistent relationship to measures of their productivity (Herzberg, et al., 1957). Subjective estimates by college men of how much their dates at a dance liked them had almost no relationship to how their dates actually liked them (Walster, Aronson, and Abraham, 1966). Subjective estimates by psychologists of how much psychotherapy had increased their research productivity had no relationship to actual increases in their productivity (Wispé, 1965).

What is to be made of this chaos where no kind of understanding seems to be related to any other kind? A clue lies in the one major positive finding of the Kurtz and Grummon (1971) study. The benefits of therapy for the clients were measured in six different ways: (1) improvements in self-esteem as measured by the Tennessee Self Concept Scale, (2) reduction in the number of signs of psychological disturbance as measured by the same scale, (3) improvements on MMPI scores as estimated by independent raters, (4) ratings of the success of therapy by the counselor, (5) ratings of the success of therapy by the client, and (6) a composite score. The ratings by the counselors of their understanding had no correlation with any of the measures of improvement. Neither of the two measures of sensitivity had any relationship to any of the measures of improvement. The ratings by the independent judges were significantly related to only one of the six measures. However, the ratings by the client of his counselor's understanding of him were related to *all* the measures. The combined measure of improvement had a correlation of .55 with client ratings of counselor.

Theories of psychotherapy have uniformly stressed the overriding importance of the client perceiving his therapist as a warm and understanding person (Fromm-Reichman, 1950; May, 1939; Rogers, 1957; Truax and Carkhuff, 1967; Tyler, 1969).

Truax and Carkhuff, in their extensive review of research on the effects of psychotherapy, reach the following conclusion: "The weight of the evidence, involving large numbers of clients or therapists, suggests that the average effects of therapeutic intervention (with the average therapist or counselor) are approximately equivalent to the random effects of normal living . . . ." They do not conclude that therapy has no influence. They conclude that the help given by good therapists balances the harm done by bad therapists. That is, the positive results achieved by the therapist whose clients perceive him as warm and understanding are canceled by the negative results achieved by the therapist whose clients perceive him as cold and not understanding. It is vital, therefore, not only for therapists but for people in general, to relate to others in such ways that they are perceived as being close to, sympathetic with, and understanding of others.

A THEORETICAL SOLUTION

What do we do that leads others to perceive us as being understanding? The answer given by the theoretical model in Figure 3 is this: The more considerate and responsible we are toward a person, the more he will perceive us as having a rationalistic understanding of him, i.e., of being close to him, sympathetic with him, and understanding of him.

Nearly everyone agrees on the importance of consideration and responsibility, for they rate high on the list of desirable qualities.

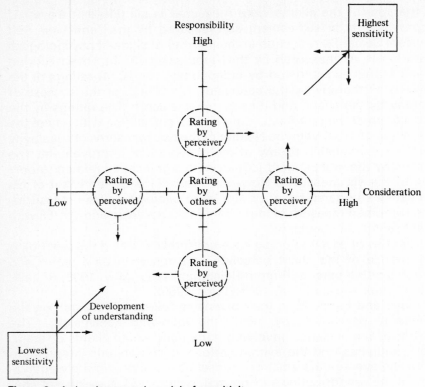

Figure 3 A developmental model of sensitivity

Nearly everyone, however, disagrees about their measurement. In particular, a perceiver is likely to rate himself high on the consideration and responsibility he is showing toward the person he is perceiving. The perceived, however, is likely to rate him lower. Impartial observers of the relationship between the perceiver and perceived are likely to rate the consideration and responsibility somewhere between the self-rating of the perceiver and the perceived person's rating of him. In general, there is no predictable relationship between the ratings made from these three different points of view.

The dotted circles in the figure picture these relationships. The "rating by perceiver" circles are high on both the consideration and responsibility scales and lead the perceiver to conclude that he has a good understanding of the person he is perceiving. The "rating by perceived" circles, on the other hand, are low on both dimensions and, therefore, reflect the perceived's impression that the perceiver has a poor understanding of him. The "rating by others" circle is placed in the middle to suggest that ratings by those outside a relationship are likely to be more moderate than those inside it.

The model does *not* hypothesize that our *feeling* of understanding a person is related to his feeling of being understood. It does not hypothesize that our *feeling* of understanding a person is related to the accuracy of our predictions about him. And it does not hypothesize that our *feeling* that we are being considerate and responsible is related to either his feeling of being understood or our sensitivity to him. It *does* hypothesize that the more considerate and responsible our *behavior* toward him, the more likely he is to perceive us as understanding him. It does hypothesize that the more considerate and responsible our *behavior,* the more accurate our predictions about him are likely to be and the more likely we are to become idiographically sensitive to him. And, most relevant for our purposes, it does hypothesize that the more effective training is in developing considerate and responsible *behavior,* the more sensitive the trainee will become. These assumptions demand empirical support; more, in fact, than we will be able to provide. The preliminary requirement, however, is for objective measures of consideration and responsibility.

THE MEASUREMENT OF CONSIDERATION AND RESPONSIBILITY

Fleishman (1953) set himself the task of describing as simply and realistically as possible the ways in which supervisors interact with their workers. He started with 1,800 specific kinds of behavior that supervisors display in their interactions with followers. These were sorted into ten general categories: initiation, representation, fraternization, organization, domination, recognition, production emphasis, integration, communication down, and communication up. Rating scales were then developed to measure a supervisor's position on each of them. Here, for example, is the rating scale for *initiation:*

He tries out new ideas in the group
always_____ often_____ occasionally_____ seldom_____ never_____

Supervisors rated themselves on each of the ten scales. They were also rated by their subordinates on the same scales.

Ratings of supervisors were made by their subordinates on all dimensions. These were correlated with each other and then factor analyzed. The result was that most of the variation in supervisory behavior could be described by variations along two dimensions: consideration and responsibility (Fleishman labeled the last "Initiation of Structure"). *Consideration and responsibility are independent,* i.e., how a supervisor is rated on one dimension is unrelated to how he is rated on the other.

Typical of the items in the final consideration scale were the following:

He sees that a person is rewarded for a job well done.

He makes those in the group feel at ease when talking with him.

He backs up his men in their actions.

Negative items in the scale were the following:

He refuses to give in when people disagree with him.

He changes the duties of people without first talking it over with them.

He doesn't give credit when it is due.

Fleishman and Salter (1963) describe the general quality of these items as including ". . . behavior indicating mutual trust, respect, and a certain warmth and rapport between the supervisor and his group. This does not mean that this dimension reflects a superficial 'pat-on-the-back,' 'first-name-calling' kind of human relations behavior. The meaning of this dimension goes more deeply into respect for the individual and includes such behavior as allowing subordinates more participation in decision making."

Typical items in the final responsibility scale were the following:

He offers new approaches to problems.

He asks for sacrifices for the good of the entire department.

He assigns people to particular tasks.

He criticizes poor work.

He encourages slow-working people to greater effort.

These statements are described as including ". . . behavior in which the supervisor organizes and defines group activities and his relation to the group. Thus he defines the role he expects each member to assume, plans ahead, establishes ways of getting things done, and pushes for production."

As used in practice, the two scales are completed by the subordinates of a supervisor. While each of the scales has high internal consistencies, scores on them have no relationship. These scales were developed in work situations. However, the dimensions appear not only in all leadership situations but also in all human relationships: teaching, counseling, parent-child relations, etc. With slight changes in wording, the scales can be fitted to these situations. In all these situations, however, the measurement is made by the subordinate, not by the leader; by the client, not the counselor; and, in terms used in the theoretical model, by the perceived, not the perceiver.

Can the perceiver, himself, identify where he stands in his consideration and responsibility toward the perceived? Direct ratings are worthless. In the first place, consideration and responsibility are highly desirable qualities, and people tend to ascribe such qualities to themselves. Those who don't rate themselves high on these qualities may, in fact, be perceived by others as having more of these qualities than those who do rate themselves high on them.

In the second place, people who rate themselves high may be convinced that they are really considerate and responsible. On the one hand, they may confuse their intentions with their actual behavior. On the other hand, they may define being considerate and responsible as the way in which they behave. Perceiver ratings, then, must control for the goodness factor and be based on the same standards that the perceived uses in determining the consideration and responsibility of the perceiver.

Doré (1960) tried to meet these requirements in developing self-rating scales of consideration and responsibility. He started with the same items used by Fleishman. However, he presented them as forced-choice pairs where each member of the pair had been judged as desirable as its mate. The original form of his questionnaire had 120 forced-choice questions. In a revised form, the pairs were reduced to sixty (Smith, 1968).

In the further revised form shown in Table 9-1, Attitudes Toward Leadership, the first sixteen items provide a measure of "consideration" and the second sixteen provide a measure of "responsibility". Both scales have internal consistencies above .80. They have a slight but negative correlation ($r = -.30$). That is, those who are high in consideration have a slight tendency to be lower in responsibility. Women score higher than men in consideration; men score higher than women in responsibility.

TABLE 9-1
Attitudes toward Leadership

DIRECTIONS: In each question are two statements of things that a leader can do. Choose the one you feel it is more *important* for him to do. If you feel that both alternatives are poor, choose the one you think is *less* poor.

It is more important for a leader:

Consideration

1. (1) To make decisions independently of the group.
   (2) To really be a part of his work group.*
2. (1) To let workers take time out from the monotony when they wish.*
   (2) To allow workers to make decisions only when given explicit authority by the leader.
3. (1) To take an interest in the worker as a person.*
   (2) To maintain definite standards of performance.
4. (1) To have his workers do their work the way they think is best.*
   (2) To rule with a firm hand.

*Indicates high-consideration response.

TABLE 9-1, continued

5.   (1) To decide in detail how the work shall be done by the workers.
     (2) To let workers make decisions whenever they feel competent.*
6.   (1) To make it clear that he is the leader of the group.
     (2) To have workers settle by themselves most of their job problems.*
7.   (1) To have the workers settle by themselves most problems.*
     (2) To have scheduled rest periods.
8.   (1) To have his workers do their work the way they think is best.*
     (2) To assign specific responsibilities and duties daily.
9.   (1) To do the important jobs himself.
     (2) To have workers take their rest periods when they wish.*
10. (1) To feel he belongs in his group.*
     (2) To reward the good worker.
11. (1) To have his workers do the work the way they think is best.*
     (2) To have the worker depend upon him to make decisions.
12. (1) To get the work done on time.
     (2) To be friendly toward his workers.*
13. (1) To act as he thinks best, regardless of the views of his workers.
     (2) To be proud of his work group.*
14. (1) To give the workers the power to act independently of him.*
     (2) To assign workers to particular tasks.
15. (1) To do the important jobs himself.
     (2) To let the workers decide how to do each task.*
16. (1) To leave it up to each worker to get his share of the work done.*
     (2) To set up most projects himself.

Responsibility

17. (1) To call the group together to discuss the work.†
     (2) To work right alongside the workers.
18. (1) To pitch right in with the workers.
     (2) To plan the work carefully.†
19. (1) To explain carefully each worker's duties to him.†
     (2) To spend some of his time helping get the work done.
20. (1) To work hard himself.
     (2) To schedule the work of the men carefully.†
21. (1) To be an authority in the type of work the group does.
     (2) To tell poor workers when their work isn't measuring up to what it should
          be.†
22. (1) To do the same work as his men whenever time allows.
     (2) To plan how his men will do the job.†
23. (1) To call the group together to discuss the work.†
     (2) To attempt to make his work not too different from the work of his men.
24. (1) To be respected as a man of high technical skill in his field.
     (2) To spend over half his time in supervisory activities such as planning and
          scheduling.†
25. (1) To let his workers know how they are doing on their jobs.†
     (2) To spend some of his time helping get the work done.
26. (1) To pass along to his workers information from higher management.†
     (2) To help get the work done.
27. (1) To be known as a man of great technical skill in the field.
     (2) To schedule the work to be done.†

*Indicates high-consideration response.
†Indicates high-responsibility response.

TABLE 9-1, continued

28. (1) To meet with the workers to consider proposed changes.†
    (2) To pitch right in with the workers to help make changes.
29. (1) To explain the duties of each worker's job to him until he really understands them.†
    (2) To pitch right in with the workers.
30. (1) To perform the same work as the workers whenever possible.
    (2) To plan his day's activities in considerable detail.†
31. (1) To be known as a skillful trainer.†
    (2) To set an example by working hard himself.
32. (1) To work right alongside his workers.
    (2) To try out new ideas on the work group.†

†Indicates high-responsibility response.

If consideration is such a desirable trait, what causes students to differ so widely in their scores on this scale? An inspection of the items shows that some people feel strongly that a leader should stress the job to be done and others feel equally strongly that a leader should stress consideration of those who are to do it.

If responsibility is such a desirable trait, what causes students to differ so widely in their scores on this scale? They differ in the degree to which they think a leader should play a "differentiated role." Some stress that a leader should play an undifferentiated role, should himself always act like a follower, should "work right alongside of his workers." At the other extreme, some stress that the leader should not try to act like a follower and do the same things he does. Rather, they believe that he should take on tasks that his followers cannot do as well: organizing the work, planning on-the-job training, and informing subordinates about policies.

What is the *best* place for one to be on the consideration and responsibility scales? People have firm positions on their answers that they defend with conviction and, what they consider convincing examples. Our view is a pragmatic one. James (1955) advanced pragmatism as a method for mediatating between rationalistic and empirical views. Pragmatism, he said (pp. 42–47), is:

> The attitude of looking away from first things, principles, "categories," supposed necessities; and of looking towards last things, fruits, consequences, facts . . . . *What difference would it practically make to any one if this notion rather than that notion were true? If no practical difference can be traced, then the alternatives mean practically the same thing, and all dispute is idle . . . . There can be no difference anywhere that doesn't* make a difference elsewhere—no difference in abstract truth that doesn't make a difference in concrete fact.

What difference does it make where a leader is rated by his followers on consideration and responsibility? What difference does it make whether a person feels that a leader should stress the work or the worker, should be like or different from his followers?

EFFECTIVENESS OF THE CONSIDERATE AND RESPONSIBLE

A growing body of evidence indicates that people who are considerate and responsible are more successful leaders and more successful in their interpersonal relationships. A study of leadership in the college classroom by Dawson (1970) clearly reveals the typical results. He taught the same course at the same time to four different groups under four different styles of leadership: HIGH consideration, HIGH responsibility; HIGH consideration, LOW responsibility; LOW consideration, HIGH responsibility; and LOW consideration, LOW responsibility. At the end of the course his students rated him on the following kinds of statements:

Low Consideration
He treats his students without considering their feelings.

He refuses to explain his actions.

He acts without consulting his students first.

High Consideration

He puts suggestions that are made by students into operation.

He is willing to make changes.

He makes students feel at ease when talking with him.

Low Responsibility

He lets students do their work in the way they think best.

He does not criticize poor work.

He does not emphasize quantity of work.

High Responsibility

He insists that his students follow a standard way of doing things.

He decides in detail what shall be done and how it shall be done.

He emphasizes meeting deadlines.

His student ratings on the statements consistently fitted his intended style. In addition, the low-consideration and low-responsibility style was least successful; the high-consideration and high-responsibility style was most successful. The students in the latter class reported higher satisfaction, did better on objective examinations, and volunteered for outside work more frequently.

Schafer and Bayley (1963) studied the relationships between more than fifty mothers and their sons and daughters over a period of eighteen years. The study began with observations made by pediatricians when the children were born and finished with ratings made by psychologists when the children were adolescents. An analysis of the relationships between mother and child found a dimension comparable to low and high consideration (hostility versus love) and a dimension comparable to low and high responsibility (autonomy versus control). The higher a mother's rating on the love scale, the happier, calmer, and more constructive her child. The results with high-control mothers were inconsistent. The more the mother controlled her infant child, the more constructive the behavior of the infant; the more the mother controlled her adolescent child, the *less* constructive the behavior of the adolescent. Conclusion: "The child's need for a positive relationship remains constant but his need for autonomy varies from birth to maturity." The most responsible mother is one who is permissive or restrictive depending upon the needs of the child.

Gagné and Fleishman (1959) report studies using their Supervisory Behavior Description Questionnaire of such diverse groups as bomber crews and university faculties. Groups under leaders high in consideration had higher productivity, lower rates of absence, and fewer accidents. Supervisors who were high in structuring tended to have employees who were high producers. Their employees, however, were more often absent, more likely to be hurt, more likely to submit grievances, and more likely to quit. With the supervisors, as with the mothers, the determining influence seems to be not how much structure he initiates but why he initiates it. If his aim is to achieve his own personal goals regardless of the impact upon his followers, his efforts are likely to fail. If his aim is to assist his followers in achieving their common goals, then his efforts are likely to succeed. It is for this reason that we use responsibility rather than initiation of structure. Responsibility stresses a feeling of accountability for what happens to the other person.

In regard to psychotherapy, Rogers (1961) comments: "I have long had the strong conviction—some might say it was an obsession— that the therapeutic relationship is only a special instance of interpersonal relationships in general, and that the same lawfulness governs all such relationships." The positive correlations reported by Truax and Carkhuff (1967) between improvement in therapy and unpossessive warmth, authenticity, and empathy suggest that consideration and responsibility are an important element of this "lawfulness."

SENSITIVITY OF THE CONSIDERATE AND RESPONSIBLE

Fleishman and Salter (1963) had twelve supervisors on the Yale University Campus fill out a Self-Description Questionnaire as they thought their twenty-four subordinates had filled it out. Their sensitivity score was the accuracy of their predictions about how their subordinates would respond. The subordinates described their supervisors as they saw him by filling out a Supervisory Behavior Description Questionnaire. The sensitivity scores of the supervisors were correlated with their consideration and responsibility ratings. The sensitivity of a supervisor was positively but not significantly related to his score on the responsibility scale ($r = .23$). His sensitivity was positively and significantly related to his score on the consideration scale ($r = .40$). As the correlation between scores on consideration and responsibility are practically zero, the supervisor who was seen as high on both consideration and responsibility would be seen still higher in sensitivity.

The author and his students have repeatedly found that measures of considerate and responsible leadership attitudes (Table 9-1) were significantly related to a wide variety of measures of sensitivity (Doré, 1960; Grossman, 1963; Johnson, 1963; Shook, 1971). A typical correlation with large groups of students is .20 with each of the scales and .30 with the combined scales. These correlations, though significant, are small. However, the scales measure motivation, not performance. Also, while measures of intelligence and classroom achievement are always related to sensitivity, they are never related to consideration and responsibility in leadership attitudes. Thus the relationship between actual considerate and responsible behavior with sensitivity among people of the same intelligence and ability would probably be much higher.

The sensitive also tend to be competent leaders. Cline and Richards (1959) found that the most sensitive participants in a T-group setting described themselves as egotistical and conceited and were described by their fellow trainees as egotistical and conceited. The authors drew the following sketch of the sensitive person in this setting:

> . . . a person who possesses a considerable amount of ego strength, self assuredness, and even conceit (probably to the point of occasionally irritating others). He is somewhat independent (emotionally) of other people and is not particularly concerned about how they regard him. He has tendencies toward leadership and dominance and has little psychic difficulty in initiating action or making decisions about things in his environment.

Chance and Meaders (1960) tape-recorded forty-five-minute interviews with two men who had previously completed the Edwards Personal Preference Schedule. Ninety-six undergraduate men, who had also completed the inventory, filled it out as they predicted the interviewed men had filled it out. An accuracy score for each student was obtained by counting the number of times predicted responses agreed with actual responses. The traits of the eighteen most accurate students were compared with the traits of the eighteen who were least accurate. From an examination of the trait differences the authors drew the following sketch of the sensitive person:

> . . . a person who is active and outgoing in social relationships, who likes other people but is not markedly dependent upon them, who is ascendant but not

hostile and competitive, and who is not given to intellectual reflections about his interpersonal relationships. The picture is one of an individual who finds significant satisfaction in social activities and carries on his daily life with a minimum of interpersonal or intrapersonal conflict.

The competence of the sensitive is also verified by studies in actual leadership situations. Squad leaders in the army were asked the following questions about each of the ten infantry trainees under them (Showel, 1960):

1 What is his first name?

2 Has he been on KP during the past week?

3 Has he been on sick call during the past week?

4 Has he had a pass during the past week?

5 What is his rifle qualification score?

6 How many years of schooling has he completed?

7 What was his job before entering the army?

8 What is his principal hobby or interest?

9 What is his ambition for a future civilian career?

The squad leaders answered similar questions for their trainee sergeant and trainee platoon guide. The correctness of their answers was determined by comparing them with the answers actually given by the trainees, the sergeant, and the guide. The accuracy score was the total number of correct answers. The leaders with the highest accuracy score were the best leaders as judged by (1) ratings by their trainees, (2) rating by the sergeant, (3) rating by the platoon leader, and (4) score on a standardized leader-reaction test.

The sensitive are also more effective in their human relationships. Dymond (1954) had fifteen married couples predict their respective spouses responses to fifty-five items on a personality inventory. Their scores were then related to the happiness of the marriage as rated by the marriage partners and by an outside judge. The happily married were more accurate in their predictions than the unhappily married: "Married love is not blind, and ignorance is not connubial bliss. The better each partner understands the other's perceptions of himself and his world, the more satisfactory the relationship."

In summary, the consideration responsibility (CR) theory assumes that a person's degree of consideration and responsibility toward a person determines how he is perceived by that person, how sensitive he will become to that person, and how effective his relationship with that person will be. A variety of facts seem to fit the theory. Thus the development of consideration and responsibility, the theory and facts imply, should receive heavy attention in idiographic training.

CHAPTER 10
IDIOGRAPHIC TRAINING

IDIOGRAPHIC sensitivity is the ability to make increasingly accurate predictions about a person with increasing exposure to him. How can differences in this ability be measured? How can training develop the considerate and responsible orientations that seem so central to the improvement of idiographic sensitivity? Can people be trained in ways that simultaneously develop observational, theoretical, and nomothetic sensitivity as well as idiographic sensitivity? This chapter proposes answers to all of these questions.

THE MEASUREMENT OF IDIOGRAPHIC SENSITIVITY

The measurement of idiographic sensitivity may be approached directly or indirectly. The direct approach is to measure predictive accuracy with varying degrees of exposure to the same person. The greater the improvement with exposure, the greater the idiographic sensitivity. The indirect approach is reductive. It assumes that idiographic sensitivity is what is left after the influences of observational, theoretical, and nomothetic sensitivity have been reduced, controlled, or, ideally, eliminated. This approach might seem unduly devious. It has, however, advantages of convenience and generality that make it worthy of serious consideration.

Table 10-1 is an indirect measure of idiographic sensitivity. In its development, Shears (1967) eliminated the influence of observational sensitivity by presenting the persons to be judged in typescript. He eliminated the influence of variations in the level and spread of goodness ratings by requiring the respondent to match each statement, whether desirable or undesirable, to one of the three men. He eliminated the influence of sex stereotypes by having the respondents differentiate between members of the same sex.

It was more difficult to reduce the powerful influence of nomothetic sensitivity. Respondents often make more accurate predictions about an individual from just knowing his group memberships ("a forty-year-old married physician with three children") than they do from more detailed information (Meehl, 1954; Stone, Leavitt, and Gage, 1957; Stelmachers and McHugh, 1964). Furthermore, apparent differences in the sensitivity of respondents to an individual often turn out to be due to differences in their nomothetic sensitivity, i.e., to differences in their knowledge of the groups to which the individual belongs.

TABLE 10-1
Test of Idiographic Sensitivity
(Shears, 1967)

DIRECTIONS: This is a test of your ability to make accurate predictions about people. You will be given information about George, Walter, and Allen. Your task is to use this information to make judgments about them. Correct answers have been obtained from attitude and personality scales filled out by each man and from ratings and sketches made on each man by his friends and relatives. The test is divided into two sections:

Section 1: Individuals

Section 2: Comparisons

SECTION 1

This part consists of brief interviews with three men followed by questions about their behavior. Follow the directions given at the beginning of each case. The interviews are given in the following order:

(1) George

(2) Walter

(3) Allen

The Case of George

George is middle-aged, married and has one child. As part of a research project on understanding people, he was given a brief interview. A typescript is given below:

Psychologist: "What sort of person are you?"
George: "Just an average person. I like the normal things most people do. I like sports, I like to dance and play around that way. Of course, I don't run around, I'd say I was getting into a stable class. I'm over the younger fling."
Psychologist: "What would you consider your greatest personality handicap?"
George: "Well, maybe too reserved."
Psychologist: "In what way?"
George: "Well, especially in business. I think I take too much of what the boss says, and do it. And, though maybe I can do it better, I do it the way he says to avoid trouble. In other words, I try to get along with people, which is good. But maybe sometimes I should say more about it to maybe help me and the others."
Psychologist: "Assert yourself a little more?"
George: "Yes."
Psychologist: "Do you ever lose your temper?"
George: "Well, very seldom with a person. I may become upset. I try my best not to let them know it."
Psychologist: "What would you do if someone told a lie about you?"
George: "Well, what kind of a lie—that I did something I didn't?"

TABLE 10-1, continued

Psychologist:	"Yes, a lie that perhaps would be damaging to your character."
George:	"Well, I don't know, but I imagine I'd try and find out why the person said it. Maybe, as far as he knew, he was telling the truth."
Psychologist:	"Would you go to him and talk to him about it?"
George:	"If it was of importance; otherwise I would forget it."
Psychologist:	"What sort of hobbies do you particularly enjoy?"
George:	"Well, I like to make things. Woodwork and hunting are the main things."
Psychologist:	"How important do you feel religion is to people in these times?"
George:	"I don't go in for religion too much. I believe that it is necessary for everybody to have a basic belief. As far as the religious part goes, in my own living I don't place that as a major issue."
Psychologist:	"Then religion is not too important to you personally?"
George:	"No."
Psychologist:	"But you do feel that people should have some sort of basic faith?"
George:	"Yes, they have to have a code to live by, and that's the best one I can think of."

George checked one alternative on each of the statements below to describe himself. *Check the alternative you think he checked.*

1. When my conscience begins to bother me . . .
   (1) I'm ashamed.
   (2) I analyze myself.
   (3) I try to do the right thing.*
2. I could hate a person who . . .
   (1) is a hypocrite and two-faced.
   (2) is cruel and ridicules others.
   (3) . . . I don't hate anybody.*
3. When they offered me help I . . .
   (1) was somewhat embarrassed.
   (2) thanked them but refused.
   (3) accepted.*
4. I boiled up when . . .
   (1) I was criticized unjustly.
   (2) I saw people hurting others.*
   (3) I was cheated.

The Case of Walter

Walter is a young married man with two children. A typescript of his interview follows.

Psychologist:	"What sort of a person are you?"
Walter:	"That's hard to determine. I'm one person to myself and another type of person to society. I'd have to give two definitions to answer that correctly—how I am to myself, and how I am to people who know me."
Psychologist:	"What sort of person are you to yourself?"
Walter:	"Well, I think I'm a person of probably over-average intelligence, with ambitions to be able to better myself and my society."
Psychologist:	"What sort of person do you feel you are to other people?"
Walter:	"Well, I hope I'm pretty nearly the same kind of person to other people as I am to myself. I get along well with most people, I don't have a great many friends; I have a few intimate friends, and with these people I'm

*Indicates correct answer.

TABLE 10-1, continued

	quite close. I get along well with these people. And I can be pretty compatible with most people."
Psychologist:	"What do you feel is your greatest personality handicap?"
Walter:	"The fact that I try too hard to do things, I believe. This hinders me from being able to do things—by being under certain tensions."
Psychologist:	"Do you ever lose your temper?"
Walter:	"Rarely."
Psychologist:	"What sort of thing would cause you to lose your temper?"
Walter:	"Well, never having lost my temper completely—I've always been able to hold my emotions pretty well in check—it would have to be a fairly devastating thing, I think, to make me lose it, or to become completely out of control of myself."
Psychologist:	"What sort of hobbies do you particularly enjoy?"
Walter:	"Golf, music, spectator sports—I am not too athletic—tennis, things such as this."
Psychologist:	"How important do you feel religion is to people in these times?"
Walter:	"That's a pretty deep subject. Not being a deeply religious man myself, it isn't too important to me. The moral teachings of religion help man be able to live better with himself, and with other people in society. I think today it's quite important for most people—not for the supernatural aspects of it, but for the moral teachings."
Psychologist:	"You don't feel that it's necessary for you?"
Walter:	"Not necessary, no."

Walter has checked one alternative on each of the statements below to describe himself. *Check the alternative you think he checked.*

5. I would go mad if . . .
   (1) somebody nagged me all the time.
   (2) I had nothing to do.*
   (3) I thought there were no purpose in life.
6. At the party, I was . . .
   (1) a little shy and reserved.
   (2) the life of the party.
   (3) quite smooth and polished.*
7. My philosophy of life is . . .
   (1) "Whatever you do, do well."*
   (2) "Enjoy today, think of tomorrow."
   (3) "Do unto others as you would have them do unto you."
8. I enjoy . . .
   (1) great music.*
   (2) being with people.
   (3) sports.
9. When I meet people, I generally feel . . .
   (1) indifferent.*
   (2) uneasy and self-conscious.
   (3) at ease and genial.

The Case of Allen

Allen is young and single. His interview follows:

Psychologist:	"Just what sort of a person are you?"
Allen:	"Well, I guess an easy-going one. I'm easy to get along with."

*Indicates correct answer.

TABLE 10-1, continued

Psychologist:	"What else can you tell me about yourself?"
Allen:	"Well, I guess that's about all. I have some temper—not much."
Psychologist:	"What would you consider your greatest personality handicap?"
Allen:	"Well, I guess just paying attention when there are people talking to me. Just paying attention to them."
Psychologist:	"Do you have difficulty paying attention when people talk to you?"
Allen:	"No, no, I don't have no difficulty, it's just that whenever I walk into a place, I just don't speak, I'm quiet."
Psychologist:	"Do you have difficulty making friends?"
Allen:	"No, no, I don't find no difficulty making friends."
Psychologist:	"After you once get to know them, then. But to begin with, you feel a little reserved, is that it?"
Allen:	"Yuh."
Psychologist:	"Well, do you ever lose your temper? What about?"
Allen:	"Once in a great while. It has to be something pretty mean, I guess, or something pretty big. One I guess is just—I don't know—couldn't tell you that until I lost my temper. Well, for instance, my little brother taking off with my car."
Psychologist:	"That would make you unhappy?"
Allen:	"Yuh."
Psychologist:	"What would you do if someone told a lie about you?"
Allen:	"I guess that would make me a little sore too, if it wasn't true."
Psychologist:	"What would you do, go to the person and talk to him about it?"
Allen:	"I wouldn't do nothing. Just sort of keep it to myself."
Psychologist:	"What sort of things do you do in your spare time?"
Allen:	"Oh, usually drive around; I like to drive around quite a bit."
Psychologist:	"Do you participate actively in sports, or are you a spectator?"
Allen:	"No, I participate in it. Basketball, for instance."
Psychologist:	"How important do you feel religion is to people in these times? How is it important to you?"
Allen:	"Yes, I really do think that religion is important. I don't know. I guess just being good, people go out, and that ain't so bad, just going out and partying, but after that, the way they gather . . ."
Psychologist:	"And you think that religion would affect that sort of thing?"
Allen:	"I think so, because of conscience—people have a conscience, and that would be on it."
Psychologist:	"In what way is religion important to you?"
Allen:	"I don't know, well, sometimes when you go out partying, you feel like doing something else, and yet you don't."
Psychologist:	"Because of your religion, is that it?"
Allen:	"Uh-huh."

Allen checked one alternative on each of the statements below to describe himself. *Check the alternative you think he checked.*

10. When I make a mistake, I . . .
       (1) don't give a damn.
       (2) am embarrassed.*
       (3) laugh it off.
11. I feel "down in the dumps" when . . .
       (1) I don't feel "down in the dumps."

*Indicates correct answer.

TABLE 10-1, continued

    (2) I say the wrong thing.*
    (3) I don't succeed.
12. When they told me what to do . . .
    (1) I did just the opposite.
    (2) I listened politely but did nothing.
    (3) I did it.*
13. At the party, I was . . .
    (1) a little shy and reserved.*
    (2) the life of the party.
    (3) quite smooth and polished.
14. Religion seems to me . . .
    (1) unnecessary.
    (2) a problem.
    (3) necessary and important.*

SECTION 2

The men in Section 1 filled out a series of attitude and personality scales. Their friends also rated them on a series of traits and gave sketches of them. The statements below are based on the answers that the men and their friends gave. If you think the answer to a particular question is:

George mark "1"

Walter mark "2"

Allen mark "3"

Go back and reread the interviews if you wish to; in any given subsection, an individual may be used more than once.

Religious Beliefs

(1) George, (2) Walter, and (3) Allen filled out a rating scale about their religious beliefs. Which one answered in the following manner?

(2)   15. Agreed that "I am unable to accept the idea of 'life after death,' at least not until we have some definite evidence there is such a thing."
(3)   16. Agreed that "God will punish those who disobey his commandments and reward those who obey Him (either in this life or a future life)."
(2)   17. Disagreed that "There exists an evil intelligence, personage, or spirit in the universe often referred to as Satan or the Devil."

Adjective Check List

The three men were each given pairs of adjectives and were asked to choose the one which they thought was a better description of themselves. In each of the pairs below, only one of the men checked the italicized adjective. Mark "1" if you think it was George, "2" if you think it was Walter, or "3" if you think it was Allen:

(2)   18. *Arrogant*—apathetic
(2)   19. *Progressive*—outgoing
(3)   20. *Shy*—assertive
(1)   21. *Steady*—spunky

*Indicates correct answer.

TABLE 10-1, continued

(1) 22. *Tolerant*—ingenious
(1) 23. *Stable*—robust
(3) 24. *Contented*—quick
(1) 25. *Warm*—forceful
(1) 26. *Moderate*—artistic
(2) 27. *Restless*—unemotional
(3) 28. *Sincere*—original
(1) 29. *Good-natured*—painstaking
(3) 30. *Kind*—insightful
(1) 31. *Changeable*—tense
(3) 32. *Loyal*—clever
(1) 33. *Foolish*—cynical

Personality Inventory Items

(1) George, (2) Walter, and (3) Allen were given a series of true-false items. Which one of the three answered *false* to these items?

(3) 34. I like to be the center of attention.
(3) 35. It is easy for me to talk to strangers.
(2) 36. At times I think I am no good at all.

Which one of the three answered *true* to these items?

(2) 37. I easily become impatient with people.
(1) 38. I take a pretty easy-going and lighthearted attitude toward life.
(3) 39. Policemen are usually honest.

Thumbnail Sketches by Friends

Friends of (1) George, (2) Walter, and (3) Allen also gave thumbnail descriptions of them. Which one was described as follows?

(2) 40. "Is in a state of rebellion against all religions."
(2) 41. "Enjoys almost all good art and music."
(3) 42. "Does quite poorly in speaking to groups."
(2) 43. "Rather fussy about what he eats and how it is prepared."
(3) 44. "Is shy and reserved at parties."
(3) 45. "Prefers going steady with one person."
(1) 46. "Is fairly easy-going with children."
(1) 47. "Raises voice a little but maintains control in family arguments."
(1) 48. "Is about average in regards to ambition."
(2) 49. "Somewhat insecure and high-strung."
(1) 50. "Is easy to get along with."
(3) 51. "Is a rather quiet and humble person."
(3) 52. "Loyal, honest, and kind."
(2) 53. "Tends to 'stew' about things, changes his mind back and forth before making final decisions."

Ratings by Friends

(1) George, (2) Walter, and (3) Allen were rated by their friends on a series of personality traits. Which one was rated as follows?
(2) 54. Least affectionate

TABLE 10-1, continued

(2)	55.	Most rebellious
(2)	56.	Least shy
(3)	57.	Least egotistical
(3)	58.	Most careful
(1)	59.	Least ambitious
(2)	60.	Most egotistical
(1)	61.	Least careful

Shears reduced the influence of differences in nomothetic sensitivity by employing a double item analysis. A hundred students took the 240-item pilot form of this test. They also took a 150-item test of nomothetic sensitivity that measured their accuracy in predicting the different interests of men and women, of young and old men, of executives and unskilled workers, and of psychologists and men in general. Each of the 240 items was tested for its ability to discriminate between those who did well from those who did not do well on the test as a whole. Each item was also tested for its *in*ability to discriminate those who did well on the nomothetic test. Shears then selected 120 items from the 240 that met these two tests. A new group took the revised test of idiographic sensitivity and the same 150-item test of nomothetic sensitivity. The scores of students on the two tests were correlated. Nomothetic sensitivity had no influence on individual sensitivity, for the correlation was zero. In spite of these drastic eliminations, the internal consistency of the test was .57.

Shears also provided some evidence for the validity of the test by making a direct comparison of the differences between students who had only nomothetic cues with those who had the nomothetic cues and individual ones. The first group were given only the group memberships of George, Walter, and Allen and asked to make the predictions in the test. They received only a chance score (18). Those who received the typescript did much better (30).

Repeated administrations of the test can be used to measure changes in the ability of trainees to utilize purely idiosyncratic cues in making predictions about people. However, it does not provide a direct measure of their ability to increase the accuracy of their predictions of a particular individual with increased knowledge of him. Such a test requires that the same trainees take the same test with varying amounts of information. No such tests exist for general use. It is impractical to expose the same person to different audiences for long periods of time. Consequently, except for a few studies of married couples, we have almost no information about sensitivity in enduring relationships. This is a very serious gap.

Table 10-2 presents items from a direct measure of idiographic sensitivity, i.e., the ability of trainees to improve their predictive

TABLE 10-2
Sample Items from a Direct Measure of Idiographic Sensitivity

You have now read, seen, heard, and interacted with the instructor for weeks. How well do you understand him and understand what he thinks of himself?

Observational Sensitivity Items

1. He weighs: (1) 155   (2) 165   (3) 175

2. His height is: (1) 5'7"   (2) 5'9"   (3) 5'11"

3. His age is: (1) 45–49   (2) 50–54   (3) 55–59

Theoretical Sensitivity Items

He completed the same personality inventory as you did. Indicate how you think his scores compared with those of the men in this class. Mark: (1) LOW: 25th percentile or less; (2) AVERAGE: 26th to the 75th percentile; (3) HIGH: 76th percentile or higher.

4. Cautious vs. BOLD

5. Unemotional vs. EMOTIONAL

6. Artistic vs. PRACTICAL

7. Present-minded vs. FUTURE-MINDED

8. Rationalistic vs. EMPIRICAL

Nomothetic Sensitivity Items

His "true" or "false" answer to the following statements were the *same* answers as those given by more than two-thirds of college men. Answer as you think both he *and* the typical man did.

9. I prefer quiet games to extremely active ones.

10. The thought of God gives me a complete sense of security.

11. Radical agitators should be allowed to make public speeches.

12. I always finish one task before taking on others.

His answers to the following statements were the *opposite* of those given by more than two-thirds of college men. Answer as you think *he* did.

13. I think I would like to decorate a room with flowers.

14. I believe that competitiveness is a necessary and desirable part of our economic life.

15. If I had the ability, I would enjoy teaching poetry at a university.

Idiographic Sensitivity Items

He filled out the Strong Vocational Interest Blank. Answer "like" for those that you think he checked "like"; "dislike" for those that you think he checked "dislike."

16. Actor

17. Architect

18. Tennis

TABLE 10-2, continued

19. Certified public accountant

20. Hunting

accuracy to their trainer with varying degrees of exposure to him. This type of test is adaptable and interesting to trainees. It can, of course, be used only by the particular trainer or investigator involved. The problem of internal consistency enters here as in all measurements. A common error in the construction of such tests is to overestimate the sensitivity of respondents. Consequently, scores on such tests are close to chance. An aspect of the same error is to require respondents to make differentiations that are too fine. Questions, for example, with three alternatives are generally more discriminating than those with five. Even with revisions, such tests may need a hundred items to obtain satisfactory reliability. With sixty items, the frequently revised test in Table 10-2 has internal consistencies of less than .60.

As the sample items indicate, such direct tests may provide measures of all the sensitivity components. The problem with observational items is to find those that are stable (weight may change significantly over a semester) and sufficiently difficult. Sensitivity to age seems an interesting problem for investigation. Students vary widely in their ability to judge it and the ability seems to be related to general sensitivity. It is also an easy problem for investigation, for the criterion is nearly perfect. The only need is for subjects of varying sex and ages.

In the theoretical section of this test the investigator may plug in items from any theory. It must be borne in mind, however, that trainees may find it extremely difficult to apply even the simplest theory with accuracy. In the nomothetic section, the biggest problem is to find items with adequate normative data. Manuals for the MMPI and the Strong Vocational Interest Blank have item-by-item norms for men and women. Interest items are numerous, brief, and readily understandable. A final general problem with such instruments is to make them sufficiently sensitive to change, i.e., to include items that trainees have a chance of improving on over the course of training.

CR FEEDBACK

The CR (consideration + responsibility) theory states a basic aim of idiographic training but does not state it concretely nor indicate how it is to be achieved. It states that increased sensitivity is a by-product of increased consideration and increased responsibility and that it is these increases, therefore, which should be a primary aim of training.

But how does a person *behave* in a considerate and responsible way in a specific situation? How can the frequency of such behaviors be increased? It is to these questions that the work of Daw and Gage (1967) addressed itself in a practical, comprehensive, and successful way. Their research is discussed here in some detail, for it not only outlines a simple way of increasing considerate and responsible behavior in a school situation but also provides a general procedure for increasing such behavior in other situations.

The aim of the program was to develop the consideration and responsibility that 151 elementary school principals showed in their relationships with their teachers. The first critical task was to define considerate and responsible behavior in this situation in a realistic fashion. The authors sought statements that would

> . . . deal with behaviors that could be expected to occur frequently, that could be briefly described without qualifying phrases, and could be changed by the principal within the time span of the research in a way that could be recognized by the teachers.

The seventy items originally written were reduced to the final twelve on the basis of ratings of their importance, improvability, and noticeability; the ratings were made by psychologists, professors of educational administration, teachers, and principals.

Though the authors did not refer to the concepts of consideration and responsibility, they are presented here under these headings.

Consideration

1 Encourages teachers with a friendly remark or smile.

2 Gives enough credit to teachers for their contribution.

3 Does not force opinions on teachers.

4 Demonstrates interest in pupil progress.

5 Interrupts the classroom infrequently.

6 Displays much interest in teachers' ideas.

Responsibility

7 Enforces rules consistently.

8 Criticizes without disparaging the efforts of teachers.

9 Informs teachers of decisions or actions which affect their work.

10 Gives concrete suggestions for improving classroom instruction.

11 Enlists sufficient participation by teachers in making decisions.

12 Acts promptly in fulfilling teacher requests.

For a CR program to be effective in any situation, it would seem necessary that similar steps be followed: (1) select behaviors reflecting consideration and responsibility, (2) stress those behaviors that occur most frequently, (3) stress those that are most modifiable, (4) stress those that are most identifiable, and (5) stress those that are most relevant to consideration and responsibility in that situation.

Feedback from teachers to principals was the only method Daw and Gage used to change behaviors. It was assumed that principals would change their inconsiderate and irresponsible behaviors after they had been alerted to these problems by their teachers. The assumption was based on an awareness that a wide variety of theories converge on this principle. Heider stresses that the learner is motivated to correct an *imbalance;* Newcomb, to remove an asymmetry; Osgood and Tannenbaum, an incongruity; Festinger, a dissonance; and others, to maximize self-esteem.

Before feedback from the teachers was given, the principals rated themselves on each of the twelve items from "very much unlike me" to "very much like me." They also rated how their ideal principal would be rated. Two weeks after the principal's teachers had made their ratings of him, he received a report of the discrepancies between the ratings his teachers gave him and the ratings they gave their ideal principal. Half of the principals received only the median ratings made by their teachers; the other half, the median-plus-distribution of ratings. Later analysis showed that differences in the form of feedback made no difference in how much the principals changed. Practically all those who reported said that they found the feedback interesting, understandable, and informative.

The form met the general requirements for effectiveness in feedback: (1) the feedback was not in the form of self-estimates or ratings by nonparticipating experts—it was given by those directly involved; (2) the feedback did not concern vague estimates of likeability, goodness, or effectiveness—it involved specific, observable, and significant kinds of behavior; and (3) it involved matters about which the principals were deeply concerned.

The feedback worked. The teachers rated their principals again several months later. The principals had shifted their behavior toward the teacher's ideal on all twelve of the items, significantly so on all but "Demonstrates interest in pupil progress" and "Interrupts class infrequently." The authors concluded: "All in all, the results indicate that the feedback affected changes in the principals' behavior . . . . The behavior of teachers, principals, and persons in many similar roles could be made more effective by applying the results . . . ."

The experimenters based their conclusions on the results of using the basic experimental design shown in Table 10-3. Feedback group A consisted of the 151 principals who were first rated by their teachers, then given feedback, and then rated again. Might not the

TABLE 10-3
The Basic Design of the Principal Study
(Adapted from Daw and Gage, 1967)

Group	Initial Rating	Feedback?	Final Rating?	Differ- ence?
Feedback Group A	Yes	Yes	Yes	Yes
Control Group B	Yes	No	Yes	Yes
Control Group C	No	No	Yes	No

principals have changed as much even if they had not been given feedback? The 143 principals in control group B provided an answer to this question, for they were rated initially and finally but were given no feedback from their teachers. It was the feedback that made the difference, for group A improved more on every one of the twelve kinds of behavior than did group B. Did groups A and B become sensitized to their inconsiderate and irresponsible behaviors just from filling out the initial form? The 161 principals in control group C who did not complete the initial rating were rated by their teachers at the end. The ratings that their teachers made of them were no different from the ratings of the principals in group B. Thus feedback in this situation worked. It not only worked, but it worked fast. The principals in the experimental and control groups were assigned at random to either a six-week or a twelve-week interval group. The principals who were rated again six weeks after they received feedback had changed as much as those who were rated again after twelve weeks.

Adequate feedback, it seems clear, is sufficient to increase the considerate and responsible behaviors of those who want to be more considerate and responsible. The critical problem here is to define consideration and responsibility in realistic behavioral terms. A person's consideration is a tendency to know and respect the rights and feelings of others; his responsibility, his tendency to hold himself accountable for what happens in a situation to a person. But it is what he *does* that indicates to others his knowledge, respect, and feeling of accountability to them. What he does varies from person to person and from home, to school, to work, to clinic, to public office. Consequently, the terms must be defined to fit the particular situations.

Some people, however, have little desire to become more considerate and responsible. A child does not know the meaning of the words. Consideration and responsibility develop slowly and are often arrested. The motivation is weak in the autistic, the impulse-ridden, or opportunists like Owen Simons:

Owen is a twenty-five-year-old graduate student. He is good-looking and always neatly dressed. He is intelligent, fluent in speaking, forceful in writing, and ambitious to achieve a high status in his chosen field. He is keenly aware of the rules governing his advancement toward this status—a high grade-point average, politeness in dealing with his teachers, etc. However, his use of the rules is consistently expedient. He copies the work of others into his papers without acknowledging the source. He distorts the opinions of others when he thinks it is to his advantage. He manipulates others to do his work. When caught breaking the rules, he gives fervent lip service to the ideals of consideration and responsibility. He asserts that "he didn't understand" that what he had done was either inconsiderate or irresponsible and asks: "Why didn't someone tell me?" He assumes an air of contriteness and humility. He appeals to the sympathies of others when he thinks appeals will work; he makes forceful demands that his rights be protected when he thinks force will work. He is generally disliked and avoided by his fellow students. His best friends state that Owen often makes him "want to punch him in the nose."

Even for such an individual, however, the training problem may be viewed as one of defining considerate and responsible behaviors that are appropriate to his stage of personality development.

Unlike rationalistic understanding, idiographic sensitivity peaks early. We quickly reach the limit of the information that we can or want to use to improve our sensitivity. We do not look at people with the dispassionate curiosity of a mechanic looking at a motor and trying to find out what "makes it tick." It is closer to the truth to say that we strive to understand as little as we can about a person—and still get from him what we want. Our thoughts are generally dominated by such questions as: What can he do for me? What can he do for us? It is only occasionally that the question becomes: What does he really think of himself, why does he think so, and how is he likely to feel, think, and behave in the future? The more considerate and responsible the person, the more likely he is to have this last question in mind.

Increased consideration and responsibility lead to idiographic sensitivity; increased sensitivity leads to increased consideration and responsibility. Feedback from the person tells him which of his efforts to be considerate have failed because of his lack of sensitivity. The success or failure of his efforts to do things for the person or have him do things for himself gives him even more incisive feedback. Consideration, responsibility, and sensitivity interact to increase his motivation to learn more effective general ways of understanding people.

People, however, are considerate and responsible objectively and not subjectively, concretely and not abstractly. A person can *behave* in a considerate and responsible way toward only a limited number of people in a limited number of ways. Training can only hope to expand these limits, not to eliminate them.

THE PROGRAMMED CASE METHOD

Even the considerate and responsible make slow and unsteady progress in improving their sensitivity to a person. How can this progress be accelerated? Adler advocated a two-step approach. First, a person should form an impression of the life style through intuitive guessing. Second, he should verify this general impression through checking the various expressions of the individual from early life to the present, comparing them with his initial impression (Ansbacher and Ansbacher, 1956, p. 332):

> We are provided with a vast store of material. Every word, thought, feeling, or gesture contributes to our understanding. Any mistake we might make in considering one expression too hastily can be checked and corrected by a thousand other expressions. . . . In a way we are like archaeologists who find fragments . . . and from these fragments proceed to infer the life of a whole city which has perished. Only we are dealing not with something which has perished, but with the inter-organized aspects of a human being, a living personality which can continuously set before us new manifestations of its own meaning . . .

He felt that people in general and clinicians in particular improve their sensitivity through making judgments and then receiving feedback about their correctness (Adler, 1927, p. 16):

> Error is followed quickly by punishment, and the correct understanding of the ailment is crowned by success in the treatment. In other words, a very effective test of our knowledge of human nature occurs in psychiatric practice. In ordinary life, an error in the judgment of another human being need not be followed by dramatic consequences, for these may occur so long after the mistake has been made that the connection is not obvious.

Adler's approach, impeccable in theory, fails in practice: The predictions made by those with clinical training are no better than those with ordinary life experiences. Why? Because, in general, the predictions that the clinician makes are not actually susceptible to being "checked and corrected by a thousand other experiences." Even when they can be checked, there is nothing to check them against. Rorer (1965) lists some of the kinds of predictions made by clinicians that are not susceptible to proof or disproof, though they believe they are:

SELECTIVE PREDICTIONS   The clinician, like everyone else, remembers what makes him comfortable and forgets what does not. He remembers what fits his beliefs and forgets what does not. That is, he remembers his accurate predictions; he forgets his inaccurate ones.

UNIVERSAL PREDICTIONS   The clinician often makes predictions about a specific person that are likely to be right for anyone. Phrenologists, palm readers, and astrologers make deliberate use of such predictions. But everyone can and does sometimes use it:

You prefer a certain amount of change and variety and become dissatisfied when hemmed in by restrictions and limitations.

While you have some personality weaknesses, you are generally able to compensate for them.

You have a great need for others to like and admire you.

You get depressed from time to time.

The person is likely to say "you are right." Nine out of ten people agree that each of these is an accurate description of themselves.

REVERSIBLE PREDICTIONS   The clinician sometimes makes predictions that he can interpret as accurate no matter what the person is or does. He says: "This person has a tendency to act out, but it will probably be held in check by his dependency needs." If he does "act out," score "right." If he does not act out, score "right." ("His dependency runs so deep that you could tell that he was too frightened to get out of line.")

PARTLY CLOUDY PREDICTIONS   Suppose we predict that tomorrow will be partly cloudy. We are almost certain to be correct, for we count it correct if either a patch of blue or a patch of cloud appears at any time during the day. If the clinician predicts that a person is "intelligent," he can count it correct if any evidence of intelligence is assumed to be a verification. That is, the clinician's lack of quantification, his failure to specify "how much," enhances his apparent predictive accuracy.

FUZZY PREDICTIONS   We predict that a person is "sincere." How can the prediction be checked? We predict that he is "phony." How can this be checked? The clinician predicts that a client is a "latent homosexual." How can this be checked? Making ambiguous or unverifiable predictions is probably the most pervasive of all methods of enhancing confidence in the validity of subjective impressions.

Yet clinicians persist in making such predictions and in retaining their confidence in them. Meehl (1960) comments: "Personally, I find the cultural lag between what the published research shows and what clinicians persist in claiming to do with their favorite devices even more disheartening than the adverse evidence itself." What is the solution to this problem? Chapman and Chapman (1967), after still another study showing that clinicians were no better than naive judges, suggest:

Each graduate student in clinical psychology could be asked to serve, during his training, as an observer in a task like those used in the present studies, and he could be shown the source of the illusory correlates which he reports. He would then probably have a keener awareness of the difficulties of making such observations, and he would be better able to guard against them in his future clinical practice. Hopefully, he would also be more receptive to relevant research evidence as a result of such training, and would be less inclined to rely solely on his own clinical observations. He would also be aware that "consensual validation" may reflect shared systematic error rather than shared accuracy.

However, the authors are doubtful that such training will be tried and modest in their hopes for it if it is.

Dailey (1966a, 1966b) offers a more radical solution to the problems of idiographic training. His programmed case method provides frequent, immediate, precise, factual, and meaningful feedback to trainees.

His cases are life stories arranged chronologically in episodes. The trainee guesses at each step what the next episode will be (choosing from among three alternatives, two of which are plausible but wrong). He is given feedback on the accuracy of his prediction. The method is designed to be used by an individual. However, it lends itself readily to group discussion. The typical case is about 1,500 words in length and contains fifteen episodes or events spanning an individual's life history. Here is the beginning of one case (1966a).

> This man is an industrialist. You will be reading a short account of his life. However, instead of reading an ordinary, straightforward life history, you will follow a special procedure designed to help you see how well you understand him as a human being.
>
> On each page there are several incidents, lettered A, B, and C. Any one of these incidents could plausibly have occurred in his life. Your job is to decide which incident *did* happen.
>
> It is necessary that you not read ahead, and that you make a decision before you go on to each next page. Then at the top of each page, you will be told which of the incidents which you just reviewed on the preceding page was actually true of the person's life.
>
> As a result of this procedure, you will experience a gradual improvement in understanding this man. However, do not be discouraged if your understanding is inaccurate during the first few pages.
>
> If the procedure is clear to you, please turn the page and begin.
>
> PLEASE TRY TO CHOOSE THE TRUE EPISODE

A.   As a child, he never took well to studies. Fascinated by carnivals, he left school early in high school to join a carnival troupe. He traveled about the country with them for several years, doing every possible type of labor but developing no special talent.

B.   His parents were poor and he left school at eleven to help support himself and them. He ran errands for the local photographer. By the end of his teens he had learned the trade and saved enough to buy out his employer. He spent winters in Florida and summers at Lake Placid, New York, photographing the tourist trade.

C.   His academic interests showed early signs of scientific talent. He spent hours by himself, searching for species of butterflies, bugs, and plants to add to his various collections.

MAKE YOUR CHOICE BEFORE YOU TURN THE PAGE

IF YOU CHOSE B: You were correct. His parents were poor and he left school at eleven to help support himself and them. He ran errands for the local photographer. By the end of his teens he had learned the trade and saved enough to buy out his employer. He spent winters in Florida and summers at Lake Placid, New York, photographing the tourist trade.

The developed cases include twenty-two biographies and seventeen case histories. The biographical cases are based on events in published biographies which describe what the person did or said in particular situation, time, and place. The biographies include Henry Ford, Senator McClellan, Alec Guiness, and Edward R. Murrow. The cases include three Colombians, ten sales managers, two printers, a trucking supervisor, and a woman executive. While these are generally of normal persons, they include undertones of emotional difficulties including bouts with alcoholism, compulsive cleanliness, and paranoid tendencies.

A "programmed case laboratory" is made up of ten or more programmed cases. During such a laboratory, the typical trainee does improve. In the first third of twelve programmed cases, 100 undergraduates had an average predictive accuracy of 40 percent; in the middle third, 54 percent; in the final third, 64 percent. Trainees generalize what they learn from one case to other cases. The average accuracy score of eighty-five undergraduates and forty-three industrial managers on their first two cases was 44 percent. By the time they had reached their fifth and sixth cases, their accuracy was 55 percent. By the eleventh and twelfth cases, 61 percent. Indirect evidence indicates that what is learned in the training generalizes to life situations. Dailey (1966) concludes:

> May we not hope that the appreciation of human behavior in its natural concreteness, and the measurement of understanding of that appreciation by the young clinician, will of necessity put the study of individuals in its rightful place in the professional curriculum?

THE TYPICAL CASE METHOD

The programmed case method throws out the baby with the bath. It concentrates successfully upon the development of idiographic sensitivity. However, it throws away the contributions that observational, theoretical, and nomothetic sensitivity may make to the development of general sensitivity. Is it possible to develop programmed cases that develop idiographic sensitivity and, simultaneously, contribute to the development of observational, theoretical, or nomothetic sensitivity? If possible, how could it be done?

The results of the training evaluation of Wakeley (1961) provide a hopeful clue. His study compared the effectiveness of different methods of improving sensitivity. The six methods were (1) *pooling:* "Use the information which you have about people whom you know well when you are making judgments about people whom you know less well"; (2) *observing the self:* "Pay attention to yourself"; (3) *observing others:* "Pay attention to the other person"; (4) *individual differences:* "Everyone is different from everyone else"; (5) *recording-rating:* "Avoid level and spread errors"; and (6) *combination* of the above methods.

Only the pooling method produced significant improvement. Part of the ten-minute instructions given the trainees using the pooling method follows:

> In the course of your living you have obtained a great deal of information about many people. The pooling principle simply suggests that you use this information when making inferences about a person with whom you have had little contact. When you are attempting to make inferences about a person whom you do not know well, one of the things which you can do is to form a pool of people whom you do know well who are like the unknown person. You take what you do know about the person, form a pool of people you know well, and then make your predictions or judgments based on the pool. The important things to remember in making these pools are to use people you know well and to use all the information you have about the person you are trying to judge. You may form a pool that leads to wrong predictions if you use just one piece of information about the person, such as his skin color, his religious preferences or any other single piece of information. You may also form some pools that lead to wrong predictions if you use people whom you do not know well.

Essentially, these pooling instructions advised the trainees to (1) observe the groups to which the individual belongs, as, for example, "a young Catholic mother with an eighth-grade education whose husband is a carpenter"; (2) pick from people that you know well those who most closely match this person; and (3) assume that the person will think, feel, and behave as the average person in this matched pool would think, feel, and behave.

Each of the six groups of twenty members met for three hours. Only one hour, however, was devoted to instruction and practice. The first and last hours were devoted to taking a film test of sensitivity. During the hour of training the trainees were not only told about the principle they were to use, but were also given about forty-five minutes of practice in applying it with feedback. A control group had no training but took the pretest and the endtest. Only the "pooling" group made significant improvement over their initial performance and over the control group. In a follow-up study, older businessmen made similar improvements using the same method.

Wakeley's pooling method probably worked because it is a method that people already use successfully. We can and do learn about people we do not know by comparing and contrasting them with people we do know. The pooling method focuses the attention of trainees upon this method. For the particular trainee, however, the method is limited by whom he happens to know and how well he knows them. The programmed case method has the same limitation, for it focuses the attention of trainees upon people who happen to have had good biographies written about them or upon people whom the investigators happen to know.

However, cases do not have to be picked by chance. They may be selected in accordance with a deliberate plan. A case, in other words, may be chosen not only to develop idiographic sensitivity but also to develop a particular observational skill, to promote use of a particular theory, or to acquaint the trainee with a particular group. Ideally, it might do all of these things.

Doctors, psychiatrists, social workers, clinical psychologists, and indeed all groups who must deal with individuals in a practical setting have long made use of typical cases. What is being advocated, therefore, is not a new method; it is the infinitely more systematic and precise use of an old method. The individual cases should be carefully selected to develop a well-defined observational skill, to develop knowledge of and the ability to use an empirically derived theory, or to develop skill in applying established characteristics of a group to members of that group. The incidents or episodes in the case would not be based on vague recollections or casual impressions but upon systematic observation. Above all, the presentation of the cases to trainees would not be in the form of written cases or lectures but in the form of a tested sequence of predictions to be made by trainees with immediate feedback and discussion. Vividly presented, such cases would then become part of the pool of cases which a trainee had learned to know well and which he could compare and contrast with people he met in his everyday life.

The procedures for selecting, developing, and using such cases now seem clear. It also seems reasonably certain that the method could succeed where other methods have failed, i.e., in the development of general sensitivity. The process of selecting, developing, and using such cases would be hard and slow, but the process should be increasingly successful.

IMPLICATIONS AND APPLICATIONS

CHAPTER 11

THE SELECTION OF SENSITIVE PEOPLE

SOME persons are much more sensitive than others. Techniques for identifying these gifted persons would be of great value in selecting clinical psychologists, psychiatrists, social workers, and, indeed, workers in most fields. Furthermore, the identification of such persons would allow us to study their methods and to communicate them to others. Promising sensitivity and personality tests are already available and the methods for improving them, though laborious, are clear. As yet, however, no one has used such tests in any practical way. The immediate reason is the lack of adequate tests to use. But the reason there are none is the lack of interest in their development.

Among college students, "understanding" rates only a half-step behind "sincere" and "honest" and ahead of "trustworthy," "dependable," and "intelligent" (Anderson, 1968). Almost all students check it as a trait that is characteristic of them. No one wants to find out that he is in the fifth percentile in understanding. Testers are also as reluctant to inform others that they lack understanding as that they lack intelligence.

Furthermore, we do not feel the need of a test to tell us what we think we can see with our own eyes. Our impressions and our predictions about a person reflect our perceptions. We do not have an opinion about a person; we have a perception of him, i.e., we "see" him for what he is. It is hard for us to believe that what we see in him could be wrong. For us, it is the reality about him. We resist empirical evidence of our insensitivity because we really cannot believe it.

The professional resists the development and use of empirical measures of sensitivity because he feels he already has a valid measure, i.e., the estimates of experts of a person's understanding. Yet, as we have seen, a judge's estimate of how well a therapist understands his client has no relation to how well the client thinks the therapist understands him.

Fish (1970) has provided a simple explanation for this confusion. He had judges listen to the tapes of twenty-four counseling interviews and rate the degree of empathy that the therapist had with the client. He also had each client rate how well his therapist understood him. As usual, there was no correlation between therapist understanding as rated by the judges and as rated by the clients ($r =$ .03). In another part of the study, each therapist was rated on how much he talked about physical symptoms accompanying emotional states, how much about behavior accompanying them, how much about sensory qualities associated with them, etc. Result: the less the therapist talked about sensations in relation to his emotions, the less empathic the judge rated him. For the client, the more the therapist talked about physical symptoms, the less empathic the client rated him. The ratings of both judges and clients seem to have nothing to do with how the therapist was relating to the client or how sensitive he was to him. Ratings of empathy were correlated with his "empathic style." Fish concludes: "It would follow that therapists could be trained directly in this verbal style, just as it is easy to train them in the monotonous patter of hypnosis." Our ratings of understanding, then, are not ratings of actual understanding. Rather, they are ratings of whether an individual has the traits and talks as we think an understanding person would. Furthermore, we differ in what traits we think an understanding person has and how we think he talks. Such ratings are not an adequate substitute for empirical measures of sensitivity.

TESTS OF SENSITIVITY

Without measures of sensitivity, as we said in Chapter 1, we cannot select those who need training, design programs to meet the need, give trainees knowledge of the progress they are making, or evaluate the effectiveness of the training they have had. We, therefore, raised the necessary questions involved in developing such measures: How should the person to be predicted be presented to the predictors? What kinds of predictions should they be asked to make? How should they record their predictions? And, most important of all, how can the goodness of the developed measures be determined? The same questions apply to the selection of sensitive people.

In answering these questions, we advocated a component view that required independent measures of observational, theoretical, nomothetic, and idiographic sensitivity. The view assumes that sensitivity is not just a difficult ability, but an ability that is a product of different and sometimes conflicting skills. It is not a 100-meter dash but a decathlon. Performance in the decathlon depends upon ability in the 100-meter dash and the 1,500-meter run, in the long jump and the high jump, in the discus throw and the javelin throw, and in the shot put and the pole vault. Similar abilities are required in throwing events, and different and somewhat conflicting abilities in running events. Overall, though, outstanding performance in one event compensates for mediocre performance in others. In a similar way, the requirements for being an astute observer may conflict with those for being an intuitive theoretician. But the person who observes everything has less need for theory, and the master of theories has less need for observations. In general, however, those who are gifted in their understanding of people are at least above average on all of the components.

The problem of selection can be approached directly by using tests of sensitivity; indirectly, by using measures of abilities, traits, or orientations that correlate with sensitivity. Shook (1971) explored both approaches. Consequently, it will be useful to consider his study and its results in each of these areas in relation to other findings. His subjects were twenty-six male and forty-one female undergraduate students who completed a large battery of sensitivity, ability, personality, and orientation tests.

Shook assumed that the best measure of sensitivity would be one which combined scores from tests of different components. As a measure of nomothetic sensitivity, he used the Men and Women Test (Table 8-1). He also used the Instructor Test (Table 10-2). This test involved the ability to apply the trait theory to an individual after weeks of exposure to him so that it combined elements of both theoretical and idiographic sensitivity.

He developed the Zolton Test (Table 11-1) to have a measure saturated with the observation component. Observational accuracy can be measured directly by testing how well a person can remember what he saw and heard. However, such measures have the weakness of stressing deliberate rather than incidental observation, the latter probably being closer to the core aspect of this component. The Zolton Test requires the respondent to make predictions, not to report observations. However, these predictions must be based on observations made about Zolton during a five-minute interview. The fact that the adjective alternatives in each question are roughly equated for social desirability reduces the influence of individual differences in level and spread of goodness ratings as well as the influence of nomothetic elements. Shook showed his students Zolton in a filmed test and also gave them the typescript of the filmed interview. In other studies, the test has been used with just the interview with comparable validities.

The intercorrelations between scores on the Men and Women, the Instructor, and the Zolton Tests supported the component view. Scores were independent of each other, the median correlation being .11. Raw scores on the three tests were translated into standard scores and then added. This composite measure of sensitivity, therefore, gave equal weight to the three different tests.

TABLE 11-1
The Zolton Test

Here is the typescript of a brief interview with Zolton, an unmarried man of twenty-one. After reading about Zolton make the predictions indicated in the instructions that follow the interview.

Psychologist:	"Just what sort of person are you?"
Zolton:	"Well, I guess an easy-going one. I'm easy to get along with."
Psychologist:	"Well, what else can you tell me about yourself?"
Zolton:	"Well, I guess that's about all. I have some temper—not much."
Psychologist:	"What would you consider to be your greatest personality handicap?"
Zolton:	"Well, I guess just paying attention when there are people talking to me. Just paying attention to them."
Psychologist:	"Do you have difficulty paying attention to people?"
Zolton:	"No, no, I don't have no difficulty, it's just that whenever I walk into a place, I just don't speak, I'm quiet."
Psychologist:	"Do you have difficulty making friends?"
Zolton:	"No, no, I don't find no difficulty making friends."
Psychologist:	"But to begin with, you feel a little reserved about it, is that it?"
Zolton:	"Yuh."
Psychologist:	"What sort of thing would cause you to lose your temper?
Zolton:	"Once in a great while. It has to be something pretty mean, I guess, or something pretty big. One I guess is just—I don't know—couldn't tell you that until I lost my temper. Well, for instance, my little brother taking off with my car."
Psychologist:	"That would make you unhappy?"
Zolton:	"Yuh."
Psychologist:	"What would you do if someone told a lie about you?"
Zolton:	"I guess that would make me a little sore too, if it wasn't true."
Psychologist:	"Would you go to the person and talk to him about it?
Zolton:	"I wouldn't do nothing. Just sort of keep it to myself."
Psychologist:	"Well, how would you feel and what would you do if someone gave you a million dollars?"
Zolton:	"I'd be pretty happy, I guess. I guess I've never thought about what I'd do with it. I'd spend it I guess."
Psychologist:	"What sort of things do you do in your spare time?"
Zolton:	"Oh, usually drive around; I like to drive around quite a bit."
Psychologist:	"Do you participate actively in any sports, or are you a spectator?"
Zolton:	"No, I participate in it. Basketball, for instance."
Psychologist:	"How important do you feel religion is to people in these times?"
Zolton:	"Yes, I really do think that religion is important, I don't know, I guess just being good, people go out, and that ain't so bad, just going out and partying, but after that, the way they gather . . ."
Psychologist:	"And you think that religion would affect that sort of thing?"
Zolton:	"I think so, because of conscience—people have a conscience, and that would be on it."
Psychologist:	"In what way is religion important to you?"
Zolton:	"I don't know, well, sometimes when you go out partying, you feel like doing something else, and yet you don't."
Psychologist:	"Because of your religion, is that it?"
Zolton:	"Uh-huh."

At three different times Zolton checked from the Gough Adjective Check List those adjectives that he considered self-descriptive. In each of the following groups of

TABLE 11-1, continued

adjectives Zolton checked *one* of the adjectives every time; the other two he never checked at all.

Mark on the separate answer sheet the number before the adjective that you think he chose in each group.

1.	(1) affectionate*	(2) clever	(3) autocratic
2.	(1) alert*	(2) inventive	(3) deceitful
3.	(1) aloof	(2) apathetic	(3) ambitious*
4.	(1) irresponsible	(2) opportunistic	(3) confident*
5.	(1) anxious*	(2) show-off	(3) self-centered
6.	(1) cautious*	(2) outgoing	(3) inhibited
7.	(1) pessimistic	(2) defensive*	(3) dissatisfied
8.	(1) wholesome	(2) considerate*	(3) conscientious
9.	(1) adventurous	(2) contented*	(3) insightful
10.	(1) obliging	(2) natural	(3) cooperative*
11.	(1) blustery	(2) boastful	(3) forgetful*
12.	(1) courageous*	(2) charming	(3) commonplace
13.	(1) complicated	(2) confused	(3) nervous*
14.	(1) curious*	(2) precise	(3) severe
15.	(1) jolly	(2) dependable*	(3) idealistic
16.	(1) unassuming	(2) stable	(3) forgiving*
17.	(1) shy*	(2) dreamy	(3) reflective
18.	(1) irritable	(2) silent*	(3) preoccupied
19.	(1) evasive	(2) stubborn*	(3) shallow
20.	(1) generous*	(2) versatile	(3) quick
21.	(1) fault-finding	(2) hardheaded*	(3) rattlebrained
22.	(1) natural	(2) outgoing	(3) honest*
23.	(1) absent-minded*	(2) sulky	(3) thankless
24.	(1) coarse	(2) arrogant*	(3) hostile
25.	(1) high-strung	(2) peculiar	(3) changeable*
26.	(1) modest*	(2) formal	(3) inhibited
27.	(1) discreet	(2) peaceable*	(3) foresighted
28.	(1) stable	(2) sincere*	(3) unaffected
29.	(1) awkward	(2) impatient	(3) moody*
30.	(1) quarrelsome*	(2) cynical	(3) deceitful
31.	(1) hasty	(2) indifferent	(3) timid*
32.	(1) conscientious	(2) individualistic	(3) understanding*

*Indicates correct answer.

The subtests have unsatisfactory reliabilities. While the Men and Women Test had an internal consistency of .71, the consistency of the Instructor Test was .59 and the Zolton Test only .53. The effort to increase reliabilities in such measures should be vigorously pursued in order to eliminate questions that are too easy, too hard, or too ambiguous.

However, low internal consistency does not inevitably mean that the test has no validity. For example, scores of beginning clinical graduate students on a sensitivity test of near-zero reliability correlated more highly with later success as a clinical psychologist than other measures having much higher reliabilities (Kelly and Fiske, 1951). The explanation lies in the homogeneity or heterogeneity of parts of the test. The test of highest reliability is one that is completely homogeneous, i.e., every item is a repetition of the first item. The test of lowest reliability is completely heterogeneous, i.e., every item in the test measures something completely different from every other one. However, a test can be completely heterogeneous and yet have high validity if every one of the independent items is really measuring a different aspect of one thing. The components of sensitivity illustrate exactly this point on a larger scale, i.e., they are completely independent of each other, but each measures a different aspect of the same thing—sensitivity.

A test does not have validity; it has validities. The validity of a measure is determined by the degree to which it measures what it is assumed to measure. A test, however, may be assumed to measure quite different things, and these assumptions may vary in their validity. Thus it might be assumed that composite scores on the Shook battery are a valid predictor of a personnel interviewer's ability to assess job candidates, of a squad leader's knowledge of his men, of a therapist's understanding of his client, and of a husband's understanding of his wife. One of these assumptions might have no validity; another, a little; and still another, a lot.

Who do you want to understand what about whom? The answer determines what test of validity is to be made. We want, for example, first-grade teachers to understand first-graders. A test of general sensitivity like the Shook battery might be valid for this purpose. It is certain, however, that sensitivity tests designed for this specific purpose would be more valid. Such a battery might include a test of their accuracy in observing what six-year-olds looked like and said; a test of their ability to identify where a particular child stood in relation to his primary mental abilities; a test of their knowledge of the interests and attitudes of the typical six-year-old; and a test of their ability to learn about a child as the school year progressed.

The process of developing specific sensitivity tests is laborious: more films, more cases, more item analyses, and more checks of internal consistency. However, the tests would not only contribute to the selection of more sensitive people for specific situations but also clarify the goals and improve the methods of sensitivity training for specific situations. Thus teachers who do not pay attention to children need observational training; those who have a poor understanding of the typical child need nomothetic training; and those who do not continue to learn about their children need idiographic training.

Shook, however, was not only interested in developing tests of the components of sensitivity but also in exploring the correlates of sensitivity. For this purpose, he was striving to develop a test of sensitivity that was as general as possible.

PERSONALITY TESTS

If we knew the traits of the sensitive person, we could bypass the measurement of sensitivity. To find out the traits of the sensitive person, however, we need at least: (1) scores on an adequate test of sensitivity, (2) scores on possibly related personality traits, and (3) an adequate number of subjects for whom we have both so that relationships can be established between sensitivity and traits. Only a handful of studies have met these minimum requirements. Still, the consistency of findings provide a rough picture of the sensitive personality and hope that the details can soon be filled in.

Shook is the only investigator who has used component measures of sensitivity. Thus his results not only indicate some of the qualities of the generally sensitive person but also suggest some of the different qualities related to the different components of sensitivity.

Skill in Symbolic Representation

As a person matures, he becomes more skillful in repr esenting the psychological worlds of himself and others by symbols. His symbols may be words, numbers, maps, pictures, or music. Words, however, are the most common symbols used in forming impressions of people and making predictions about them. The adult is thus more sensitive to more things about others than is the child with his limited vocabulary. Since adults differ widely in their symbolic skills, we can safely assume that these differences are related to sensitivity.

Shook fully verified the assumption. As measures of symbolic skills, he used scores on an arithmetic test, a reading comprehension test, course grades based on objective tests, and a mathematics test. All were significantly related to the sensitivity scores of his sixty-five students: arithmetic (.46), reading (.45), course grade (.35), and mathematics (.25). While all the correlations with the three component tests were positive, only reading scores were significantly related to all three. The correlations were lowest with the Men and Women Test, though it was the most reliable of the component tests.

In general, measures of symbolic skill, particularly skill in the use of words, are the most certain correlates of sensitivity. Of more than two dozen studies relating sensitivity to various measures of symbolic skill done since 1915, all were positive and the median correlation was .30. It is evident that the use of an intelligence test stressing verbal comprehension as well as sensitivity tests would improve the process of selecting sensitive people. It is likely that such tests constructed around words used in describing and explaining people would have even higher validity.

Empiricism

The sixty-five students who took Shook's battery of sensitivity tests also completed the five trait scales measuring boldness, emotionality, practicality, future-mindedness, and empiricism (Table 5-1). Scores on these scales were correlated with each of the three component measures of sensitivity as well as with the composite score. None of the sensitivity measures were related to boldness, practicality, or future-mindedness scores. The more emotional scored lower on all the components, although the overall correlation was not significant ($-.19$). Only the rationalistic-versus-empirical scores were significantly related (.28), the nonconforming, independent, and religiously skeptical empiricists obtaining higher sensitivity scores.

The greater sensitivity of the empirical is supported by a variety of other studies. Johnson (1963) found that liberalism was the only one of twenty-four traits related to a composite measure of nomothetic sensitivity. Grossman (1963) found those who had the highest readiness for change and the most humanitarian religious values were highest in idiographic sensitivity. Cline (1955), using films to present the persons to be judged, found antifascistic, tolerant, and liberal scales most highly related to sensitivity. Both Jacoby (1971) and Gabennesch and Hunt (1971) found that the open-minded and nonauthoritarian were more sensitive than the closed-minded and authoritarian.

The Sensitive Pattern

The items in the Sensitive Pattern (Table 11-2) result from a quite different approach to defining the sensitive personality. Instead of correlating scores on broad traits each of which consists of a cluster of sub-traits, this approach seeks specific questions which sensitive persons consistently answer differently from the insensitive. The author felt that an examination of such discriminating items might give a clearer picture of the personality structure of the sensitive person.

Three independent groups were employed. Each group was tested by several measures of sensitivity, the measures varying from group to group. The first group of several hundred students answered the

200 statements of the five trait scales (Table 5-1). From them, twenty-five were selected who did consistently well. Each of the twenty-five was matched for sex and intelligence with a student who did consistently poorly. The answers of the low and high group to each statement were compared and the fifty most discriminating items selected. A second group answered these fifty statements and completed a second battery of sensitivity tests. Low and high sensitivity groups were again matched for sex and intelligence and the discriminating value of the fifty statements again compared. A third group completed the thirty-six statements that retained their discriminating value in the second group, and took a third battery of sensitivity tests. A low and high group were again separated, but this time the individuals were *not matched* for sex and intelligence. The twenty items that most discriminated in this final analysis are those shown in Table 11-2, arranged under the trait scale from which they are derived.

TABLE 11-2
The Sensitive Pattern

Three large groups of students answered the items from the same personality inventory but completed different tests of Sensitivity to People. Those who scored high on these sensitivity tests consistently answered the items below differently from those who scored low. The statements are arranged under the trait scales in which they appear. The answers in parentheses were given more often by the sensitive group.

Cautious vs. Bold

(F)   1. Some people can look forward to a happier life than I can.
(T)   2. I am extremely active in my everyday life.
(F)   3. I am somewhat more shy than the average person.
(F)   4. I have quite a few fears about my future.
(T)   5. I am always taking on added social responsibility.
(T)   6. I am quite self-confident.

Emotional vs. Calm

(F)   7. I have sometimes corrected others, not because they were wrong, but only because they irritated me.
(F)   8. I am seldom excited or thrilled.

Artistic vs. Practical

(F)   9. In a discussion, I tend to lose interest if we talk about serious literature.
(T) 10. Artistic experiences are of great importance in my life.
(T) 11. I am more interested in general ideas than specific facts.

Present-Minded vs. Future-Minded

(T) 12. I am not particularly methodical in my everyday life.
(T) 13. I always keep control of myself in an emergency situation.

TABLE 11-2, continued

(F)   14. I really don't like to drink alcoholic beverages.
(T)   15. I almost never lose my head.
(F)   16. I consider most matters very carefully before I form an opinion.
(T)   17. I am a fairly impulsive person.

Rationalistic vs. Empirical

(F)   18. It is as important for a person to be reverent as it is for him to be sympathetic.
(T)   19. Compared to your own self-respect, the respect of others means little.
(T)   20. Radical agitators should be encouraged to make public speeches.

What do these twenty independent clues say about the person who is generally a good predictor of others? They strongly suggest, first of all, that the sensitive are bold, but with a powerful reservation. "Boldness" is defined and measured by an interrelated cluster of traits: dominance, self-confidence, optimism, physical energy, and gregariousness. Dominance is the central trait in this cluster and accounts for twelve of the forty items in the scale: "I enjoy speaking in public," "I have frequently assumed the leadership of groups," etc. Yet answers to none of these statements separate the sensitive from the insensitive. The sensitive are energetic, self-confident, and optimistic; they are not dominating or gregarious. They do not submit or dominate, run or fight; they interact. The pattern also strongly suggests that the sensitive are able to pay attention to others because they are not chronically preoccupied with their own inner conflicts and fears.

The sensitive are present-minded, but with even more reservations. The present-minded are unambitious, unorganized, and impulsive; the future-minded, ambitious, organized, and controlled. Ambition is the central trait in this cluster, accounting for fifteen of the forty statements: "I set very difficult goals for myself," "I am extremely ambitious," etc. None of these statements, however, separated the sensitive from the insensitive. Again, the impulsive statements in the scale indicate that the impulsive have difficulty concentrating and are likely to lose their head in an emergency. Statements of the former type do not distinguish the sensitive, and they answer statements of the latter type in the reverse direction, i.e., the sensitive do *not* lose their head in an emergency. Rather, they seem especially capable of focusing upon another person in an open-minded and flexible way.

The items from the empirical scale indicate that the sensitive person is open-minded, independent, and concerned about people. In sum, the pattern suggests that he is active, serious, attentive, and has a realistic concern for others.

The twenty items have incapacitating limitations as a device for the selection of the sensitive. The relatively few items in the scale have a low internal consistency. As a consequence, the range of scores on the scale is small. Practically, the scale might be used to eliminate the few who would score very low on it (five or less in the sensitive direction) or to chose the very few who would score high (fifteen or more). However, the scale is best viewed as a starting point for the development of measures that would focus on these apparently central aspects of the sensitive person.

Psychological Differentiation

The sensitive are intelligent empiricists. Sensitivity, however, involves the abilities to observe, to theorize, to accumulate knowledge about, and to grow in understanding of *people*. The orientations that one takes toward people, therefore, should be most directly related to how well one understands them and should have value for the selection of sensitive people. In fact, a variety of orientation tests that seem to be related to sensitivity have already been introduced and discussed.

The Test of Perceptual Style (Table 4-2) asks the respondent to choose from two possible impressions, one observational ("wearing a coat") and one emotional ("is sincere") the statement that was more like their impression of the two persons shown in silent colored films. Differences in scores are wide and reliable, indicating that some people consistently perceive a dominating affective and expressive quality in people while the perceptions of others are relatively unemotional and factual.

The Orientation Test (Table 6-3) asks the respondent to choose from two possible reactions the one he thinks each individual did have. One alternative was self-oriented, indicating that the person was wondering what the other person was thinking of him. The second alternative was other-oriented, indicating that the person was thinking about what the other person was thinking of himself. Since the persons and incidents in the test are ambiguous, it is assumed that the respondent will project his own dominantly self-oriented or other-oriented attitudes into the situation.

The Consideration and Responsibility Test (Table 9-1) asks the respondent to choose from two possible things that a leader might do, the one that he thinks is more important. In the consideration scale, one alternative indicates that the leader is primarily oriented toward the worker and his problems while the other indicates that he is oriented toward the work and getting it done. In the responsibility scale, one alternative indicates that the leader is oriented toward playing the same role as his followers while the other indicates that he is oriented toward playing a differentiated role, i.e., guiding the workers and planning and organizing their work.

Are these orientations related to sensitivity? Shook (1971) administered the battery of tests to his sixty-five students in less than an hour. He correlated scores on each as well as the composite score on all of them to his measures of sensitivity. The pattern of correlates varied with the particular orientation and the particular test. Thus the perceptual style scores were most highly related to scores on the Zolton Test; the Orientation Test to scores on the Men and Women Test; the Consideration Scale to scores on the Instructor Test; and the Responsibility Scale to scores on the Zolton Test. This shifting pattern was to be expected, for scores on the sensitivity tests are independent of each other. Furthermore, scores on the orientation scales were also independent, except that those who delegate responsibility tend to play an undifferentiated role.

However, the correlation between the composite measure of general sensitivity with the composite measure of orientation was .30. Thus scores on the latter test could be used as a predictor of sensitivity. Its usefulness is enhanced for selection purposes because of its independence of other possible predictors of sensitivity. Thus neither the separate orientation measures nor the composite score were related to any of the measures of symbolic skill (course grade, reading comprehension, arithmetic, and mathematics). Nor were the orientation measures related to scores on the empiricism scale. Thus the composite orientation score would add a new element to a predictive battery that included a measure of intelligence and a measure of empiricism.

Scores on the perceptual style, self-other orientation, consideration, and responsibility scales are almost independent. Is it possible, however, that all of them are related to differences in some more fundamental orientation? If so, might measures of this orientation lead to a better understanding of sensitivity as well as a better selection of sensitive people in the future? Variations in the psychological differentiation of "self" from "other" and their measurement may be the positive answer to both of these questions.

The theory of psychological differentiation proposed by Witkin (1965) conceives of differences in perception as dominated by a field dependence-independence dimension. The field dependent mode of perception is dominated by the overall organization of the field, with the parts of the perceptual field "fused." In a field independent mode of perceiving, parts of the field are experienced as discrete. Considerable evidence supports the conclusion that a tendency toward one or the other ways of perceiving is a pervasive characteristic of an individual's perception. For example, field-independent individuals have greater articulation of body concept than do field-dependent individuals. This and other evidence suggesting the generality of the field dependence–independence dimension leads Witkin to the following conclusion:

. . . at one extreme there is a consistent tendency for experience to be global and diffuse—the organization of the field as a whole dictates the manner in which its parts are experienced. At the other extreme there is a tendency for experience to be delineated and structured—parts of a field are experienced as discrete and the field as a whole organized. To the opposite poles of the cognitive style we may apply the labels "global" and "articulated."

Do the "global" types who have difficulty differentiating themselves from the physical world also have difficulty differentiating themselves from other people? Wegner (1971) reviewed evidence that they do. Field-dependent people are more submissive, more conforming, and more attentive to others. He himself found that those who do not differentiate the parts of the physical world do not differentiate between themselves and others. He gave sixty-three undergraduates three tests of field dependence (the Embedded Figures Test, the Closure Flexibility Test, and the Block Design Test). He also gave them two tests of their tendency to differentiate between themselves and others. One of these was the Empathy Test (Table 3-2). The other utilized a list of fifteen roles from the Role Construct Repertory Test (Kelly, 1955). The students were first asked to fill in the name of a personal acquaintance who fitted each role definition. He was then asked to name those who were similar to him and those who were dissimilar to him. The total number listed as dissimilar was the measure of self-other differentiation.

The internal consistency of the Empathy Test was .64; of the Role Similarity Form, .28. The two tests were positively but not significantly correlated. In spite of these attenuating facts, scores on both tests of self-other differentiation were related to all three tests of field dependence–independence, significantly in four out of six comparisons. That is, those who had difficulty differentiating themselves from the physical world also had difficulty differentiating their feelings and thoughts from the feelings and thoughts of other people. Global perceivers of the world are global perceivers of others; perceivers of the world are articulated perceivers of others.

Those who find it hard to differentiate themselves from the physical world also find it hard to differentiate themselves from other people. How are these two kinds of differentiation related to sensitivity? Wegner related measures of both kinds of differentiation to accuracy scores on the Empathy Test (Table 3–2). He found that the *less* people differentiated between themselves and others, the *more* accurate they were (r-.38). However, those who obtained average scores in field independence were significantly more accurate than those who obtained either low or high scores. It seems that those who see only small differences between themselves and others are more likely to pay attention to and to observe others than those who see large differences. On the other hand, the extremely field dependent may find it hard to find differences between themselves and others while the extremely field independent may find it hard to find similarities. From the point of selecting sensitive people, these results suggest the desirability of eliminating both the extremely dependent and the extremely independent.

THE SELECTION OF TRAINEES

If we could select people who are already gifted in their sensitivity, we would not need to go to the expense of sensitivity training. In any training program, some learn and some do not. If we selected trainees who would benefit from training, a great deal of fruitless effort would also be saved. In general, we don't try. Students in psychology classes are not selected for their ability to learn about people, for the development of sensitivity is never an important goal of the training. Graduate training in clinical psychology aims to improve sensitivity, but students are selected on the basis of their undergraduate grade-point average, their scholastic aptitude and their Graduate Record scores.

In contrast, the T-group movement has directed considerable effort at solving the selection problem. However, it is a complex one, as the following summary of the research evidence by Stock (1964, p. 434) indicates:

> What the individual is like when he comes to the laboratory seems to have a great deal to do with the learnings he takes away with him. In separate studies, Stock and Mathis suggest that conflict or some internal awareness of lack of fit or consistency have something to do with readiness for learning. But Watson, et al. suggested that there is some ceiling on this: highly anxious persons learn little. Consistent with this, Harrison has hypothesized that individuals so threatened by confrontation with dissonance that they must defend against it with rejection of the laboratory, distortion, and so on, are likely to close themselves off from opportunities to learn. Miles, too, found that threat-oriented individuals were less receptive to feedback of certain kinds. Mathis suggests that tendencies toward pairing and flight make for readiness to learn, while tendencies toward dependency and flight work against learning. This seems consistent with some of the findings of Watson, et al. that responsive, outgoing persons are more likely to apply laboratory learnings. Miles found that the personality characteristics of ego strength, flexibility, and need-affiliation are relevant in that they facilitated unfreezing, involvement, and the reception of feedback, and these in turn influenced learning.

Self-selection is the easiest answer to the selection question. Yet there is no evidence that those who select themselves for training learn any more than those assigned to training by force or chance. Miles (1960), for example, found no relationship between interest in attending T-group training and improvement as a result of training: "If anything the relationship was inverse . . . a high wish to change in this sample was a kind of defense protestation." In a classroom setting, Spier (1969) found no relationship between subjective estimates of improvement by trainees and objective measures of their actual improvement in a nomothetic training program.

It is by no means evident that selecting as trainees those who score high on sensitivity tests is a valid way of picking good learners. Mietus (1969) found that trainees who were in the lowest third at the beginning of training improved the most; those in the middle third improved only half as much; and those in the top third did not improve at all. Spier (1969) found correlations ranging from −.40 to −.68 between initial score and improvement. The most likely explanation is the low ceiling of the tests, i.e., the criteria provide too little room for the improvement of the best. It may be that trainees who are informed that they are good to begin with have too little motivation to improve. It may also be that the training method informs the poor trainees of things that the good ones already know. At any rate, present tests of initial sensitivity are no good for the selection of those who will benefit the most from sensitivity training.

Assume, however, that trainees are equally sensitive at the beginning. What are the qualities of those who improve the most? Trying to answer the question, we began with more than a hundred students in a 1967 program. Their improvement was determined by noting their gains on a measure of general sensitivity given before and after the training. Each member of a group of twenty-five who improved a great deal during the training was matched with one of the same sex and intelligence who improved little but who had the *same* pretest score. All the students completed the five-trait inventory (Table 5-1). Items that discriminated between improvers and nonimprovers in both the first and second programs were given to a third group in 1969. The procedure was again repeated.

The Good-learner Scale (Table 11-3) includes the twenty-five statements that improvers in all three groups answered in the same way and differently from nonimprovers. The items are placed under the trait scale from which they were derived. Under each trait, they are arranged in the order of their discriminating value.

TABLE 11-3
The Good-learner Scale

Three large groups of students answered items from the same personality inventory but participated in different training programs. *Those who improved during these programs consistently answered the items below differently from those who did not improve.* Since each of the trait scales has forty items, the number of discriminating items from a scale suggests the relative importance of that trait in learning to improve sensitivity. The answers in parentheses are those given more often by the improvers.

Cautious vs. Bold

(T)   1. I am seldom the center of attention in a group.
(F)   2. I enjoy speaking in public.

TABLE 11-3, continued

Emotional vs. Calm

(T)   3. I find that my life moves along at an even tenor without many ups and downs.
(T)   4. I usually do things in a leisurely sort of way, seldom getting excited.
(F)   5. I am moderate in my tastes and sentiments.
(F)   6. I experience frequent pleasant and unpleasant moods.
(T)   7. I have sometimes got so angry that I feel like throwing and breaking things.
(T)   8. I almost always do about as well as I expected in competition.

Artistic vs. Practical

(F)   9. I would particularly enjoy meeting people who have made a success in business.
(F)   10. I would rather see a movie than read a book.
(F)   11. I am an extremely practical person.
(F)   12. I am really only interested in what is useful.
(F)   13. I can deal much better with actual situations than with ideas.
(T)   14. Some of my friends think my ideas are a bit wild and impractical.
(T)   15. I like ballet performances.

Present-Minded vs. Future-Minded

(F)   16. I believe that what a person does about a thing is more important than what he feels about it.
(F)   17. I keep my workplace very neat and orderly.
(F)   18. I always keep control of myself in an emergency situation.
(T)   19. I like to be with people who are not preoccupied with the future.
(F)   20. I am not particularly methodical in my daily life.

Rationalistic vs. Empirical

(F)   21. My faith in God is complete for "though he slay me, yet will I trust him."
(F)   22. I consider the close observance of social customs and manners as an essential aspect of life.
(T)   23. I believe that we should have less censorship of speech and press than we do now.
(F)   24. A person should develop his greatest loyalty toward his religious faith.
(F)   25. The thought of God gives me a complete sense of security.

The unobtrusiveness of the good learner (items 1 and 2) probably is a product of the large college classes from which all the data were collected. By contrast, Cline and Richards (1959) found that the best learners in a T-group setting described themselves and were described by other members as egotistical and conceited. Learning about people in many settings requires boldness—a willingness to approach people, ask questions, and express feelings.

The calm and realistic, though not bovine, qualities of the good learner (items 3 through 8) are probably more general, for they suggest the perspective of those with an observational style. The artistic view consistently dominates the perspective of the good learner (items 9 through 15). The composite sketch of those with superior aesthetic judgment reported by Child (1965) also seems to fit those who improve with training:

> ... A person of actively inquiring mind, seeking out experience, that may be challenging because of complexity or novelty, ever alert to the potential experience offered by stimuli not already in the focus of attention, interested in understanding each experience thoroughly and for its own sake rather than contemplating it superficially and promptly filing it away in a category, and able to do all this with respect to the world inside himself as well as the world outside.

The minor signs of impulsivity in the good learner (items 16 through 20) may reflect the degree of flexibility and attentiveness to the learning setting required to learn new things about people. The empirical not only are more sensitive to begin with but also learn more than the rationalistic. This commonality probably accounts for the fact that the Good Learner Scale correlates ($r = .45$) with the pattern (Table 11-2) of traits characterizing the sensitive person. Good learners also seem to be more psychologically differentiated, for scores on the scale also negatively correlate with the empathic personality scale (Table 3-3).

The scale for selecting trainees has the merits of being empirically derived and of having a five-minute test time. It has the demerits of narrow range, low reliability, and inadequate trial.

Anthony and Wain (1971) suggest a quite different approach to the selection problem. Their trainees were thirty-one Army medical corpsmen who completed eight hours of role playing designed to increase their sensitivity. Two methods were used to predict how well they would do in training. The first required them to respond in writing to fifteen taped remarks of patients. Their responses were rated for empathy and correlated with their post-training scores. Result: $r = .45$. The second method involved rating the trainees after the first forty-five minutes of training. These ratings were much more highly correlated with post-training sensitivity ($r = .61$). Conclusion: "The ability to take tests may predict the ability to take more tests; the ability to profit from empathy training may predict the ability to profit from further empathy training." The method is simple and practical and has wide generality. It involves giving all applicants a bit of training and then selecting those who do well for more training. The problems in application are only administrative: What is to be done with the trainees who are rejected for further training?

CHAPTER 12
REVIEW AND PREVIEW

WE HAVE NOW looked at the details of a component approach to sensitivity. How did this approach arise? Every type of training involves a method, has a theoretical basis, and is directed at solving a learning problem. Each, however, has its own origins and focus. Most center upon a method. Thus the T group began with the method of unstructured interactions in small groups and has only recently become concerned with articulating a theory about it and defining the problems it can solve. Many center upon a theory. Thus programmed learning is a new by-product of an old behavior theory. The present approach began with a problem: objective evaluations invariably showed that no type of training had any measurable influence on the development of sensitivity. It was only after several decades of tinkering with methods of solving this problem that the component theory was formulated. Consequently, the principles and actions summarized in this chapter are viewed as only promising steps toward the solution of the basic problem of developing the ability to understand people.

PRINCIPLES OF SENSITIVITY TRAINING

Our theme has been that the failures of T groups, psychology instruction, and clinical training arise from a fogginess about what sensitivity is, why it develops, and how it can be increased by training. As a consequence there has been much talk of means, little of ends; much discussion of training methods, little of training goals. The principles that we have discussed have tried to clarify these goals.

Concentrate on Sensitivity as a Goal

The goal of sensitivity training, we have emphasized, should be the development of sensitivity: to improve the trainee's ability to predict the feelings, thoughts, and behavior of other people. Thus the degree to which a trainee feels close to and sympathetic with others is only considered as a means, or an obstacle, to achieving this end. The degree to which he is aware of the visual, audible, and tangible aspects of a person are also only seen as a means to it. And the degree of his practical influence over others is not viewed as an end but as one possible test of his sensitivity.

The goal is a scientific one, for it aims at stabilizing and consolidating the trainee's perceptions, thoughts, and predictions about people. The ability to take a scientific view has been a late step in man's mental development and is a refined product that only develops under special conditions. Consequently, predictive accuracy as a goal is hard to grasp and to accept.

By contrast, rationalistic understanding as a goal is easily understood and accepted. Everyone enjoys feeling close to others. They like to feel sympathy for others and to feel that others sympathize with them. They want to feel that they understand others and that others understand them. The desire for rationalistic understanding and the ability to experience it appears to be one of the firmest foundations of both primitive and advanced religions.

Empirical and rationalistic understanding are two entirely different kinds of thinking. People who are dominantly empirical and those who are dominantly rationalistic don't like each other, as William James (1955, pp. 22–23) was well aware:

> They have a low opinion of each other. . . . Their mutual reaction is very much like that that takes place when Bostonian tourists mingle with a population like that of Cripple Creek. Each type believes the other to be inferior to itself; but disdain in the one case is mingled with amusement, in other, it has a dash of fear.

Rationalistic and empirical understanding have different goals and are achieved by different means. Man, however, has and needs both kinds. Furthermore, sensitivity depends upon rationalistic understanding, for without some consideration or responsibility toward another person, man has no effective motive for becoming sensitive to him. However, rationalistic understanding does not depend upon sensitivity. It is possible to feel very close to and sympathetic with a person and to be insensitive to him, i.e., to have little or no ability to predict what he is feeling and thinking or what he will do next.

As a scientist, the psychologist has no alternative except to pursue the goal of sensitivity, for predictive accuracy is the only test of scientific understanding. Rationalistic understanding develops naturally in relationships with parents, friends, spouse, children, and fellow workers. The development of sensitivity requires effective training.

Analyze the Goal into Components

Once the empirical understanding of a person is clearly separated from an artistic, practical, and, particularly, rationalistic understanding of him, the question becomes: Is sensitivity one component or many? A component is a separable part of a whole that fits with other parts to determine the whole. We concluded that there were at least four such components of sensitivity:

Observational sensitivity: The ability to look at and listen to another person and remember what he looked like and said.

Theoretical sensitivity: The ability to select and use theories to make more accurate predictions about others.

Nomothetic sensitivity: The ability to learn about the typical member of a group and to use this knowledge in making more accurate predictions about individuals in that group.

Idiographic sensitivity: The ability to use increasing exposure to and information about a person in making increasingly accurate predictions about him.

Training has to begin at some point with some specific goal. In a sense, therefore, if there were no components they would have to be invented. There is, however, considerable evidence of the existence and independence of these component abilities. Tests measuring each of them show wide and reliable individual differences, but scores on these tests are unrelated to each other. Furthermore, the components fit recognizable and traditional training patterns.

Specify Goals for Each Component

How is the ability to make observations, to use theories, to learn about groups, and to learn about others in intimate relationships to be developed? We have examined the nature of person perception for hints about observational training, mythic versus scientific thinking for hints about theoretical training, group perception for hints about nomothetic training, and the process by which understanding develops for hints about idiographic training. The search concluded with a statement of four specific training goals.

The goal of observational training should be to develop the trainee's ability to discriminate sensory from expressive qualities. The critical problem in observational training is not that we make poor observations that lead to faulty inferences; it is that we do not make observations or inferences at all. We do not merely see or hear a person, we perceive a quality in the person (Chapter 3). This quality is not an appendage to a perception that is added and that can be subtracted. It is not the result of an intellectual process; it is an original and central part of perceptual experience. We do not see a redhead and hear a loud voice; we perceive an "interesting," "intelligent," and "level-headed" person or one who is "narrow-minded," "irritating," and "insincere."

The expressive quality that a person has for us dominates our perceptions of him. The quality, however, is far from constant. The person we perceive as friendly one minute may be seen as unfriendly the next. Furthermore, different people looking at the same person may perceive entirely different qualities, one perceiving him as "friendly" and the other as "unfriendly." What the person actually looked like and said is remembered, forgotten, or distorted to fit the expressive quality that we almost instantly perceive. These complex and fluctuating expressive qualities are dominated by their position on a good-bad dimension. In turn, the position of the quality on this dimension is heavily influenced by empathy, i.e., by the degree to which we see a person as like or unlike us.

This quality is not felt to be merely an inference, an attitude, or an opinion about a person. It is a perception of him. To the perceiver, nothing is more "real" about another person than his expressive quality. From the point of view of sensitivity, nothing is less real. The power of those qualities leads to endless erroneous predictions about how the other person feels about himself, how he feels about others, and how he will behave. The quality perceived is an undecipherable interaction between the visual and auditory cues given out by the perceived and the feelings projected into him.

It is the fundamental task of sensitivity training to develop the trainee's ability to discriminate between sensory cues and expressive qualities. For diagnosing a trainee's observational problems, giving him feedback during training, and evaluating the effectiveness of training itself, it is essential that useful measures of observational accuracy be developed. Trainees do differ markedly in their pretraining ability to make such discriminations. It is relatively easy to make trainees momentarily aware of the difference between sensory and expressive qualities. It is more difficult and more important to train him to play the observer role with skill. It is still more difficult to train him to maintain this role in stressful interpersonal reactions.

The goal of theoretical training should be to develop the trainee's ability to use other-oriented and empirically derived theories. Chapter 5 contrasted the differences between mythic and scientific theories. Mythic theories reflect perceptions of inner states; scientific theories, perceptions of the outer world. Mythic concepts are as vague and fluid as the emotional states they reflect. Scientific concepts, on the other hand, are explicit, stable, and measurable. The concepts of mythic theories are intimately interdependent, one being readily substituted for others. The concepts of scientific theories are autonomous and related to each other in formal and explicit ways.

Chapter 5 also reviewed the evidence that trained psychologists are no more sensitive than those who are not trained and that psychologists cannot beat the sensitivity of their own empirically derived instruments. Analyses of the processes by which the trained and the untrained make predictions about others show that both go through identical processes and make identical kinds of mythical errors. The most obvious of these processes is the use of "illusory correlations," i.e., assuming that things are related which are, in fact, not related.

The best way out of this impasse is to stress theories that have characteristics that lead to predictive accuracy. One of these characteristics is the "other-orientation" of a theory, i.e., the degree to which it is ultimately tested by what the other person says about himself rather than by what the theorizer thinks he is "really" like. Most dynamic theories violate this criterion, for they are based on the assumption that what the person says about himself is hopelessly distorted by his repressions and other mechanisms. However, the judgments of the psychologist of what a person is like seem to be as hopelessly distorted by the psychologist's own mechanisms. Regardless of the details of other-oriented theories, they all force their user to take the point of view of the person he is trying to understand.

A second characteristic of a useful theory is that it be empirically derived. A trait that is a generalization covering specific differences in the way people describe themselves is an example of such a theory. However, a trait approach requires the use of specific traits that fit the particular kinds of people the trainees want to understand. A trait that would be helpful for mothers trying to understand their children would not be for graduate students trying to understand hospitalized patients. In general, the traits must be derived from particular groups. They cannot be effortlessly deduced from a master theory.

Whether other-oriented and empirically derived trait theories are better, in the absolute, than other kinds is uncertain. It is certain, however, that they have immense advantages in training. Their narrowness permits the setting of limited but realistic theoretical training goals. These goals can be more readily communicated than the more abstract goals of comprehensive theoretical "systems." The stress upon the other person's impressions of himself provide valuable and practical measures of predictive accuracy. These, in turn, facilitate the giving of feedback to trainees.

It is easy to learn a theory. It is hard to use it to increase sensitivity. For example, strenuous practice and feedback on a simple trait theory resulted in only modest improvements (Chapter 6). Trainees resist substituting the neutral traits of empirical theories for the emotionally loaded traits of their mythic theories. The influence of goodness and empathy remain powerful and training techniques need to be devised to reduce their influence.

The goal of nomothetic training should be to develop the trainee's ability to differentiate himself accurately from others. We form impressions of groups as we form them of individuals: we form an instant whole impression, we differentiate within this whole, but the whole is dominated by the expressive quality that the group has for us. As with individual impressions, the goodness in group impressions is largely determined by the empathy we have with the group.

Empathy is the degree of similarity we assume between ourselves and a group. But how do we make such assumptions? Lipps (Cassirer, 1957) in 1905 answered, "The other psychological individual is . . . made by myself out of myself. His inner being is taken from mine." The fundamental error in his answer is that it accepts the splitting of reality into an outside and inside. It assumes that an individual can separate himself and others. The infant cannot. He only slowly and uncertainly learns to differentiate himself from others. Wegner (1971), for example, found wide differences even among college students in their differentiating tendencies and also found that these differences were related to their field independence, i.e., their ability to differentiate themselves from the physical world. Thus the major goal of training is not to train people to assume more similarity. Rather, it is to get them to assume less. More exactly, the goal is to develop the trainee's ability to discriminate the ways in which he is actually like and, more difficult, the ways in which he is not like an individual or another member of his group.

The problem of differentiating oneself from others seems to be a special case of the more general problem of differentiating oneself from one's group. The members of a group assume, without any particular thought, that they are like other members of their group; they assume that other members of the group are like them. When a group member knows what he is like, he assumes that other members are like him. When he knows what another member is like, he assumes that he is like that member. In general, the more closely he feels identified with the group, the more similarity he assumes; the less closely identified, the less similarity. At the negative extreme, he assumes no similarity to a member of an enemy group.

Nomothetic sensitivity is highly specific, i.e., the ability to differentiate accurately between the ways in which one is like and unlike one group is relatively independent of the ability to make this differentiation with other groups. Thus successful nomothetic training requires: (1) knowledge of what the typical member of a particular group is like (knowledge which is often hard to come by), (2) mastery of the knowledge by the trainee, and (3) skill in using the knowledge in making predictions about individuals in the group.

The goal of idiographic training should be to develop the trainee's ability to behave in ways that others perceive as considerate and responsible. Consideration is the degree to which a person understands and respects the rights and feelings of others; responsibility, the degree to which he feels and acts as if he were holding himself responsible for what happens in a situation or to a person. Chapter 9 reviews evidence that both the degree of considerate and responsible attitudes that a person reports as well as the degree that others perceive him to show are related to his sensitivity. It seems that we are best motivated to continue to learn about another person when we feel respect for him and accountable for what happens to him. Also, people reveal themselves when they perceive others as being considerate and responsible in their relationship with them.

All recognize the desirability of consideration and responsibility. What they do not recognize is that they often see themselves as behaving in considerate and responsible ways when others do not see them so. The chronic confusion arises from the fact that rationalistic and empirical understanding are so universally assumed to be merely two aspects of the same kind of understanding. When we feel we understand a person, we think we actually do. We often do not. Studies regularly show that how well a person feels he understands another individual has no relation to how well the individual feels understood or to how high independent judges rate his understanding.

The training solution is simple to state, painful to accept, and complicated in its application. It is to give trainees feedback on how considerate and responsible they are perceived to be by others. The solution may be particularly disturbing to the professional, for it takes a share of the assessment of his effectiveness out of his hands and puts it into the hands of his clients. The solution is complicated, for what is considerate and responsible behavior varies from person to person and from situation to situation. The successful effort of Daw and Gage (1967) in developing the considerate and responsible behavior of school principals shows that these complications can be solved. The study also provides a general model for their solution.

Sequence the Goals

What should be the first goal of training? The second? The third? We have assumed that training should begin at the beginning with the development of observational sensitivity, and proceed, in turn, to theoretical, nomothetic, and idiographic training. For the research psychologist, the question remains unanswered, for it remains unasked. No one has compared the effectiveness of various sequences of training.

For the trainer the question of sequencing may be answered by who he is to train, how long he will have to train them, and what physical and social setting he is to train them in. These conditions set severe limitations on what he can accomplish. Thus the realistic problem for the trainer is often not that of how to sequence a number of goals to be achieved. It is that of deciding which one is most likely to be achieved in the short time available.

Fit the Method to the Goal

The T group stresses the method of intense, unstructured interactions, the college class the lecture, and clinical training supervised practice. We have assumed, however, that the most effective method is one that is individually adapted to the achievement of a specific goal. Thus a comprehensive program would use a wide variety of methods. For example, the development of the ability to discriminate sensory from expressive qualities demands a method that exposes trainees to others under conditions of graded stress. The mastery of an empirical theory requires a combination of reading, lecture, discussion, considerable practice, and precise feedback. The development of an empirical understanding of groups can make effective use of programmed learning. The development of the ability to behave in considerate and responsible ways toward others demands relatively long and intimate contacts with others.

Observational, theoretical, nomothetic, and idiographic sensitivity are independent components. We cannot infer from their independence, however, that a training method that develops one of them will not have an influence on the development of the others. There may, in fact, be a master method to which all the methods may be subordinated. The Typical Case Method may be such a master method. However, the universality of a method cannot be assumed; it must be demonstrated. Until it is, it is prudent to assume that the development of sensitivity requires many methods.

Measure Goal Achievement

One psychology professor ends his objective examinations with the following question:

> The most universal, important, and difficult problem in any field of psychology involves the:
> (1) criterion, (2) criterion, (3) criterion, (4) criterion.

A criterion is a measure of goal achievement. If sensitivity as a goal is to have impact on training, it must be measured. The better the measure, the more successful the training is likely to be.

Criteria are necessary for activating the principle of feedback: the better training provides the trainee with knowledge of his successes and failures, the more likely he is to learn. Criteria are also necessary in formulating more realistic goals for training, sequencing these goals in the optimum manner, reducing the defensiveness of trainees, fitting training methods to the goal to be achieved, and evaluating the success of training.

If measurement is so good, why don't we have more of it? Considering the billions of dollars spent in teaching millions of students about psychology, the number of studies evaluating the consequences of this training are pitifully few. Considering the faith of many in the T-group method, their resistance to objective evaluation may seem surprising.

A comprehensive survey of the American educational system by several dozen authors showed that educational innovations are almost never evaluated on a systematic basis (Miles, 1964). They concluded that every educational researcher ought to spend his apprenticeship illuminating this text on parchment to hang over his desk:

> The creators of experimental programs have little question about the efficacy of the changes they have introduced. They know that the courses they have developed are the best possible under existing conditions; and in the light of this assumed fact, systematic evaluation seems superfluous.

If the creators do have doubts, then they and their students have fears. No teacher is hungry for proof that he has not taught; no student is hungry for proof that he has not learned.

THE T GROUP

The philosopher Whitehead in a statement in *The Aims of Education* (1929) said:

> In the history of education, the most striking phenomenon is that schools of learning, which at one epoch are alive with the ferment of genius, in a succeeding generation exhibit merely pedantry and routine. The reason is that they are overladen with inert ideas. Education with inert ideas is not only useless: it is, above all things, harmful—Corruptio optimi, pessima. Except at rare intervals of intellectual ferment, education in the past has been radically infected with inert ideas. That is the reason why uneducated clever women, who have seen much of the world, are in middle life so much the most cultured part of the community. They have been saved from this horrible burden of inert ideas. Every intellectual revolution which has ever stirred humanity into greatness has been a passionate protest against inert ideas.

The T group, with its stress upon the trainee rather than the trainer, upon the process rather than the content of training, and upon emotional rather than conceptual learning, seems to be one "passionate protest against inert ideas." Its mushrooming influence suggests that it has also stirred at least some of humanity.

Since 1946, T-group training has spread across the country and around the world. More than 100,000 Californians alone have already participated in such experiences (Allen, 1968). Between 1963 and 1968, the number of participants in T groups conducted by the National Training Laboratory Institute doubled. The method is used in classrooms, marital counseling, group psychotherapy, and church services. It has been applied to problems of race relations, police training, and executive development. It has provided the framework for a successful movie. In short, T-group training is growing, is popular, and is commercially successful.

However, it is not successful in improving sensitivity. Although the number of studies reported in Chapter 2 are few, they are consistently negative. Furthermore, T-group procedures ignore most of the principles that we have just discussed. They do not concentrate on the goal of empirical understanding. They do not train participants to discriminate sensory from expressive qualities. They eschew the use of theories, empirical or otherwise. Rather than encouraging the trainee to differentiate himself from others, the stress is in the reverse direction. Rather than fitting methods to achieve a specific goal, the T-group method *is* the goal. The T-group movement began with due attention to the desirability of measuring its achievements objectively. It has become increasingly resistant, however, to the use of such measures. Some proponents assert that it is how each individual *feels* at the end of training that is the only measure of consequence.

The T-group movement seems to have shifted its goal from the development of empirical to the development of rationalistic understanding. Increasingly, the aim of such groups is to develop in its members the feeling of being close to the other members, of being in sympathy with them, and being sympathized with by them. It is not the job of the psychologist to say what a T group should do. It is his job, however, to find out what they actually do and do not do. It seems clear that they do not increase sensitivity.

What sensitivity, transactional, interactional, encounter, nude, gestalt, and existential groups accomplish is a matter of debate rather than fact. Mintz (1971) suggests that they are a response to a cultural neurosis:

> . . . the pressures of our society produce a syndrome which, though not deviant, is intrinsically pathologic. This syndrome is marked by fear of intimacy and longing for intimacy; fear of self-exposure; difficulty in relating to others without pretense or defensiveness; conflicts around dependency and self-assertiveness; in short, a syndrome most succinctly described as alienation from others and from the self.

She suggests that such techniques as lifting and rocking, fall-catch responses, blind contact, arm wrestling, and disrobing are ways of curing the neurosis. Whether they succeed is the question. The groups concern themselves with the powerful desire for rationalistic understanding. The majority of those who attend report enthusiastic satisfaction with the experience. A few suffer serious consequences. Objective evidence of post-training benefits is nonexistent.

What could T groups do to develop sensitivity if they wanted to try? Ideally, the method should be fitted to the goal. In reality, goals are often fitted to methods. What goals are most likely to be achieved by the T-group method? Its stress upon emotional learning makes it especially unsuited for the development of theoretical sensitivity. Its stress upon the "here and now" makes it equally unsuitable for the achievement of nomothetic goals. The intense and intimate interactions encouraged by the method, however, seem especially suitable for the development of the ability to discriminate sensory from expressive qualities and for the development of considerate and responsible behavior. The radical change required for the achievement of these ends is that the groups shift from their extremely self-oriented perspective to an other-oriented one.

THE TEACHING OF PSYCHOLOGY

Of 10,000 students who take a beginning psychology course at a college or university, about 1,000 graduate with a major in psychology. About 700 of these majors apply to graduate school and 400 actually begin their graduate program. Of the 400, about 200 get their M.A. degree in psychology. Of the 200, about 100 earn a Ph.D. (Boneau, 1968). Of these 100, only fifty ever publish anything mentioned in a psychology journal. What happens to the one in fifty who has outstanding research potential? He is hired by a university to teach undergraduates, expected to do research, and rewarded for the recognition given his research by his colleagues throughout the profession.

He may teach courses in child psychology that are devoted to theories, principles, and facts about children. He may teach courses in personality or social psychology which are devoted to what psychologists know about these areas. The core of the curriculum, however, is the experimental course work in which the student learns scientific methods or statistics courses in which he learns the essential elements of statistical procedure required for doing research. The teacher may be considerate and popular with his students. In none of his courses or teaching, however, does he focus upon developing the sensitivity of his students. He is teaching his students *about* psychology, not how to use it. As a whole, the program is a watered-down and mass-produced graduate course. Its primary aim is to interest and select students who are qualified for graduate work. Its secondary aim is to keep students who are not interested or qualified for such work sufficiently satisfied so that they do not complain too strenuously.

In his nonteaching activities the instructor is preoccupied with his research and his scholarly activities. He is sometimes involved in committees concerned with curricular problems. These committees may take up a variety of matters such as adding, dropping, changing, or scheduling courses. They are rarely concerned with what a course or the program as a whole is supposed to do to the student. They are never effectively concerned with whether it, in fact, does what it is supposed to do.

Psychology instruction does not increase sensitivity (Table 2-2). It does not even try to. It does not state it as a goal, use methods adapted to its development, or measure success in its achievement. The typical instructor does not consider sensitivity a goal of his instruction, would not know how to go about achieving it if he did, and would not do it if he could, for the time and effort required would divert him from his major interest in research.

Immanuel Kant said, "Concepts without intuitions are empty; intuitions without concepts are blind." Sensitivity training is still struggling with the dilemma. Psychology courses teach theories without giving students any practice in using them; T groups give participants practice without concepts to guide them. Psychology instructors and their students are intensifying their efforts to find a solution to the dilemma. Sensitivity training in all its variations is an increasingly obvious phenomena on college campuses. "Human potential seminars" are one of the latest variants. They are highly structured. They focus on students' achievements, successes, and values. Each participant sets a goal to be reached at one meeting and its achievement evaluated at the next.

Psychology classes are especially suited to the development of theoretical and nomothetic sensitivity. In fact, most classes devote most of their time to theories and to the empirical differences between groups. The problem is that they rarely give the students any practice in using the theories and group knowledge and never give them any feedback on their success. The solution lies in the severe limitation on the number of theories and facts presented so that much more time and attention can be given to practice. If students don't learn to apply the theories and facts in the course in which they are taught, they never will. The development of effective ways of practicing them, however, will require more strenuous effort than psychology instructors customarily give to their teaching.

THE PSYCHOLOGIST AS TRAINER

Psychologists want to give psychology away. They want psychological facts and theories to be passed out freely to all who need and can use them. They want people to be their own psychologists and make their own applications. They want to be a "translator of behavioral science, busy finding ways to take knowledge out of science and to put it into the nervous system of all who can profit by that knowledge" (Sanford, 1955). Clinical psychologists represent the latest but largest group of translators. But they are having a hard time finding out how to be good ones.

The medical model represents the oldest, still dominant, but waning idea of how to be an effective translator. Terms such as "pathology," "therapy," and "diagnosis" are still ubiquitous in graduate schools of clinical psychology. The clinician who follows the medical model sees his primary job as dealing with demonstrably pathological individuals. In dealing with them, he seeks to diagnose their illness and treat it. Confidence in the model is declining, however, as evidence of its ineffectiveness has increased (Truax and Carkhuff, 1967). Also, more clinicians have become convinced that the problems with which they deal are not like the organic problems with which physicians deal but are learning problems growing out of interpersonal experiences.

The newer behavioral model of the effective translator stresses that the personal problems of the individual are learning problems. Its theories are learning theories and its methods are methods of behavior modification. Like the medical model, however, the behavior modifiers are oriented toward the diagnosis of individuals and the recommendation of learning prescriptions.

The newest model, the clinician as educator, returns him to his original roots in the educational community but on a more sophisticated level. He is no longer concerned with intellectual growth per se but with "the teaching of interpersonal skills which the individual can apply to solve present and future psychological problems and to enhance his satisfaction with life" (Guerney, 1969). Following this model, the clinician is less concerned with sick individuals than with groups that lack interpersonal skills. He is less concerned with diagnosing weaknesses than with the development of effective educational programs. He is less concerned with the solution of an immediate problem than with providing individuals with skills that will enable them to meet future problems. He is oriented toward providing the knowledge and skills desired by large numbers of the public, to help them deal with their unrealistic fears, sexual inadequacies, frustrations, and conflicts. Such problems are almost always related to insensitivity. Sensitivity training, then, is the core course to be taught by the psychologist as trainer. His first question is: Who do I want to teach what about whom? This book has tried to answer the "what" and to offer some specific course recommendations.

Finally: Psychologists are improving the accuracy of their predictions by the development and use of more and better objective measures. These measures, however, seem like canes being used by the blind. It would be better to eliminate the blindness. It would be better if we could find ways of using objective measures to improve subjective impressions. This book has been an exploration of this promising possibility.

BIBLIOGRAPHY

Adler, A. *Understanding human nature* (1927). Trans. by W. B. Wolfe. Greenwich, Conn.: Premier Books, 1965.

Albrecht, P. A., Glasser, E. M., and Marks, J. Validation of a multiple-assessment procedure for managerial personnel. *J. appl. Psychol.,* 1964, **48**, 351–360.

Allen, G. Hate therapy: sensitivity training for "planned change." *Amer. Opinion,* 1968, **11**, 73–86.

Allport, G. W. *Personality*. Boston: Houghton Mifflin, 1937.

Allport, G. W. *The nature of prejudice*. Reading, Mass.: Addison-Wesley, 1954.

Allport, G. W., and Kramer, B. M. Some roots of prejudice. *J. Psychiat.,* 1946, **22**, 9–39.

Anderson, N. H. Likeableness rating of 555 personality-trait words. *J. Pers. soc. psychol.,* 1968, **9** (3), 272–279.

Ansbacher, H. L. and Ansbacher, R. R. (eds.) *The individual psychology of Alfred Adler*. New York: Basic Books, 1956.

Anthony, W. A., and Wain, H. J. Two methods of selecting prospective helpers. *J. consult. Psychol.,* 1971, **18**, 155–156.

Argyle, M., and McHenry, R. Do spectacles affect judgements of intelligence? *British J. soc. clin. Psychol.,* 1971, **10**, 27–29.

Armour, J. B. Student attitudes in relation to classroom achievement. Unpublished master's thesis, Michigan State Univer., 1954.

Asch, S. E. Forming impressions of personality. *J. abnorm. soc. Psychol.,* 1946, **41**, 258–290.

Bagby, J. W. A cross-cultural study of perceptual predominance in binocular rivalry. *J. abnorm. soc. Psychol.,* 1957, **54**, 331–334.

Bakan, D. Clinical psychology and logic. *Amer. Psychologist,* 1956, **11**, 655–662.

Bakan, P., and Leckart, B. T. Attention, extraversion, and stimulus-personality congruence. *Perception Psychophys.,* 1966, **1**, 355–357.

Bayton, J. A., Austin, L. J., and Burke, K. R. Negro perception of negro and white personality traits. *J. pers. soc. Psychol.,* 1965, **1**, 250–253.

Beier, E. G., and Stumpf, J. Cues influencing judgment of personality characteristics. *J. consult. Psychol.,* 1959, **23**, 218–225.

Bennis, W., Burke, R., Cutter, H., Harrington, H., and Hoffman, J. A note on some problems of measurement and prediction in a training group. *Group Psychotherapy,* 1957, **10**, 326–341.

Berger, W. G. Some correlates of attitude change, retention of attitude related material, and evaluation of the communicator. Unpublished doctoral dissertation, Michigan State Univer., 1969.

Bieri, J. Changes in interpersonal perceptions following social interactions. *J. abnorm. soc. Psychol.,* 1953, **48**, 61–66.

Boneau, A. The educational base: Supply for the demand. *Amer. Psychologist,* 1968, **23**, 307–311.

Briscoe, M. E., Woodyard, H. D. and Shaw, M. E. Personality impression changes as a function of the favorableness of first impressions. *J. Pers.,* 1967, **35**, 343–357.

Brown, C. T. Introductory study of breathing as index of listening. *Speech Monogr.,* 1962, **29**, 79–83.

Bruner, J. S., and Postmann, L. J. On the perception of incongruity: A paradigm. *J. Pers.,* 1949, **18**, 206–223.

Bruner, J. S., Postman, L. J., and Rodrigues, J. Expectations and the perception of color. *Amer. J. Psychol.,* 1951, **64,** 216–227.

Bruni, E. A film test of accuracy in observing people and its correlates. Unpublished master's thesis, Michigan State Univer., 1963.

Burgess, E. W. Factors determining success or failure on parole. In A. A. Bruce (Ed.), The workings of the indeterminate sentence law and the parole system in Illinois. Springfield, Ill.: Superintendent of Public Documents, 1928.

Burnstein, E., Stotland, E., and Zander, A. Similarity to a model and self-evaluation. *J. abnorm. soc. Psychol.,* 1962, **62,** 257–264.

Byrne, D., and Clore, G. L., Jr. Effectance arousal and attraction. *J. pers. soc. Psychol.,* 1967, **6,** 1–18.

Byrne, D., Clore, G. L., Jr., and Worchel, P. Effect of economic similarity-dissimilarity on interpersonal attraction. *J. pers. soc. Psychol.,* 1966, **4,** 220–224.

Campbell, D. T. Stereotypes and the perception of group differences. *Amer. Psychologist,* 1967, **22,** 817–829.

Campbell, J. P., and Dunnette, M. D. Effectiveness of T-group experiences in managerial training and development. *Psychol. Bull.,* 1968, **70,** 73–102.

Cassirer, E. *The myth of the state.* New Haven: Yale, 1946.

Cassirer, E. *Mythic thought.* Vol. 2: The Philosophy of Symbolic Forms. New Haven: Yale, 1955.

Cassirer, E. *The phenomenology of knowledge.* Vol. 3: The Philosophy of Symbolic Forms. New Haven: Yale 1957.

Chance, J. E., and Meaders, W. Needs and interpersonal perception. *J. Pers.,* 1960, **28,** 200–210.

Chapman, L. J. Illusory correlation in observational report. *J. of Verbal Learning Verbal Behavior,* 1967, **6** (1), 151–155.

Chapman, L. J., and Chapman, J. P. Genesis of popular but erroneous psychodiagnostic observations. *J. abnorm. Psychol.,* 1967, **72,** 193–204.

Chelsea, L. A study of implicit personality theories. Unpublished manuscript, 1965.

Child, I. L. Personality correlates of aesthetic judgment in college students. *J. Pers.,* 1965, **33,** 476–511.

Cline, V. B. Ability to judge personality assessed with a stress interview and sound film technique. *J. abnorm. soc. Psychol.,* 1955, **50,** 183–187.

Cline, V. B. Person perception from the perspective of an empiricist. Symposium on interpersonal perception. American Psychological Association, San Francisco: 1968.

Cline, V. B., and Richards, J. M. Variables related to accuracy in interpersonal perception. Second Annual Report, Office of Naval Research, Contract NE 171–146, Univer. of Utah, 1959.

Cline, V. B., and Richards, J. M. Accuracy of interpersonal perception: A general trait? *J. abnorm. soc. Psychol.,* 1960, **60,** 1–7.

Cline, V. B., and Richards, J. M. Components of accuracy of interpersonal perception scores and the clinical and statistical prediction controversy. *Psychol. Rec.,* 1962, **12** (4), 373–379.

Cobb, S. Personality as affected by lesions of the brain. In J. McV. Hunt (Ed.), *Personality and the behavior disorders.* New York: Ronald, 1944. Pp. 550–581.

Cofer, C. N., and Dunn, J. T. Personality ratings as influenced by verbal stimuli. *J. Pers.,* 1952, **21,** 223–227.

Covner, B. Studies in phonographic recording of verbal material. *J. consult. Psychol.,* 1942, **6,** 105–113.

Coyle, E. Psychology and slycology. *Amer. Psychologist,* 1955, **10,** 87.

Cronbach, L. J. Processes affecting scores on "understanding of others" and "assumed similarity." *Psychol. Bull.,* 1955, **52,** 177–193.

Crow, W. J. The effect of training upon accuracy and variability in interpersonal perception. *J. abnorm. soc. Psychol.,* 1957, **55,** 355–359.

Crow, W. J., and Farson, R. E. The effect of training upon accuracy and variability in judging others. California: Western Behavioral Sciences Institute, Report No. 9, 1961.

Crow, W. J., and Hammond, K. R. The generality of accuracy and response sets in interpersonal perception. *J. abnorm. soc. Psychol.,* 1957, **54**, 384–390.

Dailey, C. A. The effects of premature conclusions upon the acquisition of understanding a person. *J. Psychol.,* 1952, **33**, 133–152.

Dailey, C. A. The experimental study of clinical guessing. *J. individ. Psychol.,* May 1966, **22**, 65–79. *(a)*

Dailey, C. A. Prejudice and decision making. *Personnel Admin.,* Sept.–Oct. 1966, 6–13. *(b)*

Daniels, H., and Otis, J. A method of analyzing employment interviews. *Personnel Psychol.,* 1950, **3**, 425–444.

Danish, S. J., and Brodsky, S. L. Training of policemen in emotional control and awareness. *Amer. Psychologist,* 1970, 368–369.

Danish, S. J., and Kagan, N. Measurement of affective sensitivity toward a valid measure of interpersonal perception. *J. counseling Psychol.,* 1971 (18), 51–54.

Daw, R. W., and Gage, N. L. Effect of feedback from teachers to principals. *J. educ. Psychol.,* 1967, **58** (3), 181–188.

Dawson, J. E. Consideration and ICS: Instructor leadership influencing student performance. Unpublished master's thesis, Michigan State Univer., 1970.

Dewey, J. *Experience and nature.* Chicago: Open Court, 1925.

Doré, R. The development and validation of forced-choice scales measuring attitudes toward leadership methods. Unpublished master's thesis, Michigan State Univer., 1960.

Doyle, A. C. *Great stories of Sherlocke Holmes.* New York: Dell, 1965.

Duncan, S., Jr. Nonverbal communication. *Psychol. Bull., 1969,* **72**, 118–137.

Dunnette, M. D. People feeling: Joy, more joy, and the "Slough of Despond". *J. appl. behavioral Sci.,* 1969, **1**, 26.

Dymond, R. F. Interpersonal perception and marital happiness. *Canad. J. Psychol.,* 1954, **8**, 164–171.

Ehrlich, H. J., and Lipsey, C. Affective style as a variable in person perception. *J. Pers.,* 1968, 522–540.

Ellsworth, P. C., and Carlsmith, J. M. Effects of eye contact and verbal content on affective response to a dyadic interaction. *J. Pers. soc. Psychol.,* 1968, **10** (1), 15–20.

Engel, E. Binocular methods in psychological research. In F. P. Kilpatrick (Ed.), *Explorations in transactional psychology.* New York: New York Univer. Press, 1961. Pp. 290–305.

Estes, S. G. Judging personality from expressive behavior. *J. abnorm. soc. Psychol.,* 1938, **33**, 217–236.

Ewart, E., Seashore, S. E., and Tiffin, J. A factor analysis of an industrial merit-rating scale. *J. appl. Psychol.,* 1941, **25**, 481–486.

Fancher, R. E., Jr. Explicit personality theories and accuracy in person perception. *J. Person.,* 1966, **34** (2), 252–261.

Fancher, R. E., Jr. Accuracy versus validity in person perception. *J. consult. Psychol.,* 1967, **31** (3), 264–269.

Fey, W. F. Correlates of certain subjective attitudes towards self and others. *J. clin. Psychol.,* 1957, **13**, 44–49.

Fish, J. M. Empathy and the reported emotional experiences of beginning psychopaths. *J. consult. clin. Psychol.,* 1970, **35**, 64–69.

Flanagan, J. C., and Burns, R. K. The employee performance record. In T. L. Whisler and S. F. Harper (Eds.), *Performance appraisal.* New York: Holt, 1962. Pp. 262–271.

Fleishman, E. A. The description of supervisory behavior. *J. appl. Psychol.,* 1953, **37**, 1–6.

Fleishman, E. A., and Salter, J. A. Relation between the leader's behavior and his empathy toward subordinates. *J. indust. Psychol.,* 1963, **1,** 79–84.

Forsythe, R. S. Assumed similarity and accuracy in observing people. Unpublished master's thesis, Michigan State Univer., 1970.

Freud, S. *Civilization and its discontents.* New York: Norton, 1961.

Fromm-Reichman, F. *Principles of intensive psychotherapy.* Chicago: Univer. of Chicago Press, 1950.

Gabennesch, H., and Hunt, L. D. The relative accuracy of interpersonal perception of high and low authoritarians. *J. exp. Res. Pers.,* 1971, **5,** 43–48.

Gage, N. L., and Exline, R. V. Social perception and effectiveness in discussion groups. *Human Relations,* 1953, **6,** 381–396.

Gagne, R. M. and Fleishman, E. A. *Psychology and human performance. New York: Holt, 1959.*

Galton, F. *Memories of my life.* New York: Dutton, 1909.

Giedt, F. H. Comparison of visual content and auditory cues in interviewing. *J. consult. Psychol.,* 1955, **19,** 407–416.

Giedt, F. H. Cues associated with accurate and inaccurate interview impressions. *Psychiatry,* 1958, **21,** 405–409.

Goldberg, L. R. Grades as motivants. *Psychol. in Sch.,* 1965, **2,** 17–24.

Golden, M. Some effects of combining psychological tests on clinical inferences. *J. consult. Psychol.,* 1964, **28,** 440–446.

Gollin, E. S. Forming impressions of personality. *J. Pers.,* 1954, **23,** 65–76.

Gollin, E. S. Organizational characteristics of social judgment: A developmental investigation. *J. Pers.,* 1958, **26,** 139–154.

Gough, H. G. *A preliminary guide for the use and interpretation of the California Institute for Personality Assessment Research, (manual), 1954.*

Gough, H. G. An exploratory cross-cultural study of interpersonal perception. Symposium on interpersonal perception. San Francisco: American Psychological Association, 1968.

Gross, C. Intrajudge consistency in ratings of heterogeneous persons. *J. abnorm. soc. Psychol.,* 1961, **62,** 606–610.

Grossman, B. A. The measurement and determinants of interpersonal sensitivity. Unpublished master's thesis, Michigan State Univer., 1963.

Grossman, B. A. Evaluation of a training program to improve the ability to differentiate between people. Unpublished master's thesis, Michigan State Univer., 1967.

Guerney, B., Jr. *Psychotherapeutic agents: New roles for nonprofessionals, parents, and teachers.* New York: Holt, 1969.

Guilford, J. S. Isolation and description of occupational stereotypes. *Occupational Psychol.,* 1967, **41,** 57–64.

Haire, M. Projective techniques in marketing research. *J. Marketing,* 1950, **14,** 649–656.

Haire, M. Role-perceptions in labor-management relations: An experimental approach. *Industr. Labor Relat. Rev.,* 1955, **8,** 204–216.

Hamid, P. N. Style of dress as a perceptual cue in impression formation. *Perceptual motor Skills,* 1968, **26,** 904–906.

Harrison, A. A. Exposure and popularity. *J. Pers.,* 1969, **37,** 359–377.

Hartlage, L. C. Differences in the listening comprehension of the blind and sighted. *Int. J. for the Educ. of the Blind,* 1963, **13,** 1–6.

Herzberg, F., Mausner, B., Peterson, R. O., and Capwell, D. F. *Job attitudes: Review of research and opinion.* Pittsburgh: Psychological Service of Pittsburgh, 1957.

Hoffman, P. J., Slovic, P., and Rorer, L. G. An analysis-of-variance model for the assessment of configural cue utilization in clinical judgment. *Psychol. Bull.,* 1968, **69,** 338–349.

Holt, R. R., and Luborsky, L. *Personality patterns of psychiatrists.* New York: Basic Books, 1958.

Hunt, W. A., Schwartz, M. L., and Walker, R. E. The correctness of diagnostic judgment as a function of diagnostic bias and population base rate. *J. clin. Psychol.,* 1964, **20,** 143–146.

Hunt, W. A., and Walker, R. E. Validity of diagnostic judgment as a function of amount of test information. *J. clin. Psychol.,* 1966, **22,** 153–155.

Jacoby, J. Interpersonal perceptional accuracy as a function of dogmatism. *J. exp. soc. Psychol.* 1971, **7,** 221–236.

James, W. *Varieties of religious experience.* New York: Modern Library, 1902.

James, W. *Pragmatism.* New York: World Publishing, 1955.

Johnson, R. L. Correlates of a test of group sensitivity. Unpublished master's thesis, Michigan State Univer., 1963.

Johnson, W. B., and Terman, L. M. Personality characteristics of happily married, unhappily married and divorced persons. *Charact. Pers.,* 1935, **3,** 290–311.

Jones, E. E., and deCharms, R. Changes in social perception as a function of the personal relevence of behavior. *Sociometry,* 1957, **20,** 75–85.

Kaess, W. A., and Witryol, S. L. Memory for names and faces: A characteristic of social intelligence? *J. appl. Psychol.,* 1955, **39,** 457–462.

Kagan, J. On the need for relativism. *Amer. Psychologist,* 1967, **22,** 131–141.

Kagan, N., and Schauble, P. G. Affect stimulation in interpersonal process recall. *J. consult. Psychol.,* 1969, **16,** 309–313.

Katz, D., and Braly, K. Racial stereotypes of one hundred college students. *J. abnorm. soc. Psychol.,* 1933, **28,** 280–290.

Kelley, H. H. Warm-cold variable in first impressions. *J. Pers.,* 1950, **18,** 431–439.

Kellogg, M. S. New angles in appraisal. In T. L. Whisler and S. F. Harper (Eds.), *Performance Appraisal.* New York: Holt, 1962. Pp. 88–95.

Kelly, E. L. Consistency of the adult personality. *Amer. Psychologist,* 1955, **10,** 659–681.

Kelly, E. L., and Fiske, D. W. The prediction of performance in clinical psychology. Ann Arbor: Univer. of Michigan Press, 1951.

Kelly, G. A. *The psychology of personal constructs.* New York: Norton, 1955.

Kepes, S. Y. Experimental evaluations of sensitivity training. Unpublished doctoral dissertation, Michigan State Univer., 1965.

Koltur, B. B. Some characteristics of intrajudge trait intercorrelations. *Psychol., Monogr.,* 1962, **76,** No. 33 (Whole No. 552).

Kurtz, R. R., and Grummon, D. L. Different approaches to the measurement of therapist empathy and their relationship to therapy outcomes. *J. consult. and clinical Psychol.,* 1971, **39,** 106–115.

Lamming, G. The pleasures of exile. *The Tamarack Review,* 1960, **14,** 32–56.

Levi-Strauss, C. *Structural Anthropology.* Translated from the French by C. Jacobson and B. Grundfest. New York; Basic Books, 1963.

Levy, B. I., and Ulman, E. Judging psychopathology from paintings. *J. abnorm Psychol.,* 1967, **72** (2), 182–187.

Lewis, W. A., and Wigel, W. Interpersonal understanding and assumed similarity. *Personnel Guidance J.,* 1964, **43** (2), 155–158.

Linden, J. The self-centered orientation in interpersonal relationships. Unpublished master's thesis, Michigan State Univer., 1965.

Lindzey, G., and Rogolsky, S. J. Prejudice and identification of minority group membership. *J. abnorm. soc. Psychol.,* 1950, **45,** 37–53.

Locke, E. A., and Bryan, J. F. Performance goals as determinants of level of performance and boredom. *J. appl. Psychol.,* 1967, **51,** 120–130.

Locke, E. A., and Bryan, J. F. The direction function of goals in task performance. *Organizational Behavior Human Performance,* 1969, **4,** 35–42.

Lohmann, K., Zenger, J. H., and Weschler, I. R. Some perceptual changes during sensitivity training. *J. educ. Res.,* 1959, **53,** 28–31.

Luft, J. Implicit hypotheses and clinical predictions. *J. Abnorm. soc. Psychol.,* 1950, **45,** 756–759.

Lundy, R. M. Assimilative projection and accuracy of prediction in interpersonal perceptions. *J. abnorm. soc. Psychol.,* 1956, **52,** 33–38.

McClelland, D. C., and Atkinson, J. W. The projective expression of needs. *J. Psychol.,* 1948, **25,** 205–222.

McKeachie, W. J. Lipstick as a determiner of first impressions of personality. *J. soc. Psychol.,* 1952, **36,** 241–244.

MacLeod, R. B. The teaching of psychology. *Amer. Psychologist,* 1971, **26,** 245–249.

Machover, K. *Personality projection in the drawing of the human figure.* Springfield, Ill.: Charles C Thomas, 1949.

Mahoney, S. C. The literature empathy test: Development of a procedure for differentiating between "good empathizers" and "poor empathizers." *Dissert. Abstr.,* 1960, **21,** 674.

Maier, N. R. F., Hoffman, L. R., and Lansky, L. Human relations training as manifested in an interview situation. *Personnel Psychol.,* 1960, **13,** 11–30.

Marrow, A. J. and French, J. R. P., Jr. Changing a stereotype in industry. *J. soc. Issues,* 1945, **1,** 37–53.

Marwell, G. Problems of operational definitions of "empathy," "identification," and related concepts. *J. soc. Psychol.,* 1964, **63,** 87–102.

Marx, M. H. The general nature of theory construction. In M. H. Marx (Ed.), Psychological theory. New York: Macmillan, 1951.

Masling, J. M. The effects of warm and cold interaction on the interpretation of a projective protocol. *J. proj. Tech.,* 1957, **21,** 337–383.

Maugham, W. S. *The summing up.* New York: Doubleday, 1938.

May, R. *The art of counseling.* New York: Abingdon, 1939.

Meehl, P. E. *Clinical versus statistical prediction.* Minneapolis: Univer. of Minnesota Press, 1954.

Meehl, P. E. When shall we use our heads instead of the formula? *J. consult. Psychol.,* 1957, **4,** 268–273.

Meehl, P. E. A comparison of clinicians with five statistical methods of identifying psychotic MMPI profiles. *J. counsel. Psychol.,* 1959, **6,** 102–109.

Meehl, P. E. The cognitive activity of the clinician. *Amer. Psychologist,* 1960, **15,** 19–27.

Mehrabian, A. Significance of posture and position in the communication of attitude and status relationships. *Psychol. Bull.,* 1969, **71,** 359.

Mettee, D. R. Changing in liking as a function of the magnitude and affect of sequential evaluations. *J. exp. soc. Psychol.,* 1971, **7,** 157–172.

Mietus, J. Evaluation of a sensitivity program with a component criterion. Unpublished master's thesis, Michigan State Univer., 1969.

Miles, M. B. Human relations training: Processes and outcomes, *J. counsel. Psychol.,* 1960, **7,** 301–306.

Miles, M. B. *Innovation in education.* New York: Teachers College, 1964.

Miller, J. W., and Rowe, P. M. Influence of favorable and unfavorable information upon assessment decisions. *J. appl. Psychol.,* 1967, **51,** 432–435.

Mintz, E. E. Therapy techniques and encounter techniques: Comparison and rationale. *Amer. J. Psychotherapy,* 1971, **25,** 104–109.

Morris, C. W. *Varieties of human value.* Chicago: Univer. of Chicago Press, 1956.

Mullin, J. Reliability and validity of a projective film test of empathy. Unpublished master's thesis, Michigan State Univer., 1962.

Muslin, H. L., Burstein, A. G., Gedo, J. E. and Sadow, L. Research in the supervisory process: I. Supervisor's appraisal of the interview data. *Arch. gen. Psychiat.,* **16,** April 1967.

Newcomb, T. M. The prediction of interpersonal attraction. *Amer. Psychologist,* 1956, **11,** 575–586.

Newcomb, T. M. Stabilities underlying changes in interpersonal attraction. *J. abnorm. soc. Psychol.,* 1963, **66,** 376–386.

Oakes, R. H., and Corsini, R. J. Social perceptions of one other self. *J. soc. Psychol.,* 1961, **53,** 235–242.

Olmsted, D. W. The accuracy of the impressions of survey interviewers. *Publ. Opin. Quart.*, 1962, **25**, 635–647.

Orwell, G. *A collection of essays.* New York: Doubleday, 1954.

Oskamp, S. W. Overconfidence in case-study judgments. *J. consult. Psychol.*, 1965, **29**, 261–265.

Peirce, C. S. *Essays in the Philosophy of Science* New York: Liberal Arts Press, 1957.

Proust, M. *Swann's way.* London: Chatto & Windus, 1922.

Rank, O. *Beyond psychology.* New York: Dover, 1941.

Reade, W. H. V. *The problem of inference.* Oxford: Clarendon, 1938.

Rogers, C. R. The necessary and sufficient conditions of therapeutic personality change. *J. consult. Psychol.*, 1957, **21**, 95–103.

Rogers, C. R. *Becoming a person.* Boston: Houghton Mifflin, 1961.

Rorer, L. A. The proper domain of prediction. Unpublished paper, Oregon Research Institute, 1965.

Sanford, F. H. Creative health and the principle of habeas mentem, *Amer. Psychologist*, 1955, **10**, 829–835.

Sarbin, T. R., Taft, R., and Bailey, D. E. *Clinical inference and cognitive theory.* New York: Holt, 1960.

Schafer, E. S., and Bayley, N. Maternal behavior, child behavior, and their intercorrelations from infancy through adolescence. *Monogr. Soc. Res. Child Develop.*, 1963, **28**, no. 3.

Schlessinger, N., Muslin, H. L., and Baittle, M. Teaching and learning psychiatric observational skills. *Arch. gen. Psychiat.*, 1968, **18**, 549–552.

Secord, P. F. Facial features and inference processes in interpersonal perception. In R. Tagiuri and L. Petrullo (Eds.), *Person perception and interpersonal behavior.* Stanford: Stanford Univer. Press, 1958.

Secord, P. F., and Berscheid, E. Stereotyping and the generality of implicit personality theory. *J. Pers.*, 1963, **31**, 65–78.

Shapiro, M. I. Teaching observational skills in child psychiatry to mental students. *Amer. J. Orthopsychiat.*, 1964, **34**, 563–568.

Shears, A. D. The development and analysis of a criterion of the ability to understand people. Unpublished master's thesis, Michigan State Univer., 1967.

Shook, J. Interpersonal orientations and the selection of sensitive people. Unpublished master's thesis, Michigan State Univer., 1971.

Showel, M. Interpersonal knowledge and rated leader potential. *J. abnorm. soc. Psychol.*, 1960, **61**, 87–92.

Siipola, E. M. A group study of some effects of preparatory set. *Psychol. Monogr.*, 1935, **46** (Whole No. 210).

Silkiner, D. S. A cross-cultural study of the measurement, determinants, and effects of stereotype accuracy. Unpublished master's thesis, Michigan State Univer., 1962.

Slovic, P. Analyzing the expert judge: A descriptive study of a stockbroker's decision processes. *Oregon Res. Inst. Bull.*, **8** (3), 1968.

Smith, H. C. *Personality Development.* New York: McGraw-Hill, 1968.

Soskin, W. F. Bias in postdiction and projective tests. *J. abnorm. soc. Psychol.*, 1954, **49**, 69–74.

Soskin, W. F. Influence of four types of data on diagnostic conceptualization in psychological testing. *J. abnorm. soc. Psychol.*, 1959, **58**, 69–78.

Spier, M. The improvement of stereotype accuracy. Unpublished doctoral dissertation, Michigan State Univer., 1969.

Steinman, A., and Fox, D. J. Male-female perceptions of the female role in the United States. *J. Psychol.*, 1966, **64**, 265–276.

Stelmachers, Z. T., and McHugh, R. B. Contribution of stereotyped and individualized information to predictive accuracy. *J. consult. Psychol.*, 1964, **28**, 234–242.

Stock, Dorothy. A survey of research on T groups. In L. P. Bradford, J. R. Gibb, and K. D.

Benne (Eds.), *T-group theory and laboratory method.* New York: Wiley, 1964. Pp. 395–411.

Stone, G. C., Leavitt, G. S., and Gage, N. L. Two kinds of accuracy in predicting another's responses. *J. soc. Psychol.,* 1957, **45**, 245–254.

Stotland, E., and Dunn, R. E. Empathy, self-esteem, and birth order. *J. abnorm. soc. Psychol.,* 1963, **66**, 532–540.

Symonds, P., and Dietrich, D. Effects of variations in the time interval between an interview and its recording. *J. abnorm. soc. Psychol.,* 1941, **36**, 593–598.

Taft, R. The ability to judge people. *Psychol. Bull.,* 1955, **52**, 1–23.

Taft, R. Accuracy of empathic judgments of acquaintances and strangers. *J. pers. soc. Psychol.,* 1966, **3**, (5), 600–604.

Tannenbaum, R., Weschler, I. R., and Massarik, F. *Leadership and organization: a behavioral science approach.* New York: McGraw-Hill, 1961.

Thornton, G. W. The effect upon judgments of personality traits of varying a single factor in a photograph. *J. soc. Psychol.,* 1943, **18**, 127–148.

Thurstone, L. L. Primary mental abilities. *Psychometr. Monogr.,* 1938, No. 1.

Toch, H. H., Rabin, A. I., and Wilkins, D. M. Factors entering into ethnic identifications: An experimental study. *Sociometry,* 1962, **25**, 297–312.

Toch, H. H., and Schulte, R. Readiness to perceive violence as a result of police training. *Brit. J. Psychol.,* 1961, **52**, 389–393.

Truax, C. B., and Carkhuff, R. R. *Toward effective counseling and psychotherapy.* Chicago: Aldine, 1967.

Trumbo, D. A. The development and analysis of a test of the ability to predict behavior. Unpublished master's thesis, Michigan State Univer., 1955.

Tyler, L. E. *The work of the counselor.* New York: Appleton-Century-Crofts, 1969.

Wakeley, J. H. The effects of special training on accuracy in judging others. Unpublished doctoral dissertation, Michigan State Univer., 1961.

Walster, E., Aronson, V., and Abrahams, D. The importance of physical attractiveness in dating behavior. *J. pers. soc. Psychol.,* 1966, **4**, 508–516.

Waly, P., and Cook, S. W. Attitude as a determinant of learning and memory: A failure to confirm. *J. pers. soc. Psychol.,* 1966, **4** (3), 280–288.

Warr, P. B., and Knapper, C. *The perception of people and events.* New York: Wiley, 1968.

Watley, D. L. Feedback training and improvement of clinical forecasting. *J. counsel. Psychol.,* 1968, **15**, 167–171.

Wedell, C., and Smith, K. V. Consistency of interview methods in appraisal of attitudes. *J. appl. Psychol.,* 1951, **35**, 392–396.

Wegner, D. Self-other differentiation: Field dependence and assumed similarity. Unpublished master's thesis, Michigan State Univer., 1971.

Weiss, J. H. Effect of professional training and amount and accuracy of information on behavioral predictions. *J. consult. Psychol.,* 1963, **27**, 257–262.

Western Electric Company. Complaints and grievances: supervisory conference material. 1938. Chicago: Hawthorne Plant.

Whitehead, A. N. *The aims of education.* New York: Macmillan, 1929.

Williams, W. C. *Autobiography.* New York: Random House, 1951.

Wispé, L. G. Impact of psychotherapy on the productivity of psychologists. *J. abnorm. Psychol.,* 1965, **70**, 188–103.

Witkin, H. A. Psychological differentiation. *J. abnorm. soc. Psychol.,* 1965, **170**, 317–332.

Witryol, S. L. and Kaess, W. A. Sex differences in social memory tasks. *J. abnorm. soc. Psychol.,* 1957, **54**, 343–346.

Yarrow, M. R., and Campbell, J. D. Person perception in children. *Merrill-Palmer Quart. Behavior Development,* 1963.

Zavala, A. A test of stereotype accuracy. Unpublished master's thesis, Michigan State Univer., 1960.

INDEXES

NAME INDEX

SUBJECT INDEX